Ancient Religious Wisdom, Spirituality, and Psychoanalysis

Other Books by Paul Marcus

Autonomy in the Extreme Situation: Bruno Bettelheim, the Nazi Concentration Camps and the Mass Society (1999)

Blacks and Jews on the Couch: Psychoanalytic Reflections on Black-Jewish Conflict *(co-edited with Alan Rosenberg)* (1998)

Psychoanalytic Versions of the Human Condition: Philosophies of Life and Their Impact on Practice *(co-edited with Alan Rosenberg)* (1998)

Into the Great Forest: A Story for Children Away from Parents for the First Time *(with Irene Wineman Marcus)* (1992)

Scary Night Visitors: A Story for Children with Bedtime Fears *(with Irene Wineman Marcus)* (1990)

Healing Their Wounds: Psychotherapy with Holocaust Survivors and Their Families *(co-edited with Alan Rosenberg)* (1989)

Psychoanalytic Reflections on the Holocaust: Selected Essays *(co-edited with Steven Luel)* (1984)

Ancient Religious Wisdom, Spirituality, and Psychoanalysis

Paul Marcus

WITHDRAWN

PRAEGER

Westport, Connecticut
London

Library of Congress Cataloging-in-Publication Data

Marcus, Paul, 1953–
    Ancient religious wisdom, spirituality, and psychoanalysis / Paul Marcus.
      p. cm.
    Includes bibliographical references and index.
    ISBN 0-275-97452-9 (alk. paper)
    1. Psychoanalysis and religion. I. Title.
    BF175.4.R44 M27 2003
    200'.1'9–dc21   2002190903

British Library Cataloguing in Publication Data is available.

Copyright © 2003 by Paul Marcus

All rights reserved. No portion of this book may be reproduced, by any process or technique, without the express written consent of the publisher.

Library of Congress Catalog Card Number: 2002190903
ISBN: 0-275-97452-9

First published in 2003

Praeger Publishers, 88 Post Road West, Westport, CT 06881
An imprint of Greenwood Publishing Group, Inc.
www.praeger.com

Printed in the United States of America

The paper used in this book complies with the Permanent Paper Standard issued by the National Information Standards Organization (Z39.48-1984).

10 9 8 7 6 5 4 3 2 1

Copyright Acknowledgments

Extracts from Burton Watson, *The Complete Works of Chuang Tzu*, copyright © 1968 by Columbia University Press. Reprinted with the permission of the publisher.

Extracts from Marcus Aurelius, *Meditations*, translated by Maxwell Staniforth, copyright © 1964 by Maxwell Staniforth (Penguin Classics, 1964). Reprinted with the permission of the publisher.

Extracts from Robert Gordis, *Koheleth: The Man and His World*, copyright © 1951 by Jewish Theological Seminary of America. Reprinted with permission.

This book is dedicated, on her eighty-fifth birthday,
to my mother, Sylvia Marcus,
from whom I have learned so much wisdom,
especially about the art of gracefully growing old.

Like Moses, may she live to be one hundred and twenty.

For every man, assuming responsibility for the Other is a way of testifying to the glory of the Infinite, and of being inspired.
Emmanuel Levinas

One pole of any identity, in any historical period, relates man to what is forever contemporary, namely eternity.
Erik H. Erikson

The Messiah will come only when he is no longer necessary; he will come only on the day after his arrival; he will come, not on the last day, but on the very last.
Franz Kafka

Contents

Acknowledgments   xi

1. Introduction: Ancient Religious Wisdom and Psychoanalysis   1

I. South Asian
2. Hinduism: The *Bhagavad Gita*   15
3. Buddhism: Buddha   35

II. East Asian
4. Confucianism: *The Analects*   59
5. Taoism: The *Chuang Tzu*   81

III. Greco-Roman Interlude
6. Stoicism: Marcus Aurelius's *Meditations*   101

IV. Western
7. Judaism: Ecclesiastes   119
8. Christianity: Saint Augustine's *Confessions*   139
9. Islam: The Koran   159
10. Conclusion: Toward a Spiritually Animated Psychoanalysis   177

Selected Bibliography   201

Index   205

Acknowledgments

I wish to thank a number of friends and colleagues for their valuable critical comments and editorial suggestions in the preparation of this book. First is my dear friend Professor William B. Helmreich, who generously took time out of his busy life to read and critique each chapter. Being a professor of sociology (and Judaic studies) gave him a unique angle of vision on my work, for which I am most grateful.

I was fortunate to find colleagues, each a highly regarded specialist in their field, who were each kind enough to read and critique a chapter, especially with an eye to making sure that the religious material was correct and the link to psychoanalysis was plausible, if not compelling. Of course, I alone take full responsibility for what is written in this book.

I therefore wish to thank the following scholars for their help:

The *Bhagavad Gita*: Steven J. Rosen, editor, *The Journal of Vaiṣṇava Studies*.
Buddha: Jeffrey B. Rubin, independent scholar on the integration of psychoanalysis and Buddhism.
The Analects: Professor Irene Bloom, Columbia University.
The *Chuang Tzu*: Professor Victor H. Mair, University of Pennsylvania.
Marcus Aurelius's *Meditations*: Professor William V. Harris, Columbia University.
Ecclesiastes: Professor Lawrence H. Schiffman, New York University.
St. Augustine's *Confessions*: Professor Philip A. Cary, Eastern College.
The Koran: Professor Meguin Yavari, Columbia University.

Finally, I wish to thank my wife, Irene, my soul-mate for life, a child and adult psychoanalyst who graciously read, critiqued, and reread every word of this book. This was a laborious and time-consuming task for someone who has a full-time psychoanalytic practice and helps raise our two lovely adolescent children, Raffi and Gabriela. My gratefulness to my wife in all her roles is impossible to put into words.

Introduction: Ancient Religious Wisdom and Psychoanalysis

> We need the courage as well as the inclination to consult, and profit from, the "wisdom traditions of mankind"
>
> E. F. Schumacher[1]

Psychoanalysis is a theory and profession in crisis. It has been consistently attacked in both the scholarly and popular literature as an obsolete, and even dangerous, theory of the human condition and behavior, as well as an ineffective and wasteful form of psychotherapy. Moreover, within the field there is little agreement about what psychoanalysis is, that is, what constitutes its core principles and received truths. For example, there are drastically different, competing, and untranslatable views on just about everything that, in the field's heyday, mainstream psychoanalysts used to regard as unarguable, accepted, and true about theory and technique. Take the bedrock concept of the unconscious. Roy Schafer's conceptualization of the unconscious differs from the (Melanie) Kleinian or object relations conceptualization and even more from the Jungian conceptualization. As Greenberg and Mitchell have pointed out, "Psychoanalytic models rest upon . . . irreconcilable claims concerning the human condition."[2]

Furthermore, contemporary psychoanalysis, says historian Fred Weinstein, "far from being a monolithic entity that can compel loyalty to a single perspective, as critics still sometimes describe it, is too fragmented to be constituted as a unified discipline." As Nathan Hale wrote in his widely acclaimed book *The Rise and Crisis of Psychoanalysis in the United States*, the "psychoanalytic crisis of the last decade" is "a crisis of clashing theories, competing modes of therapy, and uncertainties of professional identity." Marshal Edelson characterizes psychoanalysis as in a "profound malaise," while Edith Kurzweil claims that "the fragmentation of psychoanalytic theory proves . . . that the Freudians primarily are united by their profession rather than by their ideas." Finally, it is well known within psychoanalysis that there is a shortage of psychoanalytic patients (and trainees), and its causes and consequences have been discussed with great concern within the field.[3] There are, of course, many complex historical, sociological, philosophical, economic, and psychological reasons for this crisis, which have been discussed by scholars and practitioners who are either for or against psychoanalysis.

This book attempts to enhance the state of psychoanalysis as a theory of human behavior and form of psychotherapy and, hopefully, make it more relevant and appealing to potential analysands, many of whom can perhaps best be described as trapped in a spiritual malaise; in other words, they are alienated spiritual wanderers. Such persons are looking for a way out of their everyday way of being in the world, one that is mainly directed by a restrictive scientism, materialism, and consumerism that estranges them from the humanizing issues of meaning, morality, and truth, which are the focus of the great religious traditions.[4] In other words, many potential analysands are, consciously or unconsciously, in search of self-transformation and self-transcendence, that ineffable, though qualitatively different, lived perspective on being human that has been beautifully described in the wisdom traditions of the religions of the world.

In addition, while there are many potential analysands, as well as analysands who are currently in treatment, who are in a spiritual malaise, there are also many others who regard their spiritual quest and religious life, in and outside organized religion, as very relevant to their everyday life. For example, a recent *U.S. News/PBS's Religion and Ethics Newsweekly* poll reported the following results: nearly two thirds of Americans say religion is very important in their lives; about half questioned say they attend worship services at least once a week, the highest percentages since the 1960s; more than four of five Americans say they have "experienced God's presence or a spiritual force" close to them, and 46 percent say it happened many times; and voluntary giving to religious institutions is estimated at more than $55 billion annually. Other surveys have shown that belief in God and devotion to prayer are at historic highs in the United States. Richards and Bergin cite Gallup Organization polls that suggest that the level of religious belief has remained more or less steady for many decades, with about 95% of the population saying they believe in God and about 70% saying they are members of a church or synagogue. In Europe, more than 80% of the population polled assert that they have belief in, adherence to, or affiliation with one of the major theistic religions. Says pollster George Gallup, Jr., "There is a deep desire for spiritual moorings—a hunger for God." It is thus not suprising that one fairly recent survey found that 72% of 51 patients of a private mental health facility answered "somewhat to very important" when asked "How important to you is the inclusion of a spiritual focus as a part of psychotherapy process?"[5]

In light of these facts, I have taken a different approach than is usually taken in the conventional psychoanalytic literature. My approach is rooted in engaging the internal, so-called spiritual aspects of the great wisdom religions, and much less in institutional life or psychoanalyzing the religious experience or rituals. The book is mainly built on the following three assumptions:

First, the spiritual quest, especially the religiously animated spiritual quest, is a fundamental human activity. According to recent scientific neurotheology research, there may actually be a biological basis for spirituality, that is, the brain may have a spirituality circuit that mediates spiritual experience. Even E. O. Wilson, a world renowned biologist who would be delighted if religion failed the test of evolution and faded into oblivion, notes that humans seem to have a religious gene that is impossible to get rid of.[6] Thus, the most far-reaching psychic activity, the quest for self-transcendence, which, in the religious context, means the quest for transcending the limited universe such that one meets the glory of the Infinite, seems to be built into the human condition as a primary motivation.

Put in a more psychological language by psychoanalyst Alan Roland, "the spiritual as core dimension of the human psyche has rarely been acknowledged in Freudian psychoanalysis and only to a limited extent by neo-Freudian analysts." Seymour Applebaum, a psychiatrist, has a similar view: "the spiritual/religious dimension of the human personality is a vital component in human health." And Samuel Klagsburn, a psychiatrist, also recently pointed out that "religious values and backgrounds and spiritual dimensions are extremely important to people's dynamics." Moreover, while it is not my focus in this book, it should be noted that empirical studies have supported these observations. For example, a number of beneficial mental health indicators have been correlated with religion (e.g., regarding physical health, mortality, suicide, drug and alcohol abuse, delinquency and criminal behavior, divorce and marital satisfaction, well-being, health outcome, and depression). Religion has also been empirically shown to be very helpful in the coping process. Finally, Huston Smith, the great religious scholar, noted that hardwired into the human condition is a yearning for "more" than the world of everyday experience can satisfy. The reality that often inspires and fulfills the human yearning for "more" and for self-transcendence is God, regardless of the name that is used.

In this context, says Smith, since God's nature is fundamentally unintelligible at this time, God is best viewed more as a direction than an object. In fact, suggests Smith, one can make a strong argument that the desire for knowledge of the right direction, for orientation in life, is stronger than sexual instinct, the drive for power, and the lust for material possessions.[7]

These notions have hardly been adequately embraced by most mainstream psychoanalysts. As pointed out by Meissner, an analyst and a Jesuit, analysts often view "religious thinking and convictions [and spirituality] as suspect, even [holding] them in contempt at times. . . . there is a latent persuasion, not often expressed or even articulated . . . that religious ideas are inherently neurotic, self-deceptive and illusive."[8] While religiously animated spirituality can be, as Freud pointed out, an obsessional neurosis, a childhood neurosis, a form of masochism, a reaction formation against unacceptable impulses, or a delusion, it can also be a life-affirming part of a person's existence and a cultural asset. Psychoanalysis, in general (though there are some exceptions), has, unfortunately, too often thrown the baby out with the bathwater. That is, in my view, psychoanalysis is not a superior mode of understanding compared to religion, as most analysts have implied or claimed in their writings. Rather, along with religion, it is one of the two great narratives of subjectivity, which can be enhanced and deepened by engaging ancient religious wisdom.

Second, psychoanalysis is suffering from a "profound malaise," in part because it has become alienated from its parental roots, that is, from the profound and beautiful spiritual and ethical insights and moral philosophy that are contained in the ancient religious wisdom literature. In my view, psychoanalysis as a theory of human behavior, psychotherapeutic technique, and a worldview has been largely appropriated and controlled by the medical- and natural science–oriented psychiatric and psychological disciplines. As a result, psychoanalysis has been inadvertently blunted as a compelling and appealing life- and identity-defining narrative of the human condition and technique for self-transformation, self-mastery, and self-improvement. Perhaps, in part, the paucity of psychoanalytic patients is a consequence of this omission or underemphasis in psychoanalytic theory and treatment, which has probably left many potential analysands feeling that psychoanalysis does not speak to their hearts and minds in a relevant and compelling manner. That is, there are many existential questions that analysands seek answers to, which require a spiritual answer, not just the same old conventional, reductionistic psychoanalytic responses. For example, what does it mean to be a human being as we move through the life cycle; that is, how does one create the "good life" and "good society"? What is the meaning of death, especially in terms of how we live our lives? These are are only two of the tough questions that tend to be raised, directly or indirectly, in effective psychoanalysis and long-term psychotherapy, for they are the same questions that are asked by most reflective adults. An analyst who is not familiar with or sensitive to the ancient religious/spiritual sensibility and responses to these and other existential questions or their modern counterparts is unlikely to be able to respond in an empathic and helpful manner to the struggling analysands, who often find that analysts are not comfortable or in sync with them when these kind of issues come up in their therapy. This is not that suprising when one considers that while 96% of Americans have a theistic orientation to life, only 40% of psychiatrists do. The atheists were most frequently found among therapists who have completed psychoanalytic training.[9]

Third, if psychoanalysis is to avoid lapsing into the ghetto of intellectual insularity and irrelevance, constructive engagement with other traditions is perhaps the best way for the discipline to make progress. Unfortunately, while psychoanalysis has recently found some admirers in the fields of literary criticism, linguistics, and certain Continental philosophies, from my experience, these jargon-laced academics write about psychoanalysis in a way that feels strikingly removed from "real" people struggling with intense psychic pain and debilitating problems in living, who are trying to live more reasonable, harmonious, and decent lives. In other words, these scholars seem largely to be unacquainted with the real-life world of clinical psychoanalysis from the inside.

It has been more than sixty years since Freud died in 1939, and the field is in a serious crisis and has lost much of its animating influence on most Western cultures as well as its patient appeal. In contrast, the major religions discussed in this book have been thriving for thousands of years and there is no indication that this trend is slowing down (amazingly, there are currently about 3 billion religious adherents in the world). Moreover, the major religious thinkers have left perennial and universal legacies in both the religious and secular worlds.[10] Perhaps, to some extent, psychoanalysis has lost its prominent place in cultural discourse and psychotherapy because there is, in general, a lack of appreciation by many in the analytic community (except perhaps Jungians and some other individual writers, often in object relations) for the authenticity of religiously animated spirituality, especially those expressions of spirituality that attempt to deal with the fundamental questions of human existence. These are questions that, to some extent, psychoanalysis is also concerned with, such as how one achieves a modicum of happiness and peace of mind within this pain-filled existence? And, perhaps most important, how does one foster ultimate freedom, that is, self-transcendence?

THE WISDOM TRADITION

Who were the "wisdom" writers? They were ancient professional teacher-sages who were committed to developing "a realistic approach to the problems of life, including the practical skills and the technical arts of civilization."[11] For example, the sixth century B.C.E. was a watershed in the intellectual and spiritual development of the world. The Greek rationalist philosophers, the Jewish prophets, Confucius in China, and Buddha in India all illuminated human history during this epoch. These and other authors, such as Ecclesiastes, Chuang Tzu (the great Taoist poet-philosopher), and Marcus Aurelius (to name a few I discuss in this book), not only identify, with startling brilliance and poetic insight, some of the central problematics of the human condition as modern people construe it, but they offer what I believe is, in many ways, a reasonable and feasible attitude toward contemporary life. Moreover, their way of looking at life is similar to certain life attitudes and values embodied implicitly in the broadly conceived Freudian oeuvre but also possibly suggests what psychoanalysis might in part appropriate or further explore and develop to become a better narrative of the human condition and a more compelling technology for self-transformation, self-actualization, and self-improvement.

In other words, my aim is, in part, to explore some of the spiritual pearls contained in the internal, rather than institutional, realms of some of the world's great religions, with an eye to delineating their significance for psychoanalysis. By doing this I hope to encourage psychoanalysis to recognize its own doctrines and dogmas, which tend to inhibit, restrict, and blunt the discipline, and to sensitize it to some of the greatest truths to have had a claim on the human heart and imagination for thousands of years: the values, beliefs, and modes of being that allow us to flourish as people and as cultures. Psychoanalysis, as it is concerned with the "arts of living," can only benefit from an engagement with the sometimes anxiety-ridden, but always courageous, truth seekers and lovers of life who constitute the wisdom writers.

TWO IMPORTANT DEFINITIONS

Psychoanalysis

I should make it clear that I am aware that thus far I am referring to psychoanalysis in a manner that seems somewhat unusual to the typical or mainstream psychoanalyst: as more than a body of thought and a brand of psychotherapy. Rather, by psychoanalysis I mean a widely accepted theoreticopractical matrix, an intellectual technology for rendering existence thinkable and practicable.[12] Psychoanalysis is not merely a body of thought, but a certain form of life, one that gives its followers a language to articulate themselves and their own actions, to judge and evaluate their existence, to give their experience a meaning, and to act on themselves.[13] Most important, perhaps, many individuals have appropriated the life and identity-defining narrative of psychoanalysis when they seek to understand, endure, and possibly conquer the problems that assail the human condition: despair, loss, tragedy, and conflict. In effect, they try to synthesize the affectively discrepant experiences of life through a psychoanalytic calculus and ethic. In this sense, psychoanalysis is similar to what Michel Foucault called a "technique of the self" or a "practice of the self": "an exercise of the self, by which one attempts to develop and transform oneself, and to attain a certain mode of being," such as a state of happiness, purity, wisdom, perfection, or immortality.[14] In other words, according to Pierre Hadot (writing in another context), psychoanalysis can be viewed as a "spiritual exercise," a tool for living life correctly. The aim of a spiritual exercise is to foster a deep modification of the individual's way of seeing and being, a decisive change in how he or she lives his or her practical, everyday life.[15] As Joel Kovel, a psychoanalyst, wrote, "The essential spiritual place of psychoanalytic work cannot be displaced. Spirituality—and hence religion—continue to haunt psychoanalysis."[16] Perhaps psychoanalysis can be enhanced and made more robust as a self-sustaining narrative through better understanding, and possibly incorporating, aspects of the forms of life that the ancient religious wisdom writers insinuated in their enduring reflections.

Spirituality

Spirituality is a very difficult term to precisely define, and there is no agreed upon definition that I am aware of among scholars. In fact, most definitions of spirituality are only acceptable to their authors. My working definition mainly concentrates

> on the inner dimension of the person called by certain traditions "the spirit." This spiritual core is the deepest center of the person. It is here that the person is open to the transcendent dimension; it is here that the person experiences ultimate reality. [This includes] the discovery of that core, the dynamics of its development, and its journey to the ultimate goal. It deals with prayer, spiritual direction, the various maps of the spiritual journey, and the methods of advancement in the spiritual ascent.[17]

Put somewhat differently, spirituality as I use the term usually involves the transcendental relationship between an individual and a

Higher Being (e.g., God, a Realm, a Force, a Reality, etc., in whatever form), an experience that goes beyond specific religious affiliation, such as to a church, synagogue, temple, or mosque. Spirituality as I view it is mainly a subjective sacred experience, where one apprehends what lies beyond creation and infinitely transcends it. Religion, on the other hand, mainly includes living by a set of dogmas, rituals, traditions, and assumptions about the cosmos that have been codified and institutionalized. Most often in the West, secular spirituality is, knowingly or unknowingly, rooted in a religious tradition and/or outlook, but of course there are exceptions.

I want to say a brief word on the related notion of transcendence, a term that repeatedly comes up throughout this book. Transcendence, like spirituality, is impossible to clearly define such that the majority of scholars would agree with the proposed definition. Nevertheless, I want at least to hint at what I am getting at when I discuss transcendence, though each religion discussed in this book uses the term somewhat differently.

By transcendence, I mean entering into a mode of being such that one experiences a taste of ultimate reality, a glimpse of eternity, often called God or by some other roughly equivalent name. This mode of being usually comes about after effortful, long-term spiritual work on oneself through, say, Buddhist meditation, prayer, learning Torah, doing good deeds, and/or God's graciousness. Most important, such an encounter with ultimate reality is profoundly transformational, in that one begins to live a qualitatively different life, characterized by a high level of moral and ethical development and compassion toward others. In particular, transcendence as I use the term must involve a moral transformation such that one greatly diminishes, if not gives up, one's egocentric consciousness and self-centric mode of subjectivity. Rather, one embraces a mode of being mainly characterized by a Levinasian ethic of responsibility to the Other. In other words, transcendence in my view is not to be equated with the transient ego-enhancing feeling that one gets when one wins an Oscar, watches the Yankees clinch the World Series, hears Beethoven's Ninth Symphony, is involved in political activity, takes LSD, or, even, creates or encounters a beautiful work of art or literature. Rather, transcendence, in the religious sense in which I am using it, must also involve adopting, for the long term, a "for the Other," rather than for oneself, orientation in the world. Let us never forget that the experience of transcendence without the moral transformation I have insinuated can be extremely dangerous. The hordes of ordinary and educated Germans who saluted Adolph Hitler during a Nazi rally also experienced a kind of ecstatic, apocalyptic transcendence, as did the Stormtroopers who felt they were doing God's work by brutally murdering Jews and other minorities. Fundamentalist Islamic suicide bombers who murder innocent people also believe that they are doing Allah's work and will be rewarded after dying by entering a pleasurable transcendent realm. Transcendence, in other words, is thus not simply a mind-altering achievement, one that involves expanding normal consciousness in ways that link one to a symbolic or phenomenal reality beyond one's everyday experience. Rather, transcendence must bring about a deep commitment to living a life that is compassionate, loving, and altruistic toward humankind and all creation. That is, transcendence requires that one be dedicated, not only to transforming oneself, but also to transforming the world into a more humane and just place for all humankind.

SCOPE OF THE BOOK

This book assumes that there is a tremendous internal diversity in each religion discussed. While I understand that the ultimate is conceptualized differently by adherents to a particular religion and, of course, by different religions, I believe that these different conceptualizations are actually about one and the same divine reality. In other words, as the Hindu tradition declares, I perceive simultaneously diversity and unity across the religions discussed in this book. As the *Rig Veda* says, in a famous quotation, "Truth is one, but the wise speak of it in many ways."[18] Each religion, in other words, represents a different modality from which the connection between heaven and earth is realized and actualized. I therefore have usually chosen a particular text from each religious tradition that tends to have universal overtones, a more or less common set of ethics, and a modality of relationship to the transcendent, a reality that to the believer is transhistorical and nontemporal, that is most likely to resonate with the typical secular analyst and analysand who constitute the great majority of the psychoanalytic community. Anyone with a strong religious sensibility will, I hope, find the religious material in this book to be congenial to their specific religious outlook once they look beneath the obvious manifest differences among religions and perceive, or at least sense, the "transcendent unity of religion," following the title of the highly regarded book by F. Schuon.[19]

I should also perhaps indicate that this book is not about working with religious issues per se in psychotherapy or with religious patients. Rather it is mainly about how psychoanalytic discourse and therapy can become more receptive to transcendence and thereby more profoundly address the crucially important spiritual dimension in the lives of our patients and potential patients.[20]

In presenting the religious material in this book, I have opted for an approach that strives for a degree of systematicity. That is, while I am aware of the complexities, ambiguities, and contradictions in and between each religion, I have tried to present each chapter in a way that is somewhat formalized and organized into a series of propositions. As this book is mainly about the relationship between ancient religiously inspired wisdom or spirituality and psychoanalysis, I wanted the un-initiated student of ancient religious wisdom to have an accessible, though scholarly, introduction to the best of each religious tradition, that is, religion looked at with a sympathetic, positive mind-set. I leave it to others to focus on the dark side contained in most religious traditions, such as the fanaticism, dogmatism, suppression of women, and, perhaps most important, intolerance of difference, which sometimes leads to justifying murder in the name of God.

As the reader can see from the Contents page, the chapters are more or less arranged according to what Huston Smith has called "Religion's Four Families":[21] (1) South Asian: Hinduism (The *Bhagavad Gita*) and Buddhism (Buddha); (2) East Asian: Confucianism (*The Analects*) and Taoism (The *Chuang Tzu*); (3) Western: Judaism (Ecclesiastes), Christianity (St. Augustine's *Confessions*), and Islam (The Koran); and (4) Primal, Oral, and Tribal, which are not discussed in this volume.

I have taken the liberty of including a chapter emanating from the ancient Greco-Roman era, Marcus Aurelius's Stoic masterpiece, *Meditations*. To me it would be an omission if a book on ancient religious wisdom did not have at least one representative from that part of the ancient world. While Aurelius was a devout adherent to the Roman religion, he is best known as a Stoic devotee who tried to live his life according to its philosophy of life. While Aurelius was, in general, trying to cultivate an attitude of resignation without despair as he confronted the difficulties of existence, we can sense a spirituality that denies, yet at times yearns for, transcendence. In this sense, perhaps, his Stoic approach has a religious sensibility embedded in it, one that I think is in sync, at least to some extent, with many secularists' notion of spirituality.

Finally this book was written over a period of years, as I struggled as a traditional Jew and a Freudian-oriented psychoanalyst to make sense of the material. Each essay was written as a scholarly paper and as an individual unit, and only later did I realize that I had enough to say in each chapter to warrant a book on the subject. The reader may notice that there are, from time to time, some thematic repetitions. However, I have chosen to present the chapters more or less as the material struck me at the time when I wrote them, rather than narratively smoothing all the material into a seamless, unified whole that leads to a premeditated, forgone conclusion. That being said, each chapter, I hope, gives the reader a good sense of what I think is most important in each religious tradition as it pertains to psychoanalysis. Furthermore, each may insinuate the "transcendent unity of religion," at least as I interpret these religious traditions and texts. In a certain sense, all the religions are trying to help their adherents get closer to God, whatever their particular formulation of this process is and whatever name they use for the transcendent realm in which they aspire to reside. That is, the genuine striving to get closer to God, the Infinite, Heaven's Will, the Tao, the divine realm, or ultimate reality tends to foster in the individual a profound feeling of the primary connectedness of all beings[22] and things in the cosmos.

NOTES

1. Quoted in Huston Smith, *The World's Religions: Our Great Wisdom Traditions* (New York: Harper San Francisco, 1991), p. v.

2. Paul Marcus and Alan Rosenberg, *Psychoanalytic Versions of the Human Condition and Its Impact on Practice* (New York: New York University Press, 1998), pp. 1–4; Jay R. Greenberg and Stephen A. Mitchell, *Object Relations in Psychoanalytic Theory* (Cambridge, Mass.: Harvard University Press, 1983), p. 404.

3. Fred Weinstein, *History and Theory after the Fall* (Chicago: University of Chicago Press, 1990), p. 27; Nathan G. Hale, *The Rise and Crisis of Psychoanalysis in the United States* (New York: Oxford University Press, 1995), p. 360; Marshall Edelson, *Psychoanalysis: A Theory in Crisis* (Chicago: University of Chicago Press, 1988), p. xiv; Edith Kurzweil, *The Freudians: A Comparative Perspective* (New Haven, Conn.: Yale University Press, 1989), p. 283; Robert S. Wallerstein, "Where Have All the Psychoanalytic Patients Gone? They're Still Here," *Psychoanalytic Inquiry*, 20, no. 4 (2000): 503–526; George H. Allison, "The Shortage of Psychoanalytic Patients: An Inquiry into Its Causes and Consequences," *Psychoanalytic Inquiry*, 20, no. 4 (2000): 527–540.

4. Huston Smith, *Why Religion Matters: The Fate of the Human Spirit in an Age of Disbelief* (New York: Harper San Francisco, 2001), pp. 59–78.

5. Jeffery L. Sheler, "Faith in America," *U.S. News and World Report*, May 6, 2002, pp. 40–42; P. Scott Richards and Allen E. Bergin, *A Spiritual Strategy for Counseling and Psychotherapy* (Washington: American Psychological Association, 1996), pp. 7, 12; Bethesda PsychHealth, *Results of the Bethesda Professional Staff Chaplain Support Services Advisory Committee Survey of Professional Staff, Line Staff and Patients* (Denver: Author).

6. Not all forms of spirituality are necessarily directly or as obviously rooted in the major religious traditions. There are secular forms of spirituality (e.g., scientific inquiry, arts, sports, political activity, etc.), though, for reasons that I will make clear shortly, my focus is on religiously inspired spirituality. See Volume 2 of *Spirituality and the Secular Quest*, edited by Peter H. Van Ness (New York: Crossroad Publishing Company, 1996).

I should make clear that while there may be a neurological basis for spiritual/religious experience, this does not necessarily mean that the neurological changes that are correlated with spiritual experience are causing those experiences or, rather, perceiving a spiritual realm. Most important, there is no way at this time of definitively answering the question of whether our brain circuitry creates God or God created our brain circuitry. See Sharon Begley, "Religion and the Brain," *Newsweek*, May 7, 2002, pp. 50–58; and E. O. Wilson, paraphrased in Smith, *Why Religion Matters*, p. 72.

7. Alan Roland, *Cultural Pluralism and Psychoanalysis: The Asian and North American Experience* (New York: Routledge, 1996), p. 145; Seymour W.

Applebaum, "The Rediscovery of Spirituality through Psychotherapy," in *Psychotherapy of the Religious Patient*, edited by Moshe Halevi Spero (Springfield, Ill.: Charles C. Thomas, 1985), p. 140; quoted in Marek Fuchs, "Finding the Place of Faith in Psychiatric Treatment," *New York Times*, April 27, 2002, p. B6; John Gartner, "Religious Commitment, Mental Health, and Prosocial Behavior: A Review of the Empirical Literature," in *Religion and the Clinical Practice of Psychology*, edited by Edward P. Shafranske (Washington: American Psychological Association, 1996), pp. 187–214; Kenneth I. Pergament, *The Psychology of Religion and Coping: Theory, Research, Practice* (New York: Guilford Press, 1997); Smith, *Why Religion Matters*, pp. 3, 26.

8. William W. Meissner, *Psychoanalysis and Religious Experience* (New Haven, Conn.: Yale University Press, 1984), p. 5.

9. Polly Young-Eisendrath and Melvin E. Miller, eds., *The Psychology of Mature Spirituality: Integrity, Wisdom, Transcendence* (London: Routledge, 2000), p. 3; H. Bronheim, *The Body and the Soul: The Role of Object Relations in Faith, Shame and Healing* (Northvale, N.J.: Jason Aronson, 1998), p. 20.

10. In this book I am not taking up the "truth claims" of each religion. Rather, I am trying to mine each tradition for insights about the human condition and conduct for life that may be useful to enhance psychoanalysis as a theory and practice. Moreover, I am aware that nearly all the religions discussed in this book have a negative side in that they have fostered fanaticism and perpetrated some terrible crimes on nonbelievers and others. However, my emphasis is on what is positive in each of these traditions, that is, how psychoanalysts and analysands can benefit from engaging the ancient religious traditions.

11. Robert Gordis, trans. and commentator, *Koheleth—The Man and His World* (New York: Jewish Theological Seminary of America, 1951), pp. 16–17.

12. Nicholas Rose, *Inventing Our Selves* (Cambridge, U.K.: Cambridge University Press, 1996), p. 83.

13. Ibid., pp. 62, 64.

14. Michel Foucault, "The Ethics of the Concern for the Self as a Practice of Freedom," in *Foucault Live: Collected Interviews, 1961–1984*, edited by S. Lotringer (New York: Semiotexte, 1989), p. 433.

15. Pierre Hadot, *Philosophy as a Way of Life* (Oxford: Blackwell Publishers, 1997), p. 83.

16. Joel Kovel, "Beyond the Future of an Illusion: Further Reflections on Freud and Religion," *Psychoanalytic Review*, 77, no. 1 (Spring 1990): 81.

17. Ewert Cousins, Preface, in Van Ness, ed., *Spirituality and the Secular Quest*, p. xii.

18. Quoted in Diana Eck, *Great World Religions: Beliefs, Practices and Histories*, Part 5 (Course Guide) (Chantilly, Va.: The Teaching Company, 1998), p. 6.

19. Quoted in Seyyed Hossein Nasr, "Islam," in *Our Religions*, edited by Arvind Sharma (New York: Harper San Franciso, 1993), p. 522.

20. See Robert J. Lovinger, *Working with Religious Issues in Therapy* (New York: Jason Aronson, 1984); Moshe Halevi Spero, ed., *Psychotherapy of the Religious Patient* (Springfield, Ill.: Charles C. Thomas, 1985); Gary Ahlskog and Harry Sands, eds., *The Guide to Pastoral Counseling and Care* (Madison, Conn.: Psychosocial Press, 2000); P. Scott Richards and Allen E. Bergin, *A Spiritual Strategy for Counseling and Psychotherapy* (Washington: American Psychological Association, 1996); Richards and Bergin, eds., *Handbook of Psychotherapy and Religious Diversity* (Washington: American Psychological Association, 2000).

21. Huston Smith, *Religions of the World*. Tape 2: *Hinduism* (audiotape) (Boulder, Colo.: Sounds True, 1995).

22. Kovel, "Beyond the Future of an Illusion," p. 76.

South Asian

I

Hinduism: The *Bhagavad Gita*

2

> For him who has conquered the mind, the mind is the best of friends, but for one who has failed to do so, his very mind will be the greatest enemy.
>
> *Bhagavad Gita*[1]

The *Bhagavad Gita* (The song of the blessed Lord) is a philosophical, spiritual poem of great beauty and wisdom that is regarded by devout Hindus as their Gospel. Secular scholars of religion have characterized it as one of the great religious classics in world literature. The *Gita*, as it is referred to, is part of a larger Indian national epic poem, the *Mahabharata*, and has had an extraordinary appeal to all levels of Hindu society. For thousands of years the *Gita* has inspired and counseled Indian philosophers, pragmatic wisdom seekers, and ordinary people, as well as Western thinkers such as Arthur Schopenhauer, Ralph Waldo Emerson, Henry David Thoreau, T. S. Eliot, Aldous Huxley and Thomas Merton. The *Gita* is best viewed as a "timeless, practical manual for daily living."[2] It is a philosophy of salvation written in an accessible style that can assist ordinary people in their struggle for self-mastery, self-realization, and the creation of transcendent meaning and happiness in their lives. It is in this sense that the *Gita*, as a practical guide to everyday living, can perhaps enhance psychoanalytic theory and practice.

THE SETTING OF THE POEM

The *Gita*, some scholars say, was written between 200 B.C.E. and 200 C.E., though the tradition maintains that it was written much earlier. The author of the *Gita* is unknown, though eminent scholars such as

A. L. Basham believe that there were at least two main authors with very different, sometimes conflicting, philosophical perspectives. The *Gita* was written at a time when Hinduism, with its confusing and exacting Vedic sacrificial ritualism and its hard-to-grasp Upanishadic metaphysical doctrines about self-realization, lost its emotional hold on everyday people in favor of the down-to-earth philosophy of Buddhism. The *Gita*, in other words, was Hinduism's attempt to win back its adherents from Buddhism. The *Gita* is a relatively brief text, about seven hundred verses or eighteen short chapters. It is technically considered to be *smriti*, a remembered text that is based on tradition and derived from scripture, as opposed to *shruti*, spoken revelation transmitted from one generation to the next, such as the *Vedas* and the *Upanishads*. Regardless of its official status, pragmatically speaking, the *Gita* is an authoritative and revered Hindu text of spiritual instruction. Mahatma Gandhi, for example, referred to it as "Mother *Gita*," and characterized it in glowing terms in his translation and commentary as "a deity of the mind."[3]

The *Gita* takes place at the climax of the Mahabharata, the battle between the armies of the Pandavas and the Kauravas, who, though related by blood and history, are hostile, rival claimants to the throne. Arjuna, the fearless leader of the Pandavas, rides out in his chariot to inspect the battlefield but suddenly loses his motivation to fight, becoming indecisive, confused, and sorrowful. He articulates his doubts and anxieties to his charioteer Krishna, the incarnation of God, who is his *guru* (teacher, spiritual guide) of wisdom. In particular, Arjuna knows that as a member of the warrior class, he is obligated to fight; however, he feels intense ambivalence and guilt about killing his own relatives, teachers, and benefactors in order to preserve justice and law and obtain worldly power. The *Gita* is a record of the life- and identity-transforming dialogue between Arjuna (the student) and Krishna (the teacher) on the verge of this great battle. Similar to psychoanalysis, Krishna's goal is to foster in Arjuna "a higher reconciliation with himself" between seemingly irreconcilable desires.[4]

The *Gita* can be viewed as an allegory of the human condition. It is an ethical text that illuminates humanity's internal warfare, our conflicts between good and evil and between ego consciousness and selfish desires, on the one hand, and our "higher," God-inspired, for-the-Other nature, on the other. Arjuna thus faces the task of harmonizing the conflicting moral obligations imposed by *dharma*. Dharma is a key concept in Hinduism. According to Diana Eck, dharma is "the right ordering that supports the cosmos," which holds all things together, or cosmic law. Dharma is roughly the same as natural law, social order, and the sense of obligation that is connected to one's caste. Dharma is also "the right ordering of the human heart" or conscience.[5] As dharma reflects the revealed, eternal truth of Hinduism, it emanates from, and is animated by, God.

Arjuna, in other words, is in a fierce struggle to act in a way that is in sync with dharma, that is, in accord with God. Arjuna's moral problem on the battlefield, and by extension, our moral problem in everyday life, is twofold. (1) How do we *discern* dharma amid profoundly conflicting ideas, a wide range of possible courses of action, and ambiguous and ambivalent emotions? (2) How do we *sustain* dharma in day-to-day existence such that we can achieve lasting peace of mind or liberation, what Hindus call *moksha*? Moksha, the chief goal of life for the spiritual seeker, means freedom from all worldly attachments, from *karma* (the moral law of cause and effect), and *samsara*, the cycle of birth, death, and rebirth that persists as long as one is ignorant of one's identity with Brahman, "the holy power that undergirds all reality."[6] For believing Hindus, when one has achieved moksha—when one has joined with the eternal, inextinguishable Absolute, or God—one experiences a deep and abiding sense of self-harmony and peace of mind, the same overarching ideal goals of any psychoanalysis.[7]

THE AIM OF LIFE IN THE *GITA*

The way or discipline of knowledge or cognition (*jnana*), action or work (karma), and love or devotion (*bhakti*) are the three interrelated spiritual paths that lead one to realize the aim of human life as described in the *Gita*, namely, the deep self-understanding "that 'I' am not a separate, autonomous actor but that 'I' am at one with divine reality, and that my ultimate freedom comes from bringing my actions in accord with that reality."[8] That is, for the *Gita*, the goal of life is achieving God-realization in one's outlook and relations to others and all things, "to see the Lord in every creature and act accordingly," with compassion and the will to help, heal, and serve others. In part, what is involved in such all-encompassing empathy, says the *Gita*, is seeing "the self in all creatures and all creatures in the self."[9] The *Gita* suggests that such a different mode of being in the world brings an individual the liberation from the finite self, ego consciousness, and self-centeredness that prevents us from achieving what we really want in life, namely, a connection to the Infinite God, subjectively experienced as a sense of infinite being (living forever), infinite consciousness (transcendent, universalistic knowledge), and infinite bliss (joy).[10]

While the typical Western psychoanalyst might view the *Gita*'s aim for life as infantile, grandiose, unrealistic, and frankly, unreasonably asking too much from life as we rationally conceive what is humanly possible, the devout Hindu, in contrast, believes that such infinite being, knowledge, and bliss are obtainable in one's lifetime. However, to achieve these goals, a tremendously disciplined, brutally honest, and sustained self-exploration and self-transformation in the service of making contact with the Infinite God within oneself, with one's *atman*, is required. The atman, a key term in Hindu thought, is the "indestructible spiritual center of each being, and the ultimate 'Self' underlying all reality."[11] In Western terms, it is the "soul," which is tied to the body. Thus, the path to reach infinite being, knowledge, and bliss, the transcendent, universalistic state of being that is associated with atman and Brahman consciousness, requires knowing how to maintain dharma in the three domains of knowledge, action, and love. It is to these yogic paths (yoga literally means "yoke"), ways of rigging oneself to God and merging with Him in a relationship with love and devotion, that we now turn.

THE DISCIPLINE OF KNOWLEDGE (JNANA YOGA)

Arjuna is terribly upset and sorrowful about being morally obligated to kill his kin, friends, and teachers in order to rightfully claim the disputed throne. He asks many questions to Krishna meant to avoid fighting, for example, would it not be better to kill himself than to kill his kinsman, and in so doing disgrace his family, simply for the sake of obtaining a mere throne? Is not war itself immoral? Would it not be better to renounce war and retreat from the struggle into a life of solitude and meditation? Krishna offers many replies to Arjuna. Some are oversimplified and are geared to Arjuna's "lower" nature, while others are more sophisticated and meant to persuade Arjuna that it is unnecessary and undesirable to avoid fighting.[12] Ultimately, however, Krishna gradually brings Arjuna to deeper levels of self-awareness. He does this by offering him a new way of conceptualizing his practical crisis, one which has bearing on psychoanalysis in that it includes novel insights into the application of ethics and spirituality to the problems of existence.

Krishna begins his effort to get Arjuna out of his despondent mood and refocused on the challenge before him by drawing from philosophical ideas circulating at the time. In particular, he tells Arjuna that an individual's soul, or atman, is eternal and indestructible. He should not be troubled by the idea of the physical death that he might cause to the Kauravas since their souls are also indestructible. Krishna, in other words, is appealing to two well-known Hindu notions, the imperishability of the soul and the inevitability of death and reincarnation.

What Krishna is doing with Arjuna at this point is what many psychotherapists do when they have a client in a state of acute anxiety and confusion about an important decision that needs to be made in a timely manner and that has serious consequences. They attempt to persuade, advise, and reassure. Though Krishna does some of this, he is no inexperienced analyst; he knows that his appeal to Arjuna's ego or intellect and to the previously mentioned Hindu philosophical ideas concerning the soul and reincarnation will be of little help to Arjuna's practical crisis. Nor will Krishna's simplistic appeal to Arjuna's superego, his sense of caste duty and honor, and his shame at not wanting to be labeled as a coward on the eve of battle be of much use.

Instead, like a shrewd analyst, Krishna subtly hints at a notion that points Arjuna toward a higher level of awakening and self-understanding. Within the context of trying to show Arjuna the importance of doing his duty to fight, Krishna insinuates a very important insight about living, especially when life gets tough or when one is in a life and death situation like Arjuna's, namely, the need to have *svadharma*, one's own dharma or inner law, which animates one's thoughts and actions and is in sync with divine will, at least as one understands it. In Western psychological terms, this notion is roughly equated with the importance of having a strong internalized set of deeply felt, flexibly applied, transcendent moral values and beliefs (e.g., religious convictions and political ideologies) from which to draw, especially when making very important decisions in crisis. Such transcendent moral values and beliefs can, to some extent, help sustain one's autonomy and integration; they can protect one from being swayed by external pressures, extraneous considerations, and poorly thought out strategies; and they can help one to accept the inevitable with an attitude of resignation without despair.[13]

Krishna, in other words, is trying to help Arjuna to obtain what Hindus call "discriminative wisdom." Discriminative wisdom in the context of the *Gita* is the ability to distinguish the eternal (e.g., the atman) from the transient (e.g., one's body and materiality). More generally, however,[14] according to the *Gita*, the individual has two conflicting tendencies or selves in his or her makeup. On the one hand, we are part of nature; we are governed by lawlike principles and are a seething cauldron of self-centered desires and wishes. This "small" self (lower-case "s") can be viewed as superficial, as the surface, "false" self of everyday sociality, which, in the *Gita*, reflects our "lower" nature. However, we also have a "large" and "true" Self (upper-case "S"), a divine, spiritual core to our personality that, in part, constitutes our truly social, for-the-Other potentiality. This Self, the atman, tends to be hidden and reflects our "higher" spiritual nature. Throughout most of life, according to the *Gita*, we identify ourselves with our small, superficial self and ego consciousness, and we view ourselves as self-sufficiently working within the parameters of our psychophysical nature.

Krishna, however, is suggesting that Arjuna must radically change his mode of relating to himself. He must view his natural existence and ego consciousness as temporary and only significant when linked to his divine core, his Self, that is, to a spiritual perspective. Only when Arjuna has reidentified himself at a deeper level of integrated selfhood to his higher, spiritual Self, or atman, can he be said to be a truly for-the-Other social being. Moreover, such a reidentification is the basis for making compassionate and wise decisions in life, including in times of practical crisis, such as what Arjuna is faced with.

Krishna is thus teaching Arjuna the importance of cultivating a strong capacity for discernment in life.[15] The question is, how does one acquire this discriminative wisdom? More specifically, how does one realize this true Self? How does one reside in this different dimension of being that brings with it the peace of mind and happiness that our analysands long for?

Krishna tells Arjuna that one of the keys to discriminative wisdom is developing a state of equanimity, or spiritual equipoise. The wise man, Krishna says in a famous quotation, "does not waver"; he is "like a lamp sheltered from the wind."[16] Equanimity for the Hindu and Buddhist implies considerably more than the word tends to mean to the Western psychoanalyst, for whom it is simply mental composure, especially amid misfortune, and an expression of ego strength. Rather, equanimity is the ground where a person finds balance and centeredness amid the continuously shifting circumstances of life.[17] Equanimity is not detachment, not caring or blunting one's feelings, as some analysts may view it in the context of Hindu thought. Equanimity is the capacity to avoid getting bogged down in trying to repel or avoid inevitable psychic pain or grasping at pleasurable feeling states. Instead, it means balancing one's inclination to strongly connect to things, in pain or pleasure, with a clear awareness of the way things are, namely, that they are always changing. The cultivation of equanimity thus reduces the human tendencies to maintain unrealistic expectations in life and to attempt to unreasonably manipulate and control others. It does this by reminding us that we do not have ultimate control over our experience or that of others, no matter how much we obsessively try to or think we do.

According to the *Gita*, equanimity is achieved mainly through the practice of disciplined meditation. Hinduism has developed an elaborate and sophisticated form of meditation or psychophysical exercises that, to some extent, have infiltrated the West. For example, hatha yoga, a form of physical and breathing exercises that is very popular in the West, is viewed in Hinduism as only a preparatory practice for the other, spiritual types of yoga, including those that are described in the *Gita*. While a detailed discussion of Hindu meditation is beyond the scope of this chapter, it is important to note that it is based on the assumption that the attainment of equanimity requires intense practice, especially in yoga postures, which assist the mind in relaxing and entering into sustained concentration. The goal of this yogic path is to become a yogi, to become integrated and yoked with one's truest, deepest Self, the atman, and with Brahman, or God. Unfortunately, psychoanalysis has tended to mainly view the body as a vehicle to obtain pleasure and express psychopathology; it has not yet adequately integrated into its theory or practice the Hindu insight that the body is an essential instrument to help the mind come to calmness, especially a calmness that lasts.

In psychoanalytic terms, becoming yoked to one's Self is very roughly equated with having attained the highest level of integration, wholeness, and selfhood. It should be remembered that for the Hindu, the self can be conceptualized as a four-layered entity. Mainstream psychoanalysis is mostly familiar with the first three layers only. First is the body, second is the conscious layers of our minds, and third is the individual's personal unconscious. It is the fourth layer, which underlies and is related to the other three, that Hindu thought has hypothesized and which psychoanalysis does not theorize about; it is "Being Itself, infinite, unthwarted, eternal." This realm of the self is the "true self," or atman, which, the *Gita* says, when fully engaged, including in meditation practice, gives one increased self-knowledge, self-control, equanimity, and peace of mind.[18]

In general, then, in Hindu thought the discipline of knowledge, jnana yoga, is one of the four types of yogas that leads to God, mainly through intellectual analysis and abstract knowledge. It is especially through discriminative wisdom that the intellectually and reflectively inclined spiritual seeker realizes that the whole manifest world is transitory and unreal and that there is only one unchanging, deathless, eternal reality, called Brahman. In the context of the *Gita*, Krishna thus provides Arjuna with the possibility of becoming a different type of person, more integrated, better joined with his truest, deepest Self, and more autonomous, such as being capable of making more compassionate and wise decisions, including the decision to embrace his moral obligation to fight.

Perhaps most important, Krishna is suggesting that Arjuna needs to cultivate equanimity, a spiritual equipoise that will give him the empathic ability to feel everyone else's joy and sorrow just as if it were his own. This is because in this way, Arjuna will discern the Self (i.e., God within) in all beings and everywhere.[19] Arjuna will not only have achieved a high degree of personal integration and autonomy, he will have risen to such a high level of self-awareness, personhood, and moral refinement that he will become a truly social being, one in which a for-the-Other mode of being feels quite natural. Moreover, Krishna insinuates that by mastering the discipline of knowledge Arjuna's sense of self will be experienced on a deeper, more expansive and authentic level; that is, he will acquire a palpable sense of the infinite Self, a basis for increased happiness, and peace of mind.

However, we are not yet at a place in the *Gita* where Arjuna has mastered or internalized the discipline of knowledge or achieved Self-realization. As Miller points out,[20] Krishna is trying to get Arjuna to see that in a certain ironic sense, his compassion for his enemy is misdirected in the larger scheme of things, and that the practice of true duty and responsibility does not emanate from personal desire but is a constituent part of a larger cosmic realm that requires detachment in action (to be discussed in the next section). Krishna teaches Arjuna that his misguided reticence about killing his kinsman is based on the same mode of being, the same personal, worldly desire that motivates his enemy to stupidly fight for his rightful throne. As we shall see, Krishna's solution for Arjuna's conflict is thus rooted in another realm, where conflicts, contradictions, and opposites reside together within cosmic knowledge. Arjuna's duty as a warrior, or dharma, says Miller, is rooted in the awareness of the reciprocal and dialectical relationship between cosmic and human action (karma), which is essential to maintain universal and personal harmony.

THE DISCIPLINE OF ACTION

It is in the second spiritual path, that of karma yoga, which is the discipline of action or work and the form of yoga that is geared to the person who has an active inclination (as opposed to a reflective one, targeted by jnana yoga), that Krishna makes some of his most interesting points to Arjuna that have bearing on psychoanalysis.

While Arjuna is interested in Krishna's spiritual insights, which are rooted in jnana yoga, his main concern is a pragmatic one; that is, he is preoccupied with the question of what he is supposed to do next as he faces the impending battle. In other words, the *Gita* is suggesting that it is not enough to acquire knowledge and wisdom, especially by withdrawing from the world into a contemplative life, including striving for mystical contact with God. In addition to the reflective life, one needs to embrace one's worldly obligations and responsibilities, though, says the *Gita*, this must be done with the right attitude, one that is rarely emphasized in the Western tradition, including in psychoanalytic theory, namely, detachment in action, which is also later elaborated as selfless service in the *Gita*.

Says Krishna to Arjuna, in a well-known quotation: "Be intent on action, not on the fruits of action; avoid attraction to the fruits and attachment to the inaction. Perform actions, firm in discipline, relinquishing attachment; be impartial to failure and success—this equanimity is called discipline."[21]

Before commenting on this passage I need to briefly introduce an important Hindu concept, that of karma, the law of moral cause and effect, which will place these passages in a more meaningful conceptual context and assist us in linking karma to psychoanalysis.

As in psychoanalysis, it is assumed in Hindu thought that every action leads to a result, that is, every action has consequences for one's life. In other words, past actions tend to determine one's present circumstances. However, unlike psychoanalysis, but like most of the other religions discussed in this book, Hinduism believes that if our life is good, we must have done something in the past that was good, and if our life is bad, we must have done something in the past that is bad. This is a kind of mechanical reward and punishment system, though it clearly emphasizes a strong ethic of decision and personal responsibility. As Easwaran points out, one concern that developed over time in Hinduism about the concept of karma was that all actions in a sense implied imprisonment; anything a person did, bad or good, painful or pleasurable, would entrap him or her into the continuous cycle of cause and effect and thus propel him or her to be more tightly bound to the worldly life and selfish desires as opposed to cultivating the spiritual realm. In this context, the previously quoted passage from the *Gita* is Krishna's attempt to help Arjuna out of this labyrinth of moral cause and effect.[22]

Krishna tries to guide Arjuna by teaching him the best attitude toward work, one that will not create fetters (i.e., karma) and will bring him to Self-realization, to a spiritual unity with God, and give him the decisiveness and peace of mind he wants. Krishna says that such an attitude requires focusing only on one's work, on one's task, and never on its fruit or result. A person who is motivated by success or failure is not a person with equanimity animated by wisdom; rather he or she usually is anxious, worried, or preoccupied with the benefits of possible success. That person may also be inclined to adopt bad means to accomplish his goal. To be psychologically detached from one's work in the positive sense, one need not renounce work or be apathetic to what must be done; rather, one is asked to be apathetic to the fruits of one's action. That is, after taking great care to do what is right as one construes it, one must not worry about the results for, according to Krishna, one has control only over one's work, not its results.[23]

What Krishna is getting at in his doctrine of detachment in action may sound strange to the analysand, as if he were recommending abandoning consequential thinking and mindfulness of the effects of our actions on others. However, Krishna is making a more subtle point. He is suggesting that only through giving up the coils of egoism, the egoistic identification with what one does, will one find a lasting peace of mind. It is this attachment to the ego that is at the root of human unhappiness, and Krishna repeatedly tells Arjuna that it is only through acquiring this detachment to the results of his actions that he can truly be free and act wisely and effectively in his practical crisis.

Detachment concerning the fruits of one's action goes against the infantile tendencies and cultural learning of most analysands, in part because it means not getting bogged down in whether things work out the way we want. For example, within the realm of intimate relationships, it suggests that one should concentrate on the details of loving one's significant other well, skillfully as the Hindus say, rather than being preoccupied with the fruits of such an effort, that is, with whether one will be loved in return, which is typically the self-referential motivation of many analysands. Of course, one does, in some sense, love one's significant other in part because one wants a favorable result, that is, to be happy, but according to the *Gita*, any reward for one's good actions emanates from God as an act of grace, a term that the *Gita* actually uses a number of times in the concluding chapter. Says Gandhi in his commentary, "the reward [or any outcome] of work is entirely for Him [God] to give."[24]

In the work realm, say in one's job, detachment from the fruits means approaching one's work with a greater focus on the process of what one is doing than on its outcome. It means internalizing the childhood baseball motto, "It is not winning that counts, it is how you play the game." Winning is not what is most important, it is doing the right thing that really counts. As Gandhi points out, in the realm of social action, detachment from the fruits of one's action means focusing as much, if not more, on the means to achieve a goal as on the goal itself, for only then are we more likely to keep our means decent and reach our goal honorably.

Later in the *Gita*, detachment to the fruits of one's action is further developed in a most interesting and important way that is relevant to psychoanalysis. Having argued against egoism, selfish desires, and worldly attachments, Krishna tells Arjuna that it is impossible to be inactive in this world since some sort of actions are required to exist, that is, it is part of nature (*prakriti*) to act in the world. Work, in other words, cannot be avoided since the world is sustained by work. To avoid or attempt to alter this fact of existence is misguided: "avoid . . . attachment to inaction," counsels Krishna.[25]

Krishna then tells Arjuna that it is not enough to detach oneself from the fruit of one's actions or to avoid work, including one's moral obligations emanating from one's station in life, in one's wishes to break the karmic cycle and obtain happiness. Rather, what is required is that actions must be performed with an attitude of reverence, with loving attention to God. In other words, Krishna is saying that doing one's work in the right spirit, as sacrifice, as selfless service, is the best path to free oneself from karma, the chains of cause and effect in morality, and enjoy this world as well as the next.

Arjuna then asks Krishna a key question. He wants to know what enslaves us to the fruits of our actions. In other words, he wants to know why it is so hard to give up one's egoism, the knot of one's enslavement, especially since such egoism feels quite natural to Arjuna and, for that matter, to most of us. The main reasons, according to the *Gita*, why abandoning the fruits of one's action is so difficult is that one does not know how one is affected by one's lower nature. This nature is called the *gunas*, a term from Sankhya philosophy, one of the six classical orthodox schools of Indian philosophy circulating at the time the *Gita* was written.

Briefly, according to Schuhmacher and Woerner, a guna is one of the three fundamental qualities of phenomenal reality.[26] All things in the manifest world are made up of *sattva*, *rajas*, and *tamas*. In the context of the physical world, sattva manifests what is pure and subtle (e.g., sunshine), rajas manifests as activity (e.g., a tornado), and tamas manifests as heaviness and immobility (e.g., a block of stone). In terms of human consciousness, sattva is potential consciousness and is manifested as peace and serenity; rajas is the foundation of activity and is manifested as passion and restlessness; it can be bad (e.g., anger, hatred, or greed) or good (e.g., the motivation to act). Tamas, the foundation of resistance to activity, is manifested as laziness, lack of interest, insensitivity, and stupidity. According to Sankhya, a person's personality and mood are motivated at any given time by the governing gunas, though gunas constantly change their configuration and intensity. The goal for the spiritual seeker is to conquer tamas with rajas and rajas with sattva. This can best be accomplished through a form of understanding rooted in jnana, meaning intellectual analysis and philosophical reflection. The ultimate goal of jnana in this context is the transcendence of the gunas, of nature (prakriti) altogether. This includes the emotions and thoughts that feel so personal, so much of what we take to be who we are, for they, too, are transient manifestations of the gunas. Rather we must identify with the foundation of being, the Self (atman), which is at one with Brahman (the impersonal Godhead), and from here, we must engage in loving service to Bhagavan (the personal godhead), which is the ultimate goal.

In order, then, to give up one's egoism and attachment to the fruits of one's actions, one must embrace an attitude of loving devotion to God (bhakti). Work must be carried out in the spirit of sacrifice, as a way to achieve detachment. Otherwise, one is vulnerable to the disruptions of irrational passion and restlessness (rajas) or the quicksand of laziness, lack of interest, and stupidity (tamas). Elsewhere, the *Gita* speaks of other psychological forces that keep one tied to the fruits of one's action and away from harnessing oneself to atman and Brahman. "The three gates of hell," Krishna tells Arjuna, are the sources of the worst in humanity, for they destroy the Self. Selfish desire, anger, and greed must be given up.[27]

In modern psychological terms, what the *Gita* is putting forth is something like this: the best type of attitude toward work, and generally toward one's actions in the world, is one that reduces one's self-referentiality and focus on obtaining narcissistic gratification and instead promotes self-transcendence. Such a view tends to go against the prevailing psychoanalytic view of what usually constitutes the healthy person and the "good life." That is, the *Gita* is suggesting that when one approaches a task and, for that matter, life in general, one needs to relinquish the wish—usually a demand—that things should go as one wants. As Smith further points out, for devout Hindus, this is because everything a person does that is motivated by personal gain adds another defensive layer to one's ego, thickening it, and thus insulating the person more from God. Conversely, every action that is done without thought of personal gain reduces one's egoism, narcissism, and selfish desire until, finally, according to the Hindus, no obstacle remains to prevent a deep connection and identification with God.[28]

Put in less religious language, the *Gita* is saying that when actions are performed with the spirit of dedication and reverence, as opposed to that of personal gain (the fruits), they are performed in a manner that frees the self rather than burdening it. By reducing one's self-involvement in one's action, especially one's attachment to the fruits, one inevitably approaches what one is doing in a very different manner, altogether more serenely and sensibly than most analysands tend to do. Says Smith, by focusing completely and calmly on each task as it comes along, in the spirit of sacrifice and duty to either the transpersonal Absolute (the jnana mode) or personal God (the bhakti mode), there is less impatience, less need for mind-boggling excitement and constant activity, such as doing or thinking five things at once, as is typical of people in our society. Karma yogis, who are strongly identified with Brahman, tend to experience calmness even during intense activity. They are "like the center of a rapidly spinning wheel, . . . emotionally still. . . . [They possess] the stillness of absolute motion."[29] Moreover, the lack of motivation, or laziness, that is so common these days (another form of selfishness) is also diminished since one experiences one's work as a form of sacrifice to God and/or an expression of His will. The *Gita* thus greatly values the devoted performance of righteous work, done in the spirit of sacrifice, as the ideal method to achieve union with

God. Finally, a karma yogi is also more likely to deal better with the frustration, pain, shame, and loss that are part of our lives.[30] This is in part because with the finite ego and one's narcissism greatly diminished and with one's work yoked to God, one sees the value and meaning of everything relative to the supreme value of reality itself.

THE DISCIPLINE OF BHAKTI

It is in the final chapters of the *Gita* that Krishna teaches Arjuna the third yoga that leads to God realization, that of bhakti, perhaps the most important of all the yogas. Krishna recognizes that Arjuna is a man of action and that the highly intellectual and philosophical path of jnana yoga (knowledge) does not come easily to him, nor to most people. Jnana yoga, according to Hindu thought, is the most difficult path to God for it is the most abstract (God is conceived as a formless, transpersonal Godhead) and the most spiritual, and it requires the rare combination of a high degree of rationality and intense discipline and personal devotion. In contrast, bhakti yoga is the path of love and surrender to a God with attributes, which, ideally, leads to union with Him in divine service. It is regarded as the most straightforward and direct path to God. The idea put forth is one that is operative in all the major religions discussed in this book, namely, that love—dedicating your actions in the spirit of devotion to God—is the strongest motivation in the life of the spiritual aspirant.

Krishna thus teaches Arjuna the difference between God known as a transpersonal supreme reality and God known in a personal form with attributes such as omnipotence, omniscience, compassion, and wisdom. Krishna is himself a personal form of God, an *avatara* ("descent"), an incarnation of divine consciousness that descends into the world of human experience when dharma declines and *adharma* increases (adharma is the opposite of dharma, including ignorance and greed, etc.). The avatara descends in order to establish new paths for God realization and righteousness and to contour these paths to the particular era. This concept of avatara represents one of the earliest expressions of divine descent in religious literature.[31]

It should be remembered that when we first meet Arjuna he is a warrior leader with a practical crisis to attend to and he has little interest in wisdom seeking or mystical knowledge (jnana). Gradually, however, Krishna has facilitated his self-development and transformation such that he begins to grasp the real purpose and meaning of his life, namely, "to know who he is and to know also who Krishna is."[32] Arjuna then asks Krishna to reveal to him his ultimate power and fantastic form. He now wants to deeply know Krishna, and in particular to know which form of Krishna he might meditate on. This is a key moment in the *Gita*, for it is a sign of Arjuna's inner transformation, as he had never before spoken of embracing the reflective and meditative life. In the magnificent Chapter 11, Arjuna gets what he wants, a divine vision of Krishna in his totality as Vishnu, or God Almighty Himself. This vision is both radiant and terrifying, so much so that after a short while, Arjuna pleads with Krishna to return to his previous, friendly human form, which Krishna does. This "human form," according to the *Gita*, is Krishna's original and most confidential form and the source of the fantastic form he shows Arjuna.

What the *Gita* is saying to the Hindu believer seems to be this: worshipping God at a distance through psalms, hymns, and rituals offered in a mechanical manner will not bring one the liberating closeness to God, with the accompanying sense of infinite being, knowledge, and bliss that the believer desires. Rather, such peace of mind and happiness emanate from a deep and emotionally strong participation in the Eternal God. That is, only a constant consciousness and love of God, as expressed in virtuous actions, will facilitate His grace. In this context, grace is equated with a person's soul quickly becoming righteous and dwelling with God in eternal rest.[33] Moreover, the gracious God of the *Gita* is willing to forgive the repentant sinner and, perhaps most important, God's grace is viewed as the reward for the love of humanity. Psychologically, grace is experienced as a high degree of serenity and contentment. Put differently, bhakti, if practiced well, is capable of annulling karma, including its punishments. Unlike jnana yoga, which is geared more for intellectuals, it is available to all people, regardless of their stage or station in life.[34]

This last point is important, for bhakti yoga works against the caste system, even though some scholars believe that the *Gita* is a defense of the whole brahmanic social system.[35] That is, bhakti yoga is closely related to karma yoga and the renunciation of the fruits or results of one's actions. It is thus more in sync with the needs of the lower classes, the workers and servants and householders, in that the life of the renunciant ascetic who has withdrawn from the world is an unlikely realization for the average person. Through renunciation of the fruits of one's actions to God and offering all actions as sacrifices to Him, bhakti was accessible to the dharma of all classes and all stages of life.[36] Moreover, it did not matter what was sacrificed to God, what mattered was that it was done with the right attitude, performed in self-surrender, and without selfishness or attachment to the fruits. Says Krishna to Arjuna, "The leaf or flower or fruit or water that he offers with devotion, I take from the man of self-restraint in response to his devotion."[37]

In the concluding chapter, after Krishna has magnificently revealed himself in his totality as God Himself and Arjuna has progressively undergone deep inner transformation, it becomes crystal clear to Arjuna that only through love and consecrating one's actions to God can he attain the peace he longs for, the "infinite spirit," as Krishna describes it. At this point there is no need for dharmas, only selfless surrender to the compassionate God. Says Krishna, "Keep your mind on me, be my devotee, sacrificing, bow to me—you will come to me, I promise, for you are dear to me."[38]

In the end of the story, then, Krishna is reiterating to Arjuna that he deeply cares about him and reassuring him that he will be able to navigate himself through his practical crisis and in life in general, but only if he stays lovingly devoted in action and spirit to God. Says Arjuna a few verses later (now both more decisive and at peace with himself), "my delusion is destroyed, and by your grace I have regained my memory; I stand here, my doubt dispelled, ready to act on your words."[39]

A "SPIRITUALIZED" PSYCHOANALYSIS?

I have suggested that a serious engagement with the *Gita*, and Hinduism in general, can enhance psychoanalytic theory and practice in a number of ways. For example, the *Gita* and other Hindu teachings provide interesting and helpful ideas on different states of consciousness, peak experiences, self-control, consequential thinking, developmental levels, and, of course, relaxation techniques. These intriguing observations and formulations about consciousness, identity, and motivation are, to some extent, in sync with Western psychology. Indeed, the similarities, differences, and integration of Hinduism with Western psychology and psychoanalysis is a field of study that deserves more scholarly and clinical attention.[40]

As interesting and helpful as this discussion may be, it is not what is most compelling about the *Gita*, especially as it pertains to enhancing mainstream psychoanalysis. Rather, the *Gita* offers a strikingly different version of the human condition, one that mainstream psychoanalysis has hardly thought about, let alone integrated into itself. This version of the human condition points to a mode of being that Freud's "guilty man," Heinz Kohut's "tragic man," and Kleinian, relational, and Lacanian versions of the human condition tend to overlook, if not neglect, in their narratives.[41]

What the *Gita* puts forth is a much more sublime version of the human condition than does psychoanalysis, one that is deeply spiritual in nature in that it aims at transforming a person's entire "life into an act of creation."[42] That is, the *Gita*'s central teaching seems to be that doing one's work—living one's life with the right attitude, in the spirit of giving and sacrifice—requires an integrated discipline of knowledge, action, and, most important, loving self-surrender and attention to God. Such a discipline, or yoga, not only allows one to act in the world with less anxiety for the fruits, less frustration, and less worry for personal gain and safety, but it is also a spiritual pathway that brings one nearer to God. Such nearness to God tends to foster a life of greater serenity, contemplation, freedom, and contentment, the same goals that psychoanalytic treatment strives for. Moreover, teaches the *Gita*, the love and adoration of God is not simply an opportune tool disposable at the dawn of knowledge; rather, it is the very foundation of such knowledge, which, without it, is fundamentally flawed and incomplete.[43] This central teaching of the *Gita* is entirely compatible with the main teachings of other great world religions discussed in this book, in which it is believed that God has revealed Himself. It is in part for this reason that Hinduism has, at least in principle, tended to be tolerant of other religious pathways toward God. Says the *Rig Veda*, "Truth is one, but the wise speak of it in many ways."

I am aware that my summary of the *Gita*'s central teaching sounds extremely religious in tone and that such language may not resonate with the typical secular analyst or analysand. However, what the *Gita* is saying can be cast in less religious language, though not entirely so, since we are trying to describe an order of being that is beyond our familiar Western psychological categories and ordinary descriptions of consciousness.

The *Gita* is attempting to reveal universal psychological truths, what the believer would call timeless spiritual truths, which attempt to engage the ultimate, including the same ultimate questions of existence that psychoanalysis tends to grapple with. The *Gita* suggests that what people really want (their deepest motivation in life) is to experience within themselves the love and joy of the Infinite, that is, a sense of infinite being, knowledge, and bliss.

Psychoanalysis could benefit, I think, by reflecting on this notion, which the *Gita* assumes is a crucial fact of existence: the finite in humanity longs for the Infinite and we need and want to develop linkages between our limiting finite self and the transcendent reality beyond it, whether that central reality of the universe be called atman/Brahman, God, the Other, or for that matter, anything else that connotes self-transcendence, including perhaps the Unconscious. What I am suggesting is that psychoanalysis seriously consider the idea that there seems to be more to the human condition than is implied in the conventional goals of psychoanalytic treatment, conflict resolution, deficit repair, and the like. Rather, in addition to these praiseworthy goals, psychoanalysis should also consider the *Gita*'s claim that fundamentally, the mind has a spiritual cast. Indeed, the *Gita* and other Hindu teachings provide a spiritual cartography to this realm of being, which psychoanalysis can employ.

That is, the *Gita*'s spiritual cartography points to the need for psychoanalysis to enlarge its conception of human experience and what it is possible for psychoanalytic treatment to achieve. In particular, the *Gita* advocates cultivating a deep capacity for mystical participation in the world. For most psychoanalysts, the notion of mysticism conjures up images of infantile regression, apocalyptic thinking, neurosis, and even psychosis. But what the *Gita* is pointing to moves in an entirely different direction, insinuating a mode of being that I think is a highly desirable state of mind to cultivate for the average analysand, at least to some extent.

Briefly, a mystical participation in the world has what can be described as both an inward and an outward aspect. It is inward looking in that it moves consciousness away from the material world and strives toward a union with the transcendent central reality of the universe, which is often referred to by the spiritual aspirant as the Infinite, Divine, or God, though it can be called by other, less religious names. In its outward aspect, the spiritual aspirant senses a unity with the universe and with all there is; that is, the transcendent central reality is experienced as everywhere. This superconsciousness, or what Hindus and Buddhists call an enlightened state of being, is known internally in part when the person becomes aware of his or her identity with the central reality of the universe and discerns the illusory character of the world of space and time. Moreover, he or she experiences this state more as a gift (e.g., from the gracious God) than an acquisition. Externally, such an enlightened person's actions in the world reveal the Infinite, Divine, or God that resides in us. That is, the aspirant imitates God's most essential qualities by being compassionate, loving, gracious, and long-suffering, which is the ethical/moral ideal of Hinduism and all major religions. Such enlightenment reflects what analysts might describe as the highest degree of character development, personality integration, and selfhood.

Thus, according to the *Gita*'s spiritual cartography, the overarching psychoanalytic goal of treatment (as Freud said), self-knowledge in the service of developing the deep capacity for love and work, is best rooted in communion with the Infinite, that ineffable union with what mystics and poets have described as the "infinite sea of being underlying the waves of our finite selves."[44]

NOTES

1. Quoted from A. C. Bhaktivedanta Swami Prabhupada's translation of the *Bhagavad Gita*, reprinted as *Bhagavad Gita As It Is* (New York: Macmillan, 1972), p. 313.

2. Eknath Easwaran, *The Bhagavad Gita* (Tomales, Calif.: Nilgiri Press, 1985), p. 6. There are hundreds of translations (with and without commentaries) of the *Gita*. I have quoted from Barbara Stoler Miller's translation (New York: Bantam Books, 1986) throughout the rest of this chapter.

3. Mohandas K. Gandhi, *The Bhagavad Gita According to Gandhi* (Berkeley, Calif.: Berkeley Hills Books, 2000), pp. 50, 235.

4. Sri Aurobindo, *Bhagavad Gita and Its Message* (Twin Lakes, Wisc.: Lotus Light Publications, 1995), p. 12.

5. Diana Eck, *Great World Religions: Beliefs, Practices and Histories. Part V: Hindu, Buddhist, Muslim, Sikh: The Religions of India* (Chantilly, Va.: Teaching Company, 1998), p. 22.

6. Ibid., p. 37. Some scholars have claimed that *moksha* is not the ultimate goal of the spiritual aspirant, and that *bhakti* (devotion and loving surrender to God) is a higher form of spiritual development. As David Haberman points out, there are revered Hindu texts that demonstrate a conscious resistance to the experience of *moksha*, conceptualized as final absorption. As the theoreticians of *bhakti* assert, "we don't want to become sugar, we want to taste sugar." The *Gita* endorses this viewpoint. See David Haberman, "Enough Moksha! Constructions of Middle Class Hinduism," unpublished manuscript, p. 10.

7. As Dipankar Chatterjee points out, in the Hindu tradition there are two major streams of thought, one theistic (e.g., the *Gita*) and the other monistic (e.g., the *Upanishads*). In the former, God is viewed as a supreme being, to yoke oneself to through loving devotion, service to others, and rituals. In the monistic tradition, there is no God as such, that is, there is no attempt to characterize God as a supreme being with perfect attributes. Rather, it is the mystical quest for the undifferentiated One (what I have called "the eternal, inextinguishable Absolute"), the supreme reality (which is beyond name and form) that is the goal of the spiritual aspirant. Any efforts to identify the undifferentiated One with a God with attributes only serve to impose a limitation on the undifferentiated One. See Dipankar Chatterjee, "*Bhagavad Gita*," in *Philosophers and Their Works*, ed. John K. Roth (Pasadena, Calif.: Salem Press, 2000), 1: 257). While the *Gita* is mainly a theistic text, it also contains numerous passages that draw from the monistic tradition. Although I am mindful of these two different traditions as they are expressed in the *Gita*, for the purpose of this volume I view joining with the eternal, inextinguishable Absolute or with God as roughly equivalent psychological experiences.

8. Eliot Deutsch and Lee Siegel, "Bhagavadgita," in *The Encyclopedia of Religion*, ed. Mircea Eliade (New York: Macmillan Publishing Company, 1987), p. 126.

9. Easwaran, *Bhagavad Gita*, p. 6; Miller, *Bhagavad Gita*, p. 66.

10. Huston Smith, *The World's Religions* (New York: Harper San Francisco, 1991), p. 21.

11. John Renard, *Responses to 101 Questions on Hinduism* (Mahwah, N.J.: Paulist Press, 1999), pp. 159, 107. One of the major differences between Hinduism and Buddhism is that in the latter, the atman is denied. Buddhism rejects Hinduism's substantialist view of the self or anything that is named as an independent, imperishable essence. Moreover, for Buddhists, it is the letting go of the illusory belief in a substantial, abiding selfhood that in part constitutes *moksha* (liberation).

12. Thomas J. Hopkins, *The Hindu Religious Tradition* (Belmont, Calif.: Wadsworth Publishing Company, 1971), p. 90.

13. For example, I have argued that it was those concentration camp inmates with strong and consistent transcendent religious or political values and beliefs

(e.g., Jehovah's Witnesses, devout Christians, Orthodox Jews, staunch Communists) who were most able to maintain their autonomy, integration, and humanity amid the Nazi assault. See my *Autonomy in the Extreme Situation: Bruno Bettelheim, the Nazi Concentration Camps and the Mass Society* (Westport, Conn.: Praeger, 1999), especially pp. 87–116.

14. Deutsch and Siegel, "Bhagavadgita," p. 126.
15. Smith, *The World's Religions*, pp. 29–31.
16. Miller, *Bhagavad Gita*, p. 65.
17. Sharon Salzberg and Joseph Goldstein, "Equanimity," in *Insight Meditation: Correspondence Course Workbook* (Boulder, Colo.: Sounds True, 1996), pp. 59–63.
18. Smith, *The World's Religions*, pp. 42–44. I will discuss the usefulness of Vipassana (insight) meditation in the psychoanalytic context in greater detail in my chapter on Buddhism.
19. Easwaran, *Bhagavad Gita*, p. 101.
20. Miller, *Bhagavad Gita*, p. 8.
21. Ibid., p. 36.
22. Easwaran, *Bhagavad Gita*, p. 72.
23. Chatterjee, "*Bhagavad Gita*," p. 258.
24. Gandhi, *Bhagavad Gita*, p. 48. I will later comment on the *Gita*'s notion of grace.
25. Miller, *Bhagarad Gita*, p. 36.
26. Stephan Schuhmacher and Gert Woerner, eds., "Guna," in *The Encyclopedia of Eastern Philosophy and Religion* (Boston: Shambhala, 1994), p. 121.
27. Miller, *Bhagavad Gita*, p. 135.
28. Smith, *The World's Religions*, p. 38.
29. Ibid., p. 41.
30. Ibid., pp. 38–40.
31. Eck, *The Religions of India*, p. 23.
32. Easwaran, *Bhagavad Gita*, p. 147.
33. A. L. Basham, *The Origins and Development of Classical Hinduism*, ed. Kenneth G. Zysk (New York: Oxford University Press, 1989), p. 92.
34. In Hinduism there is a caste system under which each caste has its own legal and ethical implications. The social class system is made up of four major groups: the educated class of priests, philosophers, intellectuals, and religious leaders; the warrior group, made up of politicians, generals, officers, and civil authorities; the merchants and farmers; and the workers and servants. The untouchables are without caste or birth status; they are lowest level of Hindu society. Arjuna was from the warrior caste and therefore his duty—his dharma—was to fight. In seeming support of the caste system, the *Gita* says: "Your own duty done imperfectly is better than another man's done well. It is better to die in one's duty; another man's duty is perilous." See Miller, *Bhagavad Gita*, p. 46.

The stages of life are as follows: the student, who obtains worldly instruction from his parents and teachers so as to foster the mental skills and virtuous actions that lead to a high-level spiritual life; the householder, who is married and has a family so as to enlarge his or her consciousness and learn self-mastery and self-control; the forest dweller, who has met his or her obligations as a householder and has served the community and so withdraws into the forest so as to devote him- or herself completely to the study of philosophy, religious texts, and the intense practice of meditation; and the renunciant, a homeless mendicant who has given up the world and lives completely without possessions and solely committed to the realization of liberation. See Schuhmacher and Woerner, *The Encyclopedia of Eastern Philosophy and Religion*, pp. 43, 121, 400, 304.

35. A. L. Basham, *Origins and Development of Classical Hinduism*, p. 94.
36. Hopkins, *The Hindu Religious Tradition*, pp. 94–95.
37. Miller, *Bhagavad Gita*, p. 86.
38. Ibid., 152.
39. Ibid., p. 153.
40. J. David Keinzie, "The Historical Relationship between Psychiatry and the Major Religions," in *Psychiatry and Religion: The Convergence of Mind and Spirit*, edited by James K. Boehnlein (Washington: American Psychiatric Press, 2000), p. 6. Also see *Vishnu on Freud's Desk: A Reader in Psychoanalysis and Hinduism*, edited by T. G. Vaidyanathan and Jefferey J. Kripal (New York: Oxford University Press, 1999).
41. Paul Marcus and Alan Rosenberg, eds., *Psychoanalytic Versions of the Human Condition: Philosophies of Life and Their Impact on Practice* (New York: New York University Press, 1998).
42. Juan Mascaró, translator, *Bhagavad Gita* (London: Penguin Books, pp. xxxiii, xxix).
43. Chatterjee, *Bhagavad Gita*, pp. 259, 260.
44. Smith, *The World's Religions*, p. 33.

3

Buddhism: Buddha

> What are you? [they asked the Buddha]. What order of being do you belong to? What species do you represent? ... Are you a god? 'No.' An angel? 'No.' A Saint? 'No.' Then what are you? Buddha answered, 'I am awake.'
>
> Buddha[1]

Compared to the other wise moralists discussed in this book, Buddha's teachings have by far been most appropriated by psychoanalysis, though like the work of all religious thinkers, appropriated only by the fringe groups of psychoanalytic discourse and practice. Presently, however, a few thoughtful books have been published by authors conversant both in psychoanalysis and in Buddhist meditation, who attempt to compare, contrast, and integrate these two traditions.[2]

At first glance, psychoanalysis and Buddhism appear to describe very different versions of the human condition, with distinct core values and practices for achieving the ideal mode of being (the "good life") and divergent techniques for self-transformation. Nonetheless, both psychoanalysis and Buddhism focus on what seems to be an intractable problem of human existence: how to achieve freedom from personal suffering and instead develop increasing tranquillity of mind.

This chapter attempts to suggest how psychoanalytic theory and practice, conceived both as a compelling life- and identity-defining narrative of the human condition and as a technology for self-transformation, self-mastery, and self-improvement, may be enhanced by intellectually engaging Buddha's teachings.[3] I hope to acquaint both the psychoanalyst and the general reader with some of Buddha's provocative and penetrating insights into the dynamics of human desire, personal suffering, and the cultivation of tranquillity, particularly as these insights may help analysands in achieving greater autonomy, an increased capacity for love and work, and optimism and peace of mind. As both Buddha and Freud taught, ambitious goals are only achieved through a painstakingly slow and decisive redefinition and reconfiguration of subjectivity. In particular, it is in part through the modulation, if not conquering, of inordinate and unrealistic cravings for self-glorification, self-affirmation, and omnipotence (among other unreasonable narcissistic wishes) that individuals are most likely to acquire a modicum of happiness.[4]

In the first part of this chapter I will review some basic Buddhist psychological and spiritual concepts, suggesting benefits to analysands of appropriating into their own lives aspects of a Buddhist-like mode of being in the world. Moreover, individuals whose lives are animated by the spirit of Buddhism tend to engage the external world, including its harsh, adverse, and assaultive aspects, with a set of values, beliefs, and, perhaps most important, a sensibility that can be of some help to analysands who want to live a more reasonable, effective, tranquil, and decent life. In the second part of this chapter I will discuss how this Buddhist-like mode of being, or sensibility, can enrich psychoanalytic theory and technique so as to make it a more powerful and relevant narrative of the human condition, a technology for coping with neurotic anxiety, depression, and physical pain, and a discipline for achieving greater self-mastery.

BUDDHA'S VIEW OF THE HUMAN CONDITION

Gautama Siddhartha Buddha (560–477 B.C.E.) was born in South Nepal, India, in the foothills of the eastern Himalayas. As a son of the chieftain of the Shakya clan, he lived a privileged and sheltered life of pleasure. Tradition has it that at age twenty-nine, Gautama made a great renunciation of his luxurious life after the birth of his son. Leaving his family behind, for six years he unsuccessfully strove for enlightenment through extreme asceticism. Finally persuaded that enlightenment was not to be achieved in that way, he returned to the life of a pauper living on charity. It was in this phase of his life, while sitting in a meditation posture under a bo tree, facing east, and determined not to move until he had accomplished his radically transformational goal, that he became Buddha, "The Enlightened One." According to tradition, after his full enlightenment that night, Buddha remained under the tree another forty-nine days, crystallizing and refining his path-breaking insights. He then went off and began to teach, doing so until he died.

Buddha, like Freud, believed that life inevitably involves much suffering. Moreover, he believed that the task of maintaining one's autonomy, individuality, and dignity in the face of suffering is extremely difficult. Though Buddha believed that living is intrinsically painful, his inquisitive mind was nonetheless preoccupied with this most central question of human experience: Why does the human condition seem to involve so much suffering?

Buddha's answer was both simple and profound. He claimed that we suffer because of the transience, the impermanence, of human existence. As Ecclesiastes and Heraclitus, among other ancient thinkers, also emphasized, change is a fundamental characteristic of every substance: all things are in flux. Suffering, says Buddha, is ultimately caused by our misguided attitude toward our desires and cravings, since what we desire is, by its nature, impermanent, changing, and destined to fade away. Such common and obsessive human desires and cravings as sensual pleasure, fame, wealth, power, and longevity are caused by ignorance of our "true" nature and of the universe in which we reside. According to Buddha, freedom from our ignorance, that is, enlightenment, is achieved by following the moral and psychospiritual principles as described in the "Eightfold Path" to achieve nirvana. In other words, enlightenment, the ideal state of freedom and peace, or nirvana ("cessation" of selfish desires and ignorance) can be achieved through the wisdom that comes from deep and brutally honest self-scrutiny and disciplined meditation on the transitoriness of life.[5]

Enlightenment (*bodhi* in Sanskrit, meaning "awakened") is a complex, multiphasic, and powerful central idea in Buddhist thought, which deserves clarification. As I understand it, the heart of this deeply paradoxical concept is that an individual awakens to something like a felt presence of emptiness, a profound conviction that the true nature of all things, including human existence, is impermanent and devoid of an essence. This sense of emptiness is not a nihilistic experience: it is an intuitively apprehended transformational, life-affirming realization, one that scholars and Buddhists claim is very difficult, if not impossible, to describe accurately. It is "unperceivable, unthinkable, unfeelable, and endless beyond existence and nonexistence. . . . [E]mptiness is no object that could be experienced by a subject, since the subject itself is dissolved in the emptiness." Enlightenment, in other words, is a transmuting psychospiritual experience in which the individual realizes that emptiness and all phenomena, both absolute and relative, are completely one (i.e., awakens to the emptiness of dualistic thinking). This experience of "true" reality is, in fact, the experience of oneness.[6] Hence, enlightenment has been defined in the Zen tradition as "intimacy with all things," and in the Tibetan tradition, as "no unconsciousness."[7] Put in modern psychological terms, one might say that in a state of enlightenment, conventional distinctions between the perceiver, perceiving, and perceived vanish. The dualism of subject and object is resolved by admitting the reality of consciousness only. Moreover, in the most profound and complete form of enlightenment, the ego, self, or "I" (they are roughly synonymous terms in Buddhist psychology) is said to perish.

The ego perishes! For most Western trained psychoanalysts, this disruptive and counterintuitive notion is difficult to appreciate. Conversely, the doctrine of nonself is common to almost all forms of Buddhist thought,[8] though Buddha had ambiguous and, I think, also ambivalent, views about the self. For example, Nakamura has stressed that Buddha never offered a definitive answer to the question of whether a self exists. While he delineated what the self is not, Buddha did not give any clear and detailed description of what it is. Buddha, continues Nakamura, also did not categorically deny the soul. Perhaps most important to the psychoanalyst, though Buddha did not presuppose the existence of souls as metaphysical substances, he did affirm the existence of the self as the agent of action in practical and moral contexts. Buddha "seems to have acknowledged that the true self in one's existence will appear in our moral conduct conforming to universal norms."[9] Thus, the nonself notion is best viewed as a heuristic device meant to help develop a desirable mode of being, a practical, moral, spiritual, and psychological ideal, rather than a philosophical dogma concretely and literally interpreted (though it is frequently taken that way by Buddhist and non-Buddhist alike).

As I have suggested, this disruptive nonself doctrine assumes that the concept of ego, self, or "I," which is the main cause of all inordinate, unrealistic and unreasonable desires and cravings, must be eradicated. In other words, as in the Lacanian version of psychoanalysis, the ego is seen as composed of erroneous factors, as a delusion. To a Buddhist, the concept of ego emerges when the intellect assumes a dualism between I and not-I. As a consequence, we think and act as though we were entities distinct and disconnected from everything else, over and against a world that exists outside of us. As this notion of "I" becomes solidified as our personal identity, as it becomes the controlling narrative of our self-identity, it tends to generate such powerful wishes and discriminations as "I want this," "I love that," "I hate this," "This is mine, not yours." Once the mind is under the domination of an ego that is driven in this way, hatred, envy, selfish desire, and alienation, ending in suffering, are the inevitable consequences.[10]

Thus, for a Buddhist, the nonself doctrine does not literally mean that one needs to destroy the ego, self, or "I," as we tend to use the term in practical, everyday psychological and social contexts. Almost all Buddhists tend to "accept the 'relative,' 'conventional,' or 'common sense' experience of self."[11] Rather, as Epstein has noted, the aim is, not to dissipate the sense of I, which remains an essential and beneficial concept, "but to identify the self-representation as agent as a *representation*; as an image or simulacrum devoid of *inherent* existence." The idea is to experience the self as it truly is "phenomenologically and representationally, rather than as a fixed entity"; to deconstruct how "the self-concept has been fashioned out of internalized images of self and other";[12] and to analyze how it has been socially conditioned and "disciplined," as Michel Foucault says, by constraining normative and conventional values. By viewing the self as a metaphor, construct, or function rather than as a concrete, separate, or permanent thing, we undermine the self-destructive narcissism of our ego, with its restrictive, defensive, and often painful habitual modes of feeling, thinking, and acting.[13] Moreover, by giving up the notion of a fixed self, we are forced to face up to the insecurities and uncertainties that cause us to generate and cling to this notion in the first place, which impair our ability to experience ourselves more honestly and authentically.[14]

THE FOUR NOBLE TRUTHS

The first of the Four Noble Truths is that suffering is endemic to human existence, that is, the world in which we reside is characterized by suffering. Actually, the Pali word *dukkha*, which is usually translated as "suffering," has more subtle connotations. As Smith points out, the word was originally used "to refer to wheels whose axles were off-center, or bones that had slipped from their sockets (a modern metaphor might be a shopping cart we try to steer from the wrong end)," implying that life is essentially dislocated, out of joint; something has gone wrong, and it is painful.[15]

That existence is characterized by suffering is obvious. The world is marked by hunger, natural disasters, illness, violence, war, loss, and disorganizing change. Our experience tells us that our body will grow old, become sick, and perish. Moreover, greed, hatred, and delusion also seem to be intrinsic aspects of reality. Finally, as Freud noted, despite one's best intentions, it seems impossible to avoid contributing in some way to one's own suffering. Buddha also recognized that at times, perhaps due to a character flaw, for example, we are often bound to do precisely what we do not like, even if, in the long run, it is bad for us.[16]

That living is inherently painful, if not fundamentally characterized by suffering, is axiomatic for all Freudian devotees. One need only to think about Heinz Kohut's juxtaposition of Freud's picture of the "guilty man," with his own, that of the "tragic man": the guilty man struggles toward fulfillment of his drives. He lives under the sovereignty of the pleasure principle, endeavoring to reconcile intense inner conflict. However, he is often frustrated in his goal of tension reduction by his own deficits, or those of the people who raised him. Moreover, his life is lived under the shadow of his central anxiety, that of castration anxiety. The fate of the tragic man is only marginally more encouraging. He struggles toward fulfilling the aims of his nuclear self. He attempts to express the pattern of his very being, the ideals, ambitions, and self-expressive goals that transcend the pleasure principle. However, the frequent and inevitable failure to achieve empathy by the parents weakens the child's self and destines him to unhappiness. Moreover, says Kohut, it is the dread of complete disintegration that is the tragic man's central life anxiety.[17]

To Buddha, the origin of suffering, including neurotic suffering, the second of the Noble Truths, is craving the satisfaction of unreasonable desires. Buddhists call this clinging, grasping, or attachment, by which they mean clinging to modes of thinking, feeling, and acting that keep us attached to (in psychoanalytic terminology, obsessively identified with and bound to) unreasonable desires. In my understanding of this second Noble Truth, it is not the desires themselves that are necessarily the problem. For example, all individuals desire food, shelter, and some form of emotional connectedness to others. Moreover, clearly some desires, like the desire to help others or to understand Buddha's teachings, are admirable. Rather, it is one's attitude toward one's desires that is determinative, such as whether one insists on their perpetual gratification. By not accepting the natural flow of all things as arising, dwelling, changing, and passing away we become driven, frustrated, and bogged down by our insatiable desires. In classical Buddhism, these attachments or identifications to pleasures of the senses; to opinions, views, and theories; and to rites, rituals, ceremonies and tradition come at the expense of more spontaneous, open, and authentic spiritual experience. Most important, it is our attachment to our conviction that we exist as a solid permanent self, that is, that we are "tightly bound up and identified with our identity," or "the historical experience of our finite self," that causes our suffering.[18] In psychoanalytic terms, this is in part because such primitive narcissistic identifications tend to undermine ego functioning in that they pollute the very core, so to speak, of reason itself.

The third and fourth of Buddha's Noble Truths, the end of suffering and the path to the end of suffering, respectively, perhaps have the most relevance to psychoanalytic practice. According to Buddha—and herein lies Buddhist optimism—in this world, all individuals are capable of achieving nirvana, meaning the cessation of, and freedom from, suffering. In Buddhist teachings there are different levels, phases, and highly complex and, at times, contradictory formulations of nirvana. For example, Nagarjuna of the Middle Doctrine School of Mahayana Buddhism maintained that nirvana was itself an illusion![19] However, most of the traditions agree that nirvana is a state of illumination and liberation, characterized by a sense of oneness with the absolute, a transcending of all dualities (such as self and other), a reduced sense of individuality and separateness (in the positive sense of these terms), a feeling of serenity, increased clarity and knowledge about human existence, and a sense of emptiness (in the positive sense of that term). Nirvana liberates one from suffering, death, rebirth, karma (the universal moral law of cause and effect), and all worldly attachments and desires. It is the highest state of consciousness and requires the conquering of the three reality-distorting "poisons," which are destructive, narcissistically driven cravings: unreasonable desire, such as for sensual pleasure, power, or fame; hatred, including hatred rooted in envy; and delusions, for example, of being omnipotent.[20]

What is the path to ending one's suffering, to enlightenment and nirvana? It is not, as Ecclesiastes also says, making pleasures of the senses the central goal of one's life. While in the Buddhist worldview, disciplined and wholesome sensory pleasures have their role in life, when they are one's prime motivators and conscious goals, they are viewed as degrading and futile. This is in part because such self-indulgence is often rooted in idealization of the self. Nor are self-mortification and asceticism the path to ending one's suffering, as these are characterized by self-imposed suffering and regarded as lowly and ultimately pointless. For Buddhists, self-mortification is misguided in that it is rooted in unreasonable denial of appropriate and "natural" human desires. Buddha realized that, paradoxically, self-denial can be ego centered, often masking a wish for self-aggrandizement. Buddha, like the ancient Greeks, advocated avoiding all extremes and instead living according to the "Middle Way," an approach to life that is embodied in the Eightfold Path.

The Eightfold Path is the way to achieve nirvana. In psychoanalytic terms, we might loosely equate this path with a form of life characterized by elegantly crafted, finely tuned sublimations, a mode of being that is life affirming, has a for-the-Other focus rather than a for-oneself focus, and provides a modicum of personal happiness. A Buddhist is encouraged to cultivate "perfect" or "right" (1) knowledge or views, (2) outlook or thinking, (3) speech, (4) action, (5) livelihood or way of life, (6) effort or endeavor, (7) mindfulness, and (8) concentration or meditation. "Perfect" or "right" refers to action that causes no harm, penetrates through delusion (as Buddhists conceptualize reality), and demonstrates a harmonious and balanced way of working with each of these elements of the Eightfold Path.[21] In psychoanalytic terms, this is living a life that is governed by the conscious, reasoning mind rather than by the unconscious mind of a child or neurotic.[22] As Salzberg and Goldstein further describe it, right knowledge and outlook are the preliminary mind-set of the aspirant and lead to wisdom; right speech, action and livelihood foster ethical conduct; and right effort, mindfulness, and concentration characterize the psychological discipline necessary for sustained and regular formal meditation.[23] Meditation is one of the key psychospiritual practices to help achieve contemplative knowledge of the ultimate truth and the tranquillity that goes with it (enlightenment and nirvana). Theoretically and practically speaking, psychoanalysis does not have any concepts that are equivalent to enlightenment and nirvana; it lacks the necessary sophisticated psychology of transcendent states of consciousness.

As in Judaism, Christianity, and most other major humanistic religions, the most important and compelling ethical principle underlying Buddhist ethics is that all people should cultivate the passion of passions, a deep and broad attitude of unconditional compassion that is the underpinning of a for-the-Other mode of being. According to Buddha, if we cultivate such loving-kindness toward others and all living things, we are less likely to distort reality or to approach others through the artificial and delusional concepts of "self" and "other" (or "object," one of the more alienating psychoanalytic terms). Moreover, a person who has cultivated such an attitude of unconditional compassion toward others will be far less inclined to hurt him- or herself and will probably be more self-accepting than self-accusatory or self-punishing.

Thus, a Buddhist layperson should not kill, steal, lie, or engage in harsh speech, gossip or slander; he or she should refrain from unlawful sexual intercourse and from using sexuality in a manipulative or injurious manner; and he or she should not drink alcohol as it dulls the mind's ability to see reality clearly. Moreover, and most important, all personal relationships, and social life in general, should be animated by the values of kindness, charity, cooperation, and altruistic service to others. In psychoanalytic language, as Otto Kernberg has suggested, it is the transformation of one's infantile and often pathological narcissism into "normal" narcissism that is the psychoanalytic goal and, I would add, a goal that points to the Buddhist ideal (however, the Buddhist ideal strives for a "deeper" and "higher" level of self-transformation). Pathological narcissism is characterized by a person's infantile conception of, and demands upon, the self (e.g., self-inflation/grandiosity alternating with self-denigration/emptiness), excessive dependence on the affirmation of others, and inordinately self-referential, impoverished, and truncated relationships, especially with significant others. In contrast, normal narcissism is characterized by stable, realistic self-esteem and a benign, accepting self-concept, reasonable aspirations and ideals, and a robust capacity for sustained and deep relationships. The Dalai Lama, for example, seems to personify Heinz Kohut's ideal of the "mature" transformation of narcissism. He has wisdom, humor, creativity, and, perhaps most of all, a highly developed morality, which is rooted in a reverence for life and a Levinasian for-the-Other orientation.[24]

These, then, are a few of the fascinating basic ideas of Buddhist psychology and spirituality, though each of the Buddhist traditions has its own particular interpretation and development of Buddha's teachings. There is much that they disagree about. I hope I have given the reader an adequately complex sense of the Buddhist mode of being, thinking, feeling, and acting, which is different from our Western-inspired psychoanalytic mode. In the second part of this chapter, I want to connect this Buddhist mode of being and its unique sensibility with certain psychoanalytic ideas and practices. Before doing so, however, I want to describe briefly one of the core Buddhist psychospiritual practices that I alluded to earlier, which is the most relevant to psychoanalytic theory and clinical practice. This is meditation, a subject I will frequently refer to throughout the remainder of this chapter.

MEDITATION AS MINDFULNESS TRAINING

There are many different forms of Buddhist meditation, each with its own method and emphasis, which reflect their idiosyncratic historical trajectories.[25] The one I describe here is called Vipassana (clear seeing), or insight, meditation. The goal of insight meditation is the same as that of all meditation, namely, to bring the consciousness of the meditator to a state of enlightenment. This is a mode of being in which the distinction between subject and object, I and you, true and false vanishes; time and space are transcended; and the identity of life and death, the cycle of birth, death, and rebirth (samsara) and nirvana are experienced. The meditator thus becomes one with the absolute, which is experienced as tranquillity of the spirit or, as some Buddhists claim, as bliss. Enlightened individuals are noted for their kindness, gentleness, and wisdom.[26]

The basic instruction of insight meditation seems simple: to focus the mind with sustained attention upon an object, such as the breath, for an hour. In non-Buddhist, nonreligious terms,[27] the idea, according to Kabat-Zinn, is to condition the mind to observe what it is up to in the here and now on a moment to moment basis, but without becoming trapped in thoughts, emotions, or physical sensations.[28] The mental skill that is gradually developed is termed mindfulness, meaning moment to moment awareness of what one is experiencing.

The main point of mindfulness training is to learn how to more objectively observe one's thoughts and how to let go of them, regardless of how disturbing, pleasurable, or compelling they may seem. In other words, say Salzberg and Goldstein, by learning to view one's thoughts as largely insubstantial, ephemeral, impermanent, and transparent one is less inclined to become driven and overwhelmed by them.[29] In addition, says Kabat-Zinn, we learn to think differently, to make space for new ways of perceiving old problems and for viewing the interconnectedness of all things, and thus become deeply cognizant of everything being part of the natural life cycle of arising, dwelling, changing and passing away.

Through mindfulness training one also learns how to slow down the pace of one's life and cultivate tranquillity and self-acceptance, and thus to settle and relax into moments of being that foster greater awareness of our direct experience. Consequently, all forms of meditation are based on the ancient assumptions succinctly expressed in one of the most cherished of all Buddhist texts, the *Dhammapada*: "All we are is the result of what we have thought" and "all things can be mastered by mindfulness."[30] In other words, says Kabat-Zinn, mindfulness is essentially just a specific way of paying attention. It is a method "of looking deeply into oneself in the spirit of self-inquiry and self-understanding. . . . Mindfulness . . . is a powerful vehicle for . . . healing."[31] It is this central practice of the Buddhist mode of being that I now want to link to psychoanalysis.

FREEING ONESELF FROM NEUROTIC MISERY

Both Freudian psychoanalysis and Buddhist meditation are powerful psychotherapeutic techniques meant to increase one's happiness and peace of mind. They share many of the same goals, especially to open the unconscious mind and let its contents become conscious. However, they have at least one major difference: where the psychoanalyst aims to analyze and understand the content, story line, and meanings of the unconscious material, the meditator simply feels and observes the material without any judgment (e.g., pleasure/pain, good/bad, true/false, etc.) or interpretive effort (e.g., trying to understand what it means). In other words, the two systems advocate different approaches to investigating the emotions, thoughts, fantasies, and physical sensations, especially any painful and neurotic aspects, that come into consciousness during their respective practices. The important point is that both types of investigations are capable of fostering profound insights into one's life and into the dynamics of managing one's problems in living. Perhaps most important, these insights can contribute to the radical transformation of one's entire sensory, emotional, and cognitive experience, this being the ultimate ideal goal of both psychoanalysis and Buddhist meditation. In my view, though psychoanalytic and meditative approaches to existence and suffering are to some extent not translatable or even theoretically reconcilable (in part, because the same words and phrases in their disparate contexts have different meanings and uses), in certain important psychotherapeutic ways, these two approaches to dealing with neurotic misery are complementary.

NEUROTIC ANXIETY AND FEAR

Neurotic anxiety and neurotic fear are two of the most common problems for which analysands seek help. Mindfulness practice can have a beneficial effect on anxiety management in a way that is compatible with the psychoanalytic process. The basic idea is that by consciously observing anxious thoughts as they emerge in one's mind, using awareness, centeredness, and sustained attention, one will be better able to experience them as, simply, passing thoughts, as nothing substantial. By simply noting and observing one's anxious thoughts and by not reacting to them as one usually does (with judgmental awareness, self-accusation, or interpretations of their content), one may begin to view these disturbing thoughts in the same way one views all thoughts in formal meditation practice, as following the natural cycle of arising, dwelling, changing, and passing away. The goal is to develop the patience and self-discipline to observe them neutrally.[32]

Such an approach to one's anxious thoughts tends to reduce one's short- and long-term psychological and physical reactivity to them, giving one greater freedom to respond differently to the agitation of the internal world. One may then respond with greater perspective, less frightening automaticity, and with less tendency to equate oneself with one's thoughts (i.e., "thoughts exist without a thinker," says Wilfred Bion). Reducing one's narcissistic attachment to one's thoughts is what one seeks to achieve. Indeed, while researchers have reported that meditators were just as anxious as other people and had no diminution of internal conflict, they did have a "marked nondefensiveness in experiencing such conflicts," that is, they were more accepting of them.[33] Once there is a reduction of narcissistic involvement in one's thoughts and a degree of modulation and control of one's anxious and fearful reactions is established (which can be achieved mainly through sustained meditation practice), the analyst can more effectively interpret the unconscious wishes and conflicts that may be motivating a neurotic reaction, which can contribute to lasting improvement in the analysand's mode of being.

In other words, as a result of this meditation-inspired reduction of neurotic anxiety and fear, the analysand is more likely to be able to create, discover, and appropriate into real life the psychoanalytically conceptualized insights that can further direct his or her personality toward a life of "high-level" sublimation or, in Buddhist terms, a life on the way toward enlightenment. For instance, it is well known that neurotic anxiety and fear frequently mask unreasonable and strong narcissistic desires and wishes for omnipotent control, power, safety, and self-affirmation. Buddha was aware that beneath disturbing emotional states there usually were disavowed desires and aversions, though of course he did not talk about the disavowed material as it relates to neurotic anxiety and fear. As Rubin points out, Buddhism does not have a theory of child development, a developmental psychology, a developmental view of psychopathology, or a theory of self-pathology with structural deficits in the self.[34] In contrast, psychoanalysis provides a developmental context for understanding neurotic anxiety and fear and can provide a useful clarification of the personal, familial, historical, and contextual factors contributing to problems in living. Perhaps most important from a Buddhist perspective, psychoanalysis creates a powerful here and now context for the re-experiencing and working through of one's most primal anxieties and fears, that is, in the transference relationship with the analyst. In my view, the process of transference makes psychoanalysis incomparable in its ability to foster the conditions of possibility for the analysand to experience the present with mindfulness, with moment to moment awareness of his or her direct experience. This will lead to deeper understanding, which can be used as a basis to change behavior.

NEUROTIC DEPRESSION

Neurotic depression is a complex and ambiguous subject for which psychoanalysts have provided many helpful formulations and insights. Descriptively speaking, depression is manifested by feelings of sadness, hopelessness, helplessness, guilt, self-critical thoughts, and reduced interest in outside activities. Most important for this chapter, nearly all psychoanalytic theories of depression stress the collapse of self-esteem regulation as central to depression. It is a narcissistic vulnerability, often rooted in the person's early developmental history, that serves as the psychodynamic context for the adult propensity toward neurotic depression and other affective disorders.

The help that meditation practice has to offer to an analysand who suffers from neurotic depression is that it trains the person to respond differently to his or her feelings, thoughts, and physical sensations, mainly by attacking their narcissistic underpinning. All depressions are highly narcissistic, by definition, and meditation practice, says Goldstein,[35] targets the dislodging of our profoundly conditioned tendency to identify with the feelings, thoughts, and physical sensations that constitute our depression.[36] This is not easy to accomplish in formal meditation practice, let alone in the business of everyday life, in part because the feelings and thoughts that tend to promote the experience of depression are often vague. Meditation practice helps the analysand to make more precise delineations about what he or she is feeling and thinking in order to better recognize and understand his or her immediate experience. As a result of a more exacting rendering of what one is feeling, one is more likely to be able to accept one's feelings and thoughts as arising, dwelling, changing, and passing away. In other words, meditation practice facilitates the clearer identification and acceptance of one's depressing emotions, thoughts, and physical sensations, a power that frequently accelerates their disidentification and "passing away."

The other related contribution that mindfulness training can make to the psychoanalytic management of neurotic depression is in helping the analysand to make what Buddhists call a "wise discrimination" about how to respond to depressing emotions and thoughts. The depressed analysand learns from meditation practice that he or she can decide whether his or her state of mind is in the service of Eros or of Thanatos. If his or her state of mind is not life affirming (Eros), if instead it is judged as in the service of Thanatos (death), then the analysand has the inner freedom to relate to the state of mind with less identification, without the narcissistic loading that leads to clinging to one's depression and suffering. It is the difference between saying to oneself, "I am sad," and saying, instead, "This is sadness." Relating to one's depressing emotions and thoughts in the latter way, which is less personal, can give the needed freedom to change how one relates to one's experience and how one behaves. Such a practice of freedom, which is rooted in meditation practice and a Buddhist mode of being, increases one's ability to distinguish that which is transient (e.g., depressing thoughts) from what is eternal (e.g., nirvana); this constitutes discriminative wisdom.

PHYSICAL PAIN, ILLNESS, AND FACING DEATH

Acute and prolonged physical pain and illness are something that many analysands experience. Rather than be analytic, their tendency is to want to distract themselves from their experience and force the painful feelings to go away quickly. Mindfulness practice, says Kabat-

Zinn, is counterintuitive because it advocates the opposite strategy: it advocates "turning into" painful experience rather than away from it. For pain that is intense and prolonged, such an approach, continues Kabat-Zinn, has been experimentally shown to be a more effective way of diminishing the level of pain experienced than the attempt to distract oneself.[37] Turning in to the pain and illness is similar to what analysts advocate. Analysts recognize that when an analysand is in physical pain and/or ill, it often induces a psychic regression, and is therefore a potentially illuminating point of entry into the analysand's childhood experience, defensive structure, and ways of coping with stress and trauma. Moreover, analysts have almost always advocated facing up to one's psychic pain, regardless of its source, rather than running from it.

In a meditative approach to one's physical pain, the method is to observe and then let go of what one is feeling and thinking, to focus on the pain and, in effect, to accept its existence without distortion, distraction, or a wish to make it go away. Gradually, as one stays with the pain and distressing feelings, their intensity almost always dissipates, as one disidentifies with and somewhat impersonalizes one's experience. This ability to see oneself as separate from one's pain is rooted in the conviction that one is not a stable, permanent self, or "I," but rather a result of a fleeting association of aggregates. Thus, who one is in the moment goes beyond one's particular thoughts, feelings, and physical sensation.

In other words, the elusive goal is to subvert one's narcissistic attachment to one's pain-inspired self-representation. It is not "my pain" that I am feeling, it is "simply pain," an impersonal, transient cluster of sensations, feelings, and thoughts that can be managed through calm observation, not judgmental discrimination. In psychoanalytic terms we might say that it is the psychoanalytic exploration of one's pain and the attendant feeling states, thoughts, and fantasies that tends to foster the liberating, pain-reducing insight (an insight that Buddhists also strive for in their meditation practice) that there is a dimension of being that one can reside in where it is possible to transcend one's suffering. By denuding the experience of pain of its narcissistic identification, by not equating the experience with the sense of personal humiliation and degradation that people often experience because they feel their body is giving way or falling apart, one can reclaim the sense that one is still a dignified "whole" person (though a constantly changing one). Paradoxically, by losing our self—our narcissistic identification with our pain—we create a more dignified, stronger, and intact version of our self, which makes us better able to endure an ordeal.

How can a Buddhist meditational approach enhance an analysand's ability to come to terms with perhaps the central problem of life, the problem of death? Assuming, unlike a doctrinaire Buddhist, that one does not believe in reincarnation or another after-life notion, which may take some of the sting out of the idea of dying, a meditative approach to the fear of dying is recommended, as with any pain or problem. The key practice is to allow oneself to dwell mindfully on the fear of death, and by so doing, to attempt to internalize the insight that the fear of death is generated by a passing cluster of thoughts and feelings, though they are highly narcissistically invested ones. These troubling thoughts and feelings are rooted in one's refusal to accept the impermanence and insubstantiality of all things, including one's existence. As Salzberg and Goldstein point out, our existence, as known through a narrative of the "self" or "I," is not a stable, permanent thing, nor does it constitute the essence of who we are. Rather, what we take to be the self emanates from our identification with different aspects of the mind/body process.[38] Moreover, our death is a form of energy transformation, from which point of view all mental and physical states are a series of transitory states. The question for the Buddhist and for the analysand is thus the same: Will I approach my death with confusion, fear, and panic, or will I cross to the "other side"—or, as Buddhists say, move into the next part of the eternal flow of cycles—with clarity of mind, acceptance, and serenity?

ENLARGING PSYCHOANALYTIC VERSIONS OF SUBJECTIVITY IN LIGHT OF THE BUDDHA'S WISDOM

I have suggested that both the analysand and the analyst can benefit from intellectually engaging the teachings of Buddha and appropriating aspects of the Buddhist mode of being and sensibility into psychoanalytic theory and practice. I have also stressed that much in the Buddhist worldview, especially as embodied in Vipassana meditation, is compatible with the spirit of the psychoanalytic process and many of its therapeutic goals and life-affirming values.

In particular, I have indicated that the analysand or meditator can strengthen his or her self-observational, introspective and reflective capabilities, that is, his or her perceptual skills and "observing ego," as analysts call these psychological functions. In addition, an analysand can increase affect tolerance, which is the ability to feel, describe, and work with a wide range of emotions, with less defensiveness and reactivity and with increased openness and equanimity. This is most important when experiencing intense anxiety, depression, and physical pain. I have also emphasized that meditation teaches the analysand or meditator how not to assume an unreasonably self-judgmental, self-punitive, or severely self-critical stance. By learning to view oneself more reasonably and realistically, one tends to become more self-accepting, in both good and bad times. Furthermore, by learning to experience the present mindfully, one is less likely to become detached, alienated, or remote from oneself and from others.

This point is especially important for an analyst, who can become a more focused, less harshly judgmental, and more accurately empathic listener. In addition, by developing this capacity for sustained and calm attentiveness, what Bion called divesting oneself of "memory and desire," the analyst will avoid such defensive invasiveness as overtalking, overanalyzing, and being overly intolerant of silences. Psychoanalysts who meditate are less likely to be unreasonably narcissistically tied to their preferred theory, which will deepen their capacity to understand and work with what analysands tell them. Moreover, by being more detached in this way, one is less likely to engage in those internecine struggles that have undermined psychoanalysis as a discipline and profession.

In general, meditation promotes greater perceptual acumen, increased attentiveness, concentration, centeredness, and insight into psychological functioning. It also promotes insight into the process of thinking and feeling, enabling one to be better able to experience reality directly, to see things as they really are, without distortion (which is how the Buddhists conceptualize reality testing). Finally, I have pointed to the calming, tranquillity-producing effects of meditation practice.

Though the meditation-trained ego skills described here can be crucially important for one's ability to function well in life and achieve peace of mind, I do not regard this as the most novel, provocative, or important aspect of Buddha's wisdom, especially as it pertains to psychoanalysis. I say this because there are many other approaches for developing greater "ego strength," including such ego skills as concentration, attention, and self-calming ability. Some of these other approaches may well be more effective in the short term than meditation (or psychoanalysis). For example, certain cognitive-behavioral approaches, as well as medication, have been shown to quickly enhance, relatively speaking, an analysand's concentration, attention, and ability to feel more relaxed. These approaches are often less time-consuming, less expensive, and require less discipline and personal effort.

In my view, the most novel, provocative, and important contribution of Buddha was his sustained attack on what probably is the most widely accepted and lived version of the human condition in Western culture and one that has been heavily appropriated into mainstream psychoanalytic discourse. I am referring to the paradigm that views humanity as originally, fundamentally, and more-or-less irreversibly self- and ego-centered, a separate self guided largely by self-interest. It is this narcissistic mode of subjectivity, what the great French-Jewish philosopher Emmanuel Levinas calls the "for itself" mode of being,[39] and its causal relation to personal suffering and unhappiness, that the Buddha identified and illuminated with startling brilliance. Moreover, it is Buddha's claim that it is the overcoming of one's selfish cravings (infantile narcissism, in psychoanalytic terminology) by reconfiguring one's subjectivity, especially by relating oneself to a transcendental realm with a strong ethical dimension, that is the best way for achieving some happiness in this inevitably painful and disjointed world. Buddha's claim is mainly based on his key insight: that the narcissistically invested, stable, permanent, separate self is "imaginary, a false belief which has no corresponding reality," and that this fosters injurious thoughts of "me and mine," selfishness, craving, attachment, contempt, arrogance, pride, egoism, and other defilements and problems in living.[40]

This view of the fixed, ego-centered, separate self has infiltrated psychoanalytic theory in ways that have limited its theoretical power and clinical applicability. For example, ego psychology views the ego as the center of the subject and as compelled by strong biological and instinctual causes. Thus, the ego-centered subject is viewed as essentially independent, autonomous, and a nonsocial moral being. Humanity, in this view, is related to society largely externally and instrumentally, rather than being embedded in a social context that meaningfully and decisively shapes individuals.[41]

Self-psychology also has an egological bias. It views the ego as strengthening itself primarily for self-esteem, self-coherence, and self-continuity. As a result, the radically social nature of humanity is given inadequate attention in its narrative. Even relational perspectives, as Rubin points out, view the center of the self as the ego, with the Other treated reductively as an object. As a result of this reductionism, claims Rubin, there has been a failure on the part of psychoanalysis to put forth a viable, compelling theory of intimacy. Moreover, he says, psychoanalysis has an egocentric notion of responsibility in which the subject focuses on what the Other, viewed as a depersonalized "object" or thing, needs to do for the self rather than what the self might do for the Other. In other words, says Rubin, psychoanalysis tends to view relationships as secondary phenomena, largely because humans are conceived as fundamentally self-centered and driven by a thirst for pleasure and narcissistic gratification.[42] This includes viewing the Other mainly as a source for the gratification of one's relational needs, which results in two people in a doomed arrangement of mutually instrumental use.[43] Finally, by embracing this egological prejudice (with the exception of Jacques Lacan and a few others),[44] psychoanalysis has limited its models of health in that it has difficulty envisioning other paradigms that transcend the limits described by the psychoanalytic theory of what is humanly possible. In particular, psychoanalysis has very little to say about states of dereified, decommodified, non-self-centric subjectivity, and it lacks a sophisticated psychology of transcendent states, which sees such states as part of development and does not assume they are infantile, illusory, or pathological.[45] Psychoanalysis, in other words, can benefit from engaging therapeutics that draw on spiritual practices of meditation training for enhancing attentiveness and reality testing and for fostering a nonnarcissistic relation to our own thoughts, beliefs, and lives.[46]

A few Buddhist-inspired psychoanalytic scholars have emphasized the psychological benefits of embracing what is called Buddha's nonself doctrine. Bobrow, for example, describes how, by relinquishing the notion of the inherently existent separate self, we become less imprisoned in our "habitual, automatic and tenacious attachment to constricting versions of such a self and its relations to others," which otherwise animates and shapes our experience and behavior.[47] By giving up the notion of a stable, permanent, separate self, in part through sustained meditation practice, one may reduce one's narcissism and egocentricity, open and expand one's consciousness, and increase the inner space and energy available for self-transformation.

According to Buddha's nonself doctrine, and most important for psychoanalysis, though we seem fundamentally driven by infantile narcissism, selfishness, and a tendency toward egocentricity, we also long to transcend this mode of being and to strive for self-transcendence. Most important, says Buddha, we may overcome our inordinate narcissistic desires and selfish cravings by relating ourselves to a transcendental realm such as nirvana. However, for enlightenment to take place, tremendous ethical and moral refinement via the Eightfold Path is required.

Buddha advocates adopting what Levinas calls a "for-the-Other" mode of being as the condition of possibility for developing at least a modicum, if not an enduring sense of happiness.[48] Nirvana in this formulation can be viewed as a mode of being in which the distinction of self versus other and mine versus yours is eradicated such that the needs, wishes, and dignity of the Other are experienced as being just as compelling and important as are one's own. Nirvana, in other words, can be viewed as a state of release from experiencing one's narcissistic needs and desires as superordinate to the Other's needs and desires. In its highest form, nirvana implies residing in a dimension of the spirit in which the needs of the Other actually supersede one's own. This is one of the reasons why enlightened individuals are often striking in their compassion, kindness, and empathic relation to the whole cosmos.

As Levinas points out in another context, Buddhism, like all the major wisdom religions, moves toward placing the Other, as opposed to the ego or "I," in the center of the self. This Other-centered power invested in the self by the deservedness and exigency of the Other is what Levinas calls nonegocentric responsibility. It is this notion of the investiture of freedom by and for the Other that is the extraordinary insight that Buddhism and, indeed, all the major humanistic religions have pointed toward, each with its own gloss and emphasis.[49]

As Roy Schafer has pointed out, there are a number of "masternarratives" that constitute psychoanalytic versions of the human condition and tend to guide clinical practice. Freud puts forth the narrative of "the taming of the beast within," Kohut describes "the discovery of the self within," and Klein proposes the "mad person within raging about."[50] These masternarratives all tend to reflect the egological bias that limits the power, effectiveness, and aptness of psychoanalysis as a technology for the art of living in today's world. My hope is that psychoanalysis will begin to embrace another masternarrative, one that expresses the awesome spiritual power of Buddhism, as well as all of the major humanistic religions that have flourished for thousands of years. It is a masternarrative that Levinas beautifully evokes in the image of the parent who takes the bread from her mouth and the milk from her body to give to the child.[51] Kunz, in his elaboration of Levinas's image, tells a true story of a woman and child in Turkey, who were trapped for days under the rubble from an earthquake. When her child became weak from loss of nourishing fluids, the woman cut the end of her finger with broken glass so the child could drink her blood. Both survived! Says Kunz, "this is a model for all service. Helping hurts."[52]

The Buddha's revolutionary teaching is that to achieve enlightenment, one's selfish cravings and infantile narcissism must be transformed into "goodness," which is best expressed as radical altruism. Moreover, paradoxically, radical altruism tends to support mental health, in that it supports personal autonomy and integration. For example, Holocaust scholars have noted that, in general, the for-the-Other orientation in the concentration camps of Catholic priests, devout Jews, and Jehovah's Witnesses was the most effective way of staying psychologically intact and remaining human.[53] What was true in the camps is frequently true in ordinary life: the more you give to others, the more you receive. To some extent, the qualities that constitute remaining human in extreme situations can be recast in terms of ordinary life as being roughly equated with living a more decent, content, and happier life. Mainstream psychoanalysis can only benefit from further mining this Buddhist-inspired, Other-centered masternarrative of the human condition.

NOTES

1. Huston Smith, *The World's Religions: Our Great Wisdom Traditions* (New York: Harper San Francisco, 1991), p. 82.

2. Anthony Molino, ed., *The Couch and the Tree: Dialogues in Psychoanalysis and Buddhism* (New York: North Point Press, 1998); Jeffrey B. Rubin, *Psychotherapy and Buddhism: Toward an Integration* (New York: Plenum Press, 1996); Mark Epstein, *Thoughts without a Thinker* (New York: Basic Books, 1995). It is important to emphasize that Buddhism, like psychoanalysis, is not a monolithic system. There are many different versions of Buddhism just as there are many different versions of psychoanalysis.

3. A. F. Price and Wong Mou-lam, trans., *The Diamond Sutra and The Sutra of Hui-Neng* (Boston: Shambhala, 1990); Burton Watson, trans., *The Lotus Sutra* (New York: Columbia University Press, 1993); Edward Conze, trans., *Buddhist Scriptures* (Baltimore: Penguin Books, 1959); Walpola Rahula, *What the Buddha Taught* (New York: Grove Press, 1974).

4. Erich Fromm, "Psychoanalysis and Zen Buddhism," in Molino, ed., *The Couch and the Tree*, p. 67. See also Erich Fromm, D. T. Suzuki, and Richard DeMartino, *Zen Buddhism and Psychoanalysis* (New York: Harper Colophon Books, 1960). According to the Dalai Lama, freedom from suffering is roughly equated with happiness: "from my point of view, the highest happiness is when one reaches the stage of Liberation, at which there is no more suffering. That's genuine, lasting happiness." See Dalai Lama and Howard C. Cutler, *The Art of Happiness* (New York: Riverhead Books, 1998), p. 33. See also pp. 24, 64, 142.

5. Hakime Nakamura, "Buddhism," in the *Dictionary of the History of Ideas*, Philip P. Wiener, editor-in-chief (New York: Charles Scribner's Sons, 1973), 1: 250.

6. Stephan Schuhmacher and Gert Woerner, eds., *The Encyclopedia of Eastern Philosophy and Religion* (Boston: Shambhala, 1994), pp. 330, 101–102.

7. Jeffrey B. Rubin, "Close Encounters of a New Kind: An Integration of Psychoanalysis and Buddhism," *American Journal of Psychoanalysis*, 59, no. 1 (1999): 12.

8. In contrast, the ancient Vatsiputriya school advocated a concept of the person and soul.

9. Nakamura, "Buddhism," p. 250.

10. Schuhmacher and Woerner, *Encyclopedia of Eastern Philosophy and Religion*, p. 98.

11. Paul C. Cooper, "The Disavowal of the Spirit: Integration and Wholeness in Buddhism and Psychoanalysis," in Molino, ed., *The Couch and the Tree*, p. 238.

12. Mark Epstein, "Beyond the Oceanic Feeling: Psychoanalytic Study of Buddhist Meditation," in Molino, ed., *The Couch and the Tree*, p. 125.

13. Polly Young-Eisendrath, "What Suffering Teaches," in Molino, ed., *The Couch and the Tree*, p. 352; Cooper, "The Disavowal of the Spirit: Integration and Wholeness in Buddhism and Psychoanalysis," in Molino, ed., *The Couch and the Tree*, p. 238.

14. Epstein, *Thoughts without a Thinker*, pp. 50–51.

15. Smith, *The World's Religions*, p. 101.

16. Ibid., p. 102.

17. Paul Marcus and Alan Rosenberg, eds., *Psychoanalytic Versions of the Human Condition: Philosophies of Life and Their Impact on Practice* (New York: New York University Press, 1998), pp. 2, 207.

18. Sharon Salzberg and Joseph Goldstein, *Insight Meditation: Correspondence Course Workbook* (Boulder, Colo.: Sounds True, 1996), p. 46; Joseph Goldstein,

Insight Meditation: The Practice of Freedom (Boston: Shambhala, 1993), p. 96; Smith, *Religions of the World*, p. 118.

19. Nagarjuna, an Indian philosopher living between 100 and 200 and founder of the influential Shunyavada school of Buddhism, offered the following proof that nirvana is an illusion: If nirvana exists, it will follow the cycle of birth and death. If nirvana does not exist, it will rely upon existence for its status since nonexistence relies upon existence. For reasons of logical inconsistency, it cannot be both of these nor neither of them. Therefore, nirvana is an illusion. (See W. L. Reese, ed., *Dictionary of Philosophy and Religion: Eastern and Western Thought* (Atlantic Highland, N.J.: Humanities Press, 1980), p. 377.

20. John Renard, *Responses to 101 Questions on Buddhism* (Mahwah, N.J.: Paulist Press, 1999), pp. 50–51; Schuhmacher and Woerner, *The Encyclopedia of Eastern Philosophy and Religion*, pp. 44, 175, 248–249.

21. Salzberg and Goldstein, *Insight Meditation*, p. 7.

22. Joe Tom Sun, "Psychology in Primitive Buddhism," in Molino, ed., *The Couch and the Tree*, p. 6.

23. Salzberg and Goldstein, *Insight Meditation*, p. 7.

24. Dalai Lama and Cutler, *The Art of Happiness*.

25. As I will suggest in my chapter on Taoism, certain Taoist ideas and meditation practices have strongly influenced Buddhist theory and practice, especially Zen Buddhism. Moreover, Hindu notions and meditation techniques have also been liberally integrated into Buddhism.

26. I don't want to romanticize the concept of enlightenment nor overidealize the value of meditation. In recent years there have been a number of scandals involving so-called self-actualized, enlightened meditation teachers, including stealing funds from their meditation community and sexually exploiting nonconsenting female students. See Rubin, *Psychotherapy and Buddhism*, pp. 59, 67, 85, 179.

27. As Salzberg and Goldstein have indicated, one does not have to appropriate the Buddhist religious belief system in order to benefit from insight meditation. The meditation practices can support one's existing spiritual path, whether it is rooted in Christianity, Judaism, Islam, or a less structured, personal spiritual quest. See *Insight Meditation*, p. 1.

28. Jon Kabat-Zinn, *Full Catastrophe Living: Using the Wisdom of Your Body and Mind to Face Stress, Pain, and Illness* (New York: Delta, 1990), p. 20.

29. Salzberg and Goldstein, *Insight Meditation*, pp. 22–23.

30. Smith, *The World's Religions*, p. 109.

31. Kabat-Zinn, *Full Catastrophe Living*, p. 12. I have somewhat simplified the notion of mindfulness when, in fact, it is a very complex subject in Buddhist thought, where it consists of mindfulness of the body, feeling, mind, and mental objects. The method is described in the *Satipatthana-sutta* (The discourse on the awakening of mindfulness). Henepola Gunaratana's *Mindfulness in Plain English* (Boston: Wisdom Publications, 1991) is a very good secondary source on the subject.

32. For the purpose of this chapter I have uncritically accepted certain Buddhist ideas that may be troubling to a postmodern reader. For example, the idea that one can "neutrally" or "objectively" observe one's thoughts or, for that matter, reality, assumes that one is capable of unmediated experience. Buddhists seem to believe that one can experience the world outside one's socially constructed symbolic universe, a notion that seems to fly in the face of conventional social science wisdom. Says George Steiner, "There is no naked, primal, uninterpreted mode of experience . . . to perceive is to interpret, to 'translate.' " See "But Is That Enough," *Times Literary Supplement*, January 12, 2001, p. 11.

33. Cited in Epstein, *Thoughts without a Thinker*, p. 135.
34. Rubin, *Psychotherapy and Buddhism*, p. 156.
35. Goldstein, *Insight Meditation*, pp. 68–74.
36. In my discussion of neurotic depression, I have liberally relied on Goldstein's work on emotions.
37. Kabat-Zinn, *Full Catastrophe Living*, p. 291.
38. Salzberg and Goldstein, *Insight Meditation*, p. 41.
39. Emmanuel Levinas, "Prayer without Demand," in *The Levinas Reader*, ed. Sean Hand (Oxford: Blackwell, 1994), pp. 227–234.
40. Rahula, *What the Buddha Taught*, p. 51.
41. Paul Marcus, *Autonomy in the Extreme Situation: Bruno Bettelheim, the Nazi Concentration Camps and the Mass Society* (Westport, Conn.: Praeger, 1999), p. 165.
42. Rubin, *Psychotherapy and Buddhism*, pp. 175–179.
43. Paul Marcus, "The Religious Believer, the Psychoanalytic Intellectual, and the Challenge of Sustaining the Self in the Concentration Camps," *Journal for the Psychoanalysis of Culture and Society*, 3, no. 1 (Spring 1998): 61–75; Marcus, *Autonomy in the Extreme Situation*, pp. 175–201.
44. For Lacan, Freud's revolutionary discovery of the unconscious removed the ego from the central position in which Western thought had usually situated it. Lacan has argued that followers of ego psychology have betrayed Freud's transformational discovery by resituating the ego as the center of the subject (e.g., autonomous ego). Lacan, sounding very Buddhist, thought that the main therapeutic goal was to subvert the fixity of the ego, which is an alienating screen, an illusion that conceals the divided and fractured character of unconscious desire. In contrast, Lacan offered a "decentered" subject who is formed in the context of social relationships and who is characterized by the constant fragmentation and disintegration that is inflicted by the unconscious. See Marcus and Rosenberg, *Psychoanalytic Versions of the Human Condition*, p. 362.
45. Rubin, *Psychotherapy and Buddhism*, pp. 190, 8.
46. Ibid., pp. 70, 195–196.
47. Joseph Bobrow, "The Fertile Mind," in Molino, ed., *The Couch and the Tree*, p. 319.
48. Levinas, "Prayer without Demand," p. 231.
49. George Kunz, *The Paradox of Power and Weakness* (Albany: State University of New York Press, 1998), p. 105.
50. Paul A. Roth, "The Cure of Stories: Self-Deception, Danger Situations, and the Clinical Role of Narratives in Roy Schafer's Psychoanalytic Theory," in Marcus and Rosenberg, eds., *Psychoanalytic Versions of the Human Condition*, p. 327.
51. Kunz, *The Paradox of Power and Weakness*, p. 148.
52. Ibid.
53. Marcus, *Autonomy in the Extreme Situation*, p. 179.

East Asian

II

4

Confucianism: *The Analects*

> The mind of man is more perilous than mountains or rivers, harder to understand than Heaven.
>
> Confucius[1]

Confucius, a philosopher and teacher, was perhaps the most original and creative contributor to ancient Chinese wisdom. As Lau and Ames point out, Confucius is probably the most influential philosopher in history: " 'is' because taking Chinese philosophy on its own terms, he is still very much alive."[2] That is, Confucian notions about what constitute the central problematics of the human condition, what is the "good" society and "good" life, which foster social harmony, personal happiness, and peace of mind, has been the fertile breeding ground in which the Chinese cultural tradition has developed and flourished for about twenty-five hundred years. Moreover, though since the early 1900s Confucianism is no longer the reigning philosophy of China, it still has a significant influence in China as well as on people living throughout East Asia.

Confucius developed a moral philosophy, a pragmatic wisdom that focused on two general concerns: the right way to govern and the right way for people to live their daily lives. More specifically, like Freud, Confucius was interested in the development of a particular mode of being in the world and worldview that maximizes one's capacity to love, to effectively work, and, perhaps most important, to be a fully contributing, cooperating, and contented participant in a cohesive, stable society. In a manner that is in sync with the spirit of a psychoanalysis as broadly conceptualized, Confucius believed that it was through a process of self-cultivation and character building, that is, "learning to be human," that personal happiness, peace of mind, and harmonious social relations could be achieved. As Confucian scholar Tu Wei-ming further noted (sounding very psychoanalytic), "learning to be human" is "characterized by a ceaseless process of inner illumination and self-transformation," "it is basically an understanding of one's mental state and an appreciation of one's inner feelings." Moreover, learning to be human demands a rigorous development of one's "primordial awareness"; it requires, in Confucian terms, "becoming aesthetically refined, morally excellent and religiously profound."[3]

THE ANALECTS ("DISCUSSED SAYINGS")

Confucius (the latinized form of the Chinese K'ung Fu-tzu, "Master K'ung") was born in 551 B.C.E. in the state of Lu, now called China, and died in 479 B.C.E, in Qufu, also in the state of Lu. He lived during the mid-Chou dynasty, the period of the Warring States, a time of tremendous social disorder and more or less continuous warfare among rival feudal barons who were fighting for hegemony. Confucius had become a prominent teacher in middle age and gained many disciples (in fact, some scholars have claimed that he was the first teacher in China to offer private instruction). Though Confucius may have served as a low-level governmental official in Lu between 502 and 497, he was frustrated and demoralized because he never held an official position of any major responsibility or influence. Ironically, while Confucius never convinced the powerful rulers of his day to put his ideas into practice, and therefore in a certain sense may have viewed his life as a failure, his teachings that aimed at instructing the rulers on how to foster social cohesion and order became the basis for one of the most powerful philosophical and social influences in human history.

The Analects, the book that I mainly draw from, is a collection of sayings of Confucius recorded by his disciples and their students and compiled over a long period after his death (exactly when and by whom is a subject of scholarly debate). It should be mentioned that, because *The Analects* is generally viewed as an accretional text by scholars, it calls attention to the fact that possibly some of Confucius's ideas were shaded differently, perhaps even distorted, by later "recorders" and that some ideas not directly associated with the historical Confucius found their way into the text. The point is, that in surveying the tradition in the twenty-first century, we are not entitled confidently to attribute to Confucius ideas and motivations that may have been far from those that actually animated him. However, most Chinese traditionally believed that they were reading the words of Confucius.

From time to time I also draw from later Confucian formulations, in part, to give the reader a "feel" for some of the innovations contained in the later Confucian tradition that not only convey the "spirit" of Confucianism but also have some bearing on psychoanalysis. *The Analects* is viewed as something of a sacred scripture in Chinese tradition, though some scholars have claimed that there was no distinction between secular and sacred in Chinese tradition (at least prior to the advent of Buddhism). That is, for example, unlike in India where we find the distinction between *sruti* (the revealed) and *smriti* (the transmitted), the Chinese do not have such a distinction.

Most scholars believe that *The Analects* best conveys Confucian political philosophy and ethics (the latter is my main concern in this chapter). That is, my intention is to convey a few of the key ideas of Confucian moral philosophy and suggest in what way these ideas, in certain instances with some modification, can enhance psychoanalysis when conceived as a Western form of character development, moral cultivation, and inner enlightenment. Indeed, Confucius has a lot of food for thought when it comes to one of the main goals of psychoanalysis, namely, self-knowledge, self-realization, and self-improvement in the service of broadening and deepening one's human relatedness, sociality, and sense of social responsibility. Like Freud, Confucius was something of a rationalist, who believed that we could improve ourselves although it requires continuous personal struggle and efforts at self-mastery. That is, Confucius believed that only through a process of deepening self-awareness and self-understanding could one become the ideal person, the *chun-tzu* ("gentleman," "profound man," or "superior man," as opposed to the "inferior man"), as Confucius called him, or a person characterized by "inner sageliness and outer kingliness," a evocative term used by much later Confucianists. Such a person, on the one hand, was morally cultivated, humane, and loving, and on the other, was capable of knowing how to effectively negotiate through life and thus give him- or herself and others the maximum amount of happiness. This quest, or rather struggle for happiness, to be an "inner sage and outer king," is one of the key overarching goals of Confucianism and to some extent resonates with the Freudian project, at least as I construe these two different approaches to conducting one's life.

THE STRUGGLE FOR HUMAN HAPPINESS

In order to help the individual achieve relative peace of mind and happiness and to bring about a cohesive, ordered, and humane society, Confucius cast his eye back with longing to the golden age of the early

Zhou period, when the Tao, or Way, predominated (in the Confucian scheme, this roughly refers to the ideal human order or moral community and the good human life as a whole).[4] Indeed, Confucius viewed himself as a transmitter, and not an originator, of ancient wisdom, explaining, "I have been faithful to and loved the Ancients."[5] That is, Confucius viewed tradition as the vehicle from the golden past that could help stabilize and humanize his own chaotic and conflicted society. However, what Confucius actually did was to reinvent and reconfigure traditional Chinese culture and ancient wisdom, thus giving it a new meaning and value that was adaptable, not only to his own troubled historical context,[6] but, to some extent, to other historical periods for thousands of years after, including our own.

The main social goal of the Confucian project was thus to foster humane order, harmony, and justice in society, this being the social context for the individual to achieve peace of mind and happiness. Confucius felt that it was through knowledge and education, that is, moral self-cultivation and character development, that the individual would be able to achieve harmony with him- or herself, with the community, with nature, and with Heaven. Briefly, as I will explain later when I discuss the religious dimension to Confucius's thought, Heaven, at least according to one scholar, is an impersonal standard of justice, a kind of ethical providence to which one can orient one's life, though this providence is not necessarily destined to be triumphant in the world.[7]

What exactly constituted this knowledge and education of Chinese character, this inner illumination and self-transformation, that would engender the "good" society and "good" life and foster personal happiness? What aspects of the Confucian worldview are applicable to the analysand struggling to achieve a modicum of peace of mind? To give some preliminary Confucian-based answers to these questions, we need to review a few of the key ethical concepts that make up the Confucian project and worldview and then connect some of these ideas to psychoanalysis.

REN

Ren, translated as "benevolence," "human-heartedness," "goodness," or "humanity," is unquestionably the key ethical category of Confucian "virtue ethics," as A. S. Cua describes the nature of Confucian thought. The idea here is that developing the capacity for love and care for one's fellow human beings, that is, an affectionate interest for the well-being of others, is what constitutes personal integration and ethical development at the highest level. Says Confucius about the ruler who is good, who governs according to ren, "He loves men." Such an internalized achievement is in sync with the Tao, the term that Confucius equates with the ideal way of life (not to be confused with the Tao of the mystical Taoists like Chuang Tzu, who uses the same term but with a very different meaning).[8]

Ren thus stands for the ideal relationship between two individuals; it is the perfect virtue and the foundation of peace and harmony of a society. For Confucius, one who lives a life devoted to ren will treat people respectfully, kindly, and humanely, and for this person, life will tend to go well, mainly because he or she avoids interpersonal conflict with most people. However, Confucius always maintained that one should practice ren, not because it is efficacious, but rather because it is right. Ren, in other words, is not simply a theoretical and abstract concept; rather, it means loving others, showing personal integrity, and practicing altruism.[9] As Huston Smith indicates, ren involves both "a feeling of humanity towards others and respect for oneself, an indivisible sense of the dignity of human life wherever it appears." Moreover, says Smith, in the public sector ren fosters ceaseless diligence and hard work, which enhance both oneself and others. In private life, ren is manifested in unselfishness, empathy, generosity, righteousness, and courtesy, among other qualities. Ren, in a nutshell, means living a life according to what has been called the Silver Rule (the Golden Rule stated negatively) and the Golden Rule.[10] Said Confucius:

> Tzu-kung asked saying, Is there any single saying that one can act upon all day and every night? The Master said, Perhaps the saying about consideration: "Never do to others what you would not like them to do to you."
> ... [Responding to another question by Tzu-kung:] As for Goodness [ren]—you yourself desire rank and standing; then help others to get rank and standing. You want to turn your own merits to account; then help others to turn theirs to account—in fact, the ability to take one's own feelings as a guide—that is the sort of thing that lies in the direction of Goodness.[11]

As I have said, the purpose of *The Analects* was to illuminate what the ideal Chinese character should be in order to bring about the "good" society, which is characterized by harmonious social relations. Ren embodies all those moral qualities, which should animate an individual in his or her relations with another,[12] it is that which shapes a person as a moral being[13] and is, in part, the basis for individual human happiness. In Confucian language, if one develops one's ren, or humanity, and if one cultivates love of others, empathy, righteousness, respect, sincerity, loyalty, truthfulness, generosity, psychological strength, and discipline, among other virtuous moral qualities, then one is in sync with the Tao, or Way. This makes one a "gentleman." One is thus related to the social world in harmony but also to the Will of Heaven, thus providing a cosmic aspect to human existence.

It should be noted that for Confucius, ren is more than relative standards of good and bad or desirable and undesirable standards of social behavior. Rather, it involves absolute standards of right and wrong, a notion of universal virtue, never to be compromised even in a crisis, though as I shall shortly explain, they are, in part, guided by *li*, "rules of propriety," that is, most generally, the rules governing proper human relations as well as ceremonies and how to act in a given situation. In *The Analects*, Confucius does not spell out, let alone rigorously delineate, how one knows that something is right and just. Rather, it is assumed that the way that one knows that something is right is not simply by reference to a set of standards outside oneself but rather, ultimately, the rightness and justice of an act are the consequence of a person's cumulative experience, and it is against this standard that the act is to be evaluated.[14] As Confucius said in a famous quotation about the relationship between ren and li: "To subdue oneself [i.e., master oneself, have good self-control] and return to ritual [li, meaning morality or civilized behavior] is to practice humanness [ren]."[15]

Confucius was thus a firm believer that in general, people are all born more or less the same and it is their familial and social experience that makes them different and derails them from living a "good" life, that is, a life animated by ren and li. Says Confucius, "By nature, near together; by practice far apart."[16] In other words, for Confucius, basic human nature points to ren, that is, we are intrinsically social beings who are inclined to be a cooperating and responsible member of society.[17] As Wing-tsit Chan notes, Confucius was the first in Chinese philosophy to assert that human nature is originally good,[18] though, as a pragmatist, he was well aware of how difficult self-mastery is and of the human tendency toward selfishness, egoism, and inordinate narcissism. It should be emphasized, however, that for an individual to express his or her own interpretation of ren, such an expression must be modulated and guided by li. Not to do so is to violate the nature of ren. That is, ren and li are, ideally, always dialectically related; sustaining oneself and responsibility to the Other are always entwined in the Confucian project, though sometimes there are tensions between ren and li, which are worth being mindful of. For example, while ren fosters appreciation of common humanity, li tends to foster appreciation of hierarchical distinctions. The individual must therefore balance ren and li in a manner that displays good judgment, which is not always easy. The overarching goal, however, is being ren, that is, striving for moral excellence, humanness. This overarching goal is crucial for Confucius's societal experiment in social goodness to work, that is, his quasi-utopian vision of wide-ranging improvement.

LI

In the most simplistic sense, li means rules of propriety or etiquette. Li was a formalized code of behaviors for stabilizing, structuring, and disciplining our ever-shifting life circumstances. It provided models for what constituted ideal behavior in a wide range of contexts. For example, li prescribed the proper way to mourn the death of a parent (i.e., three years of mourning). Other examples could be given pertaining to sacrifices, marriage and communal festivities, conduct towards a ruler, parent, elder, teacher, sibling, friend, and guest, as well as more common social contexts, including good table manners and how to express commiseration. While all of these rules of conduct may appear rather exacting, if not obsessive and rigid, to the psychoanalyst, for the Confucian, li expresses a more profound insight than these examples might at first suggest; that is, li is more than rule-governed behavior meant to simply keep people in line. Li, when it is practiced properly and animated by ren, provides an aesthetic texturing to life, a kind of simple, elegant refinement that is striking to observers.

As A. S. Cua points out, li has a delimiting, supportive, and ennobling function for living one's everyday life.[19] The delimiting function of li is expressed in its main purpose, namely, the prevention and avoidance of conflict and disharmony between people. That is, li provides a set of controls on an individual's needs, desires, wishes, and interests, with the ultimate aim being to promote social harmony and stability. Li also has a supportive function. It provides possible modalities for satisfaction of desires within the acceptable and prescribed limits of action. Instead of repressing desires, li offers acceptable outlets for their satisfaction. Finally, the ennobling function of li is the cultivation of emotions or their transformation in sync with the spirit of ren. That is, while the concern with the form of proper behavior is still important, it is not simply a matter of adjusting to conventional social norms and structure, nor is it a matter of exacting obedience that leads to the gratification of the person's desires and wishes. Rather, the ennobling function of li entails "the elegant form for the expression of ethical character," that is, li is directed mainly to the creation of beautiful virtues. The beauty of the ethical character lies precisely in the delicate balance between emotions and form. Says Cua, "What is deemed admirable in the virtuous conduct of an ethically superior person is the harmonious fusion of elegant form and feelings. In the ideal case, a li-performance may be said to have an aesthetic dimension." For example, respect for traditional rites of mourning represents a concern with ren and li, because such practices express the Confucian ideal of humanity.

For Confucius, the main thrust of li is that it differentiates the human being from the animal, that is, it expresses our humanity, or ren. Li is thus the basis for an aesthetically refined, humane, and orderly form of living, which is a central goal of the Confucian project as I understand it. Psychologically speaking, according to Confucius, li, which helps organize, structure, and express emotions in a socially acceptable manner, tends to foster calm amid life's ups and downs, just as it prevents society from becoming unstable and chaotic.

Thus, for Confucius the goal of living is to achieve a life that integrates li and ren (among other Confucian virtues), that is, a life that fosters harmony and enjoyment for oneself and for others through acting appropriately in the roles and relationships that constitute an effective li-ren performance. It should be remembered that Confucius, the man, in contrast to the composite teaching that is the *Analects*, always held the spirit and the sincerity behind li above the formalities of li. In other words, in his view, li without ren was inauthentic. Put somewhat differently, like in psychoanalysis, the Confucian goal according to one scholar is in part, "transforming unrefined impulses into elegantly cultivated aesthetic expressions of the self." Being a cultured person, a "gentleman" is among other things to be "a fully socialized participant in the human community who has successfully sublimated his or her instinctual demands to further the public good."[20]

There are three other Confucian teachings that need to be briefly mentioned to further clarify what Confucius was getting at in his concept of li and in his overall project: the Rectification of Names, the Doctrine of the Mean, and the Five Constant Relationships (the latter is largely an idea that emerged later in the Confucian tradition).

The Rectification of Names reflects the fact that for Confucius, the name of an object and its actuality must correspond. In other words, a name is not just a representation of an object but is the very essence of the object itself. What this amounts to in practice is an attempt to generate a normative semantics, a language in which important nouns convey the meanings they should convey if life is to be stable and organized.[21] Thus, when Confucius says let the prince be a prince, the minister a minister, the father a father, and the son a son, he is saying that the first step in the rectification of names involves the prince acting like a prince. In other words, duty and title need to correspond, for there should be a harmonious correspondence between name and external reality. Therefore, it follows that every member of society must act in accordance with the duties emanating from his or her name. As Wing-tsit Chan points out, the rectification of names is in sync with

Confucius's commitment to an ordered, hierarchical, and liturgically formalized view of society.[22]

The idea of the Doctrine of the Mean (there is also a book of the same name that is important in the Confucian literature) is a familiar one to the Westerner for, according to some scholars, it is to some extent similar to the Golden Mean of Aristotle. The basic idea is that moderation is to be highly valued in life, for it tends to foster give and take in relations, a degree of personal restraint, and an appreciation of the principles of balance and harmony.

The Five Constant Relationships, described in the *Book of Mencius*, make up the foundation of the Confucian social project. Mencius studied under a disciple of the grandson of Confucius and further developed Confucius's teachings. The five relationships are between the father and son (which leads to the virtue of filial piety), husband and wife (good listeners), older and younger brother (brotherly respect), older friend and younger friend (sincerity), and ruler and subject (loyalty). The idea here is that for a society to remain stable, the important relationships need to be rightly ordered. Moreover, as noted, there is a virtue associated with each relationship that is practiced by the socially inferior person in the relationship. It is important to note, however, that while there is an upper and lower term in each relation, it was expected that each relation was reciprocal in a certain sense. For example, while sons (and daughters) should be respectful, parents should be loving; husbands should be dutiful and kind and wives should be good listeners, or "submissive"; rulers should be benevolent and subjects loyal, and so on. As Smith further points out, what Confucius is stressing is that you never act in isolation from others. Every action impacts on someone else. The five relationships form a framework in which you can create the maximum selfhood without undermining the very social fabric of life on which your own survival depends.[23]

It is not by chance that three of the Five Constant Relationships refer to the family, for in the Confucian scheme, the family is the microcosm of society and the ultimate basis of social cohesion and stability. Filial piety is thus a key Confucian virtue. While Confucius did not invent this notion, he was the first to explicate its meaning, namely, that it is incumbent on every son to serve his parents, whether alive or dead, according to li, and to show them great honor and respect. More generally, the idea is that people who honor and are kind to their parents, including and especially when their parents are old (and by extension, the elderly in general), are less likely to violate the law and order of society. They are also less likely to be self-centered and selfish, which puts them on the way to transforming themselves and becoming more human. It should be remembered that prior to Confucius, Chinese society had always viewed the family as the fundamental unit of society and respect for the elderly had a long history in Chinese society.

Thus, the Rectification of Names, the Doctrine of the Mean, and the Five Constant Relationships represent important elaborations of li and the Confucian project. In other words, li, when animated by ren, and ren, when structured by li, provide a comprehensive framework for living the correct or "good" life, a life that, according to Confucius, will maximize one's own and others' happiness.

THE RELIGIOUS DIMENSION TO THE CONFUCIAN PROJECT

The question of whether Confucianism is a religion the way Christianity or Islam are, for example, or an ethics, is one that scholars have been debating for a long time, and I have no intention of entering into the debate. In my view, there clearly is a broadly conceived religious dimension to the Confucian project, and I want to briefly describe this in order to deepen our understanding of the mode of being and outlook that Confucius was advocating as leading to the good society and the good life. In the conclusion of this chapter, I will attempt to suggest how the Confucian project, including its religious dimension as well as those spiritual values that it tends to foster, can possibly enhance psychoanalysis.

First, it should be stated that Confucius felt that Heaven had chosen him to satisfy a divine mission, to return the world to the Tao, or Way. "Heaven begat the power [or virtue] that is in me."[24] Moreover, by following the Way, that is by living one's everyday life according to ren and observing li, all of humankind can be in sync with the Will of Heaven. Incidentally, before Confucius, the Will of Heaven was thought to apply only to one who governs and not to all of humanity. Scholars differ in what they think Confucius meant by Heaven as he used the term in *The Analects*. For example Fung Yu-lan thinks "that Heaven . . . meant a purposeful Supreme Being or 'ruling Heaven,'" while other scholars have viewed Confucius's Heaven as a spontaneous, unpurposeful one or a "faceless amalgam of ancestors," rather than some transcendent Supreme Being or Creator.[25] There are passages in *The Analects*, or at least interpretations of passages by scholars, that tend to support all of these views. For our purposes, according to Confucian scholar Herrlee G. Creel, Confucius seems to have meant at least this by the word Heaven: "a vaguely conceived moral force in the universe." To Creel, the idea of Heaven (and the Will of Heaven) gave Confucius the comforting feeling, and perhaps reassurance, that somehow, somewhere, there was an invincible force or power that stood on the side of the lonely, vulnerable person who struggles for what is right.[26]

In general, then, Confucius adopted a rather modulated attitude toward the conventional religious ideas and practices of his time, though as I have insinuated, according to some scholars his silence did not necessarily imply disbelief in God or the afterlife. For example, when Confucius was asked by one of his students, Tzu-lu, "how one should serve ghosts and spirits," he replied: "Till you have learnt to serve men, how can you serve ghosts? Tzu-lu then ventured upon a question about the dead. The Master said, Till you know about the living, how are you to know about the dead?"[27]

As Ching further points out, Confucius's philosophy was mainly based in the inherited religions of Shang-ti ("the lord on high") or T'ien (Heaven), the supreme and personal gods of the Shang and Chou eras, respectively. *The Analects*, and Confucius's philosophy in general, do not contain any sustained, systematic religious reflections on God or the afterlife, although he felt that he had a heavenly mission and seemed to believe that human beings are accountable to a supreme being: ("He who has put himself in the wrong with Heaven has no means of expiation left").[28] Confucius was also not against ancestral worship, the basis for the official religion of the time, and he even included it, along with the rites of mourning, in the obligations of piety toward ancestors. Some scholars, however, claim that his respect for the official cult of ancestor worship was based mainly on ethical rather than religious beliefs, though this is debatable. Confucius also believed that it was unreasonable to ask the gods for their assistance. In his view, the Will of Heaven could not be influenced by prayers, and he was against all forms of superstition.[29]

Thus, we can at least say with some confidence that Confucius believed that somewhere there was a hard to define, overarching cosmic power that was on the side of the morally right. The living and loving of a life of kindness to others, compassion, righteousness, and goodness was therefore a cosmic imperative, it was the Will of Heaven. Being ren and observing li were thus the first thing that a "gentleman" should honor. I believe that this "anthropocosmic vision" as it has been called, involving the cultivation of empathy to include the whole universe as one's living reality,[30] is a particularly worthwhile goal for any psychoanalytic treatment.

THE CONFUCIAN PROJECT AND PSYCHOANALYSIS

As I have said, the Confucian project is one of reconfiguring oneself so that one becomes more fully human, at least as Confucius described this notion. The ideal person in the Confucian framework, or "gentleman," is one who is dedicated to continuous self-cultivation, self-realization, and self-improvement, in a word; he or she strives to be ren and observe li. Prior to the teachings of Confucius, one had to be born into gentleman status; however, Confucius saw this status as, not an issue of lineage, but an issue of moral cultivation, character development, and education. This Confucian goal of learning to be fully human via self-cultivation raises some interesting possibilities for broadening how certain aspects of psychoanalysis are conceptualized.

THE SELF AS A CENTER OF RELATIONSHIPS

It is extremely important that Confucius indicated that the project of self-cultivation could not be accomplished in isolation or personal retreat, such as in certain subgroups of other religious traditions (for example, in India). Rather, for Confucius, the self "is experientially and practically a center of relationships." It is not an encased world of private feelings and thoughts, though it does have its subjective aspect, such as its capacity for introspection, self-knowledge, and self-understanding. That is, the Confucian self is mainly shaped through its contacts with others and is, in part, constituted by the sum of its social roles. However, it is a mistake to believe that the Confucian self can be reduced to its sociality or the goal of mere social adjustment to societal norms. That is, for the Confucian, the self is contextualized, but not trapped in its sociality and social roles. This is because the texture of the dyadic relationships that constitute its social roles (e.g., the Five Constant Relationships) are never static or fixed. The self has to be repeatedly interwoven and reconfigured with the changing contexts of disappearing and emerging circumstances with which it engages in its concrete life situations.

This version of the self, conceptualized as an open, dynamic system engaged in continuous transformation, is somewhat different from some psychoanalytic views, which regard it more as a static, discrete thing. The Confucian self, in other words, is in sync with the main thrust of certain versions of psychoanalytic thinking (e.g., Roy Schafer's work), which view the self more as a dynamic and transformative process than a discrete entity.[31]

Thus, following Tu Wei-ming, the Confucian self was a center of relationships. It has a communal aspect, which was never conceptualized as an isolated or isolable thing. For the Confucian, to become fully human involves continuous interaction and communication with other human beings. Moreover, one's dignity as a person depends as much on communal involvement as on one's own sense of self-respect and autonomy. For the Confucian, one's self-cultivation is discerned by one's ability to harmonize human relationships by being ren and observing li. It is worth mentioning, in contrast to psychoanalysis, that the psychoanalytic process of permitting one's deeply-rooted private self to be probed and analyzed by another person is not part of the Confucian tradition. That is, Confucian self-cultivation assumes that the self that is worth cultivating is not the single individual's private possession but a sharable, communal experience that composes common humanity. For the Confucian, the cultivated self is not private property that we protect from infringement from the outside. The ego that has to be protected against being overwhelmed by the outside social demands is what the Confucians (Mencius in particular) refer to as the "small" self, the self that is a closed system. According to Mencius, the "great" self, in contrast, is public-spirited and communal and is an open system. As an open system, the self is expansive and always receptive and responsive to the world at large. Self-cultivation, in other words, can be understood as the broadening of the self to embrace an ever-expanding circle of human relatedness.[32]

This Confucian view of the self and the human project is rather different from most versions of psychoanalysis. For example, while Confucians value the dignity, autonomy, and independence of the person, as do psychoanalysts, they do not believe that this has to be based on individualism, as we in the West tend to think. That is, the Confucian defines the dignity and integrity of one's selfhood through communal relatedness, social bonding, and human solidarity. The assumption is that by doing so, one's individuality is not diminished, but rather one's deepest humanity is reached through communal participation and communication with others. Thus, the Confucian view of personal development can be conceptualized as an open-ended series of concentric circles, because the Confucian idea of the self is not built on the idea of individuality the way psychoanalysis tends to be. Rather, in Confucianism the self is always a center of relationships and has a strong communal thrust. This open-ended series of concentric circles points toward an ever-expanding horizon. Relationships thus become the point at which the individual's self, identity, and social commitment are merged and foster the context of meaning and integrity. Moreover, this is not merely the development of the self in relation to one's family, community, country, or significant other; it also includes a deepening process of insight, that is, of self-knowledge, self-understanding, and self-improvement.[33] Some of these Confucian ideas clearly resonate to some extent with various relational models of psychoanalysis that view relationships themselves as primary and irreducible.

For psychoanalysis, this Confucian view of the self suggests the benefits of possibly including in the goals of any successful analysis a social dimension in part characterized by greater sociality and social responsibility. That is, helping the analysand become an active participant in a living community, beginning with the family and progressing to the neighborhood, the city, the state, and the world. It further suggests that the process of analysis might well benefit by fostering filiality, brotherhood, friendship, discipleship, and loyalty, values that are at the heart of Confucian self-cultivation but are not usually part of what psychoanalysis and analysands regard as one of their main emphases. In other words, psychoanalysis might be enhanced by conceptualizing itself, in part, as an ever-deepening and -broadening awareness of the presence of the Other in one's life (and not only one's significant other and family) as one attempts to reconfigure oneself along a less narcissistic orientation and toward a more "for-the-Other" way of being in the world. In my view, this is one of the main aspects of what the Confucian is getting at by using the term *self-cultivation*. This is perhaps why the Confucian self, viewed as a center of relationships, is an open system. It is mainly through the continuous opening up of itself to others that the self can maintain an integrated personal identity. Self-centeredness, egoistic desires, selfishness, and inordinate narcissism tend to foster a closed world, which prevents self-transformation, that is, self-cultivation, or being ren and observing li. In other words, for the Confucian and, I hope, for the psychoanalytic devotee, a robust sense of self and wholesome self-development demand that we help others to enlarge and develop themselves. Selfhood always requires the participation and enhancement of the Other. This is one of the responsibilities associated with self-cultivation, one that is both altruistic and self-enhancing. As Confucius wrote, "As for Goodness [ren]—you yourself desire rank and standing; then help others to get rank and standing. You want to turn your own merits to account; then help others to turn theirs to account."[34] This kind of focus on developing a broadly conceived for-the-Other social self is not usually what psychoanalysis takes to be one of its main objectives. However, according to Confucius and all of the religious traditions discussed in this book, this clearly is, in part, what constitutes the practical wisdom that moves one closer to the goal of personal happiness.

This notion of selfhood as a creative transformative project that is potentiated by other human beings personifies the Confucian view that the individual is always lodged and contextualized in the world of human relationships, and not only with one's significant other or family, as psychoanalysis tends to emphasize. The Confucian objective is to expand the network of human relatedness that includes, not only one's family, significant other, community, state, and nation, but also nature and Heaven; that is, to view oneself as a cocreator of the cosmos. It is to this subject that I now turn.

AN ANTHROPOCOSMIC OUTLOOK

Unlike psychoanalysis, which tends to view the human being as the measure of all things, the Confucian regards such a perspective as too narrow and limited. For the Confucian, the proper measure for humanity is both anthropological and cosmological, what Tu Wei-ming calls "anthropocosmic." In this view, actualizing one's full humanity involves the cultivation of sensitivity and empathy to include the whole universe as one's lived experience, resulting in a unity of humankind with Heaven in Confucian terms.[35] In other words, self-realization is not only equated with the full realization of humanity, but involves the unity of humankind with a transcendent dimension that Confucians call Heaven. This is an important point, for, while Confucius was not religious in the conventional sense of his time, his sociologically oriented notion of the self as a center of relationships also had a spiritual or religious thrust to it. For the Confucian, says Robert Bellah: "Ontologically, selfhood, our original nature, is endowed by Heaven. It is therefore divine in its all-embracing fullness. Selfhood, in this sense, is both immanent and transcendent. It is intrinsic to us; at the same time, it belongs to Heaven."[36]

The idea here is not only that complete self-realization (an ideal that is never obtained), which is equated with fully actualizing one's humanity, involves the merging of humankind and Heaven. In addition, and more generally speaking, for Confucius there is acknowledgment of our finite, historical, and culturally specific existence, on the one hand, and the infinite, transhistorical, and universal on the other. This worldliness and the wish for self-transcendence are dialectically related in a creative tension.[37]

There are important ramifications for how one lives one's life for the Confucian who has embraced this anthropocosmic outlook. With regard to nature, for example, in the order of things, nature provides, not only sustenance for human survival, but also an inspiration for sustainable life. Implicit in the rhythm of nature, such as the changes of the four seasons, are important lessons in perpetual patterns of transformation, that is, regularity, balance, and harmony. In other words, for the Confucian, nature is held in esteem for its bountifulness, generosity, and grandeur in the nurturing environment that it gives us for our survival. Its awesome presence allows us to appreciate the fruitfulness and sanctity of our earthly "home." This sense of nature as home enables the Confucian to find ultimate meaning in ordinary, everyday human existence; to cultivate a sense of inner serenity and unity with nature, that is, a regularized, balanced, and harmonious lifestyle, and to view what other religions sometimes view as secular or profane, as sacred.[38] Such a view of nature, in which it is viewed with great respect, reverence, and gratitude, reflects the cosmic connectedness that in part, constitutes the spiritual dimension to Confucian thought.

For the Confucian, Heaven is the spiritual basis of moral creativity and excellence, existential grounding and meaning in life, and ultimate self-reconfiguration. In this sense, Confucianism can also be regarded as religious. That is, the Confucian commitment to respect for life, effortful work to improve the world, and devotion to ultimate self-transformation and improvement are rooted in this broadly conceived religious outlook.[39]

According to one scholar, the Confucian worldview assumes that Heaven is omniscient and omnipresent though not omnipotent. However, what we do in our everyday lives here on earth has ramifications for our personal lives, for our community, for nature, and for Heaven. The Will of Heaven (also referred to as the Way of Heaven, meaning, the ideal of the good human life as a whole) is intimately connected with what we do in our normal, everyday lives. If an individual attends to and nurtures the human way (i.e., self-cultivation, being ren and observing li, etc.), then he is unlikely to become alienated from the Will of Heaven. As we understand the bountifulness of everyday existence, viewing what is usually taken to be secular as sacred, we begin to apprehend that the great mystery of life is intrinsic to our common human experience of living. The Will of Heaven is, in a certain sense, lodged in human nature as Confucius viewed it. The goal then is for the individual to realize the Will of Heaven in our ordinary, everyday efforts, to make the Will of Heaven manifest by being ren and observing li. In this sense, the most profound meaning of humanity lies in assuming the responsibility of being the custodian of nature and the coproducer of the cosmos. Says Confucius, "A man can enlarge his Way; but there is no Way that can enlarge a man." Thus, the ultimate Confucian goal in terms of self-transformation is to reconfigure oneself to be more fully human by being ren and observing li, in other words, to be part of a trinity with Heaven and Earth as Confucians describe it.[40]

For psychoanalysis, this anthropocosmic view suggests the advantages of embracing an inclusive humanist outlook, one that combines personal self-cultivation with social ethics (especially a sense of social responsibility and an awareness that ultimate self-transformation is a communal act) and moral metaphysics (e.g., Heaven as immanent transcendence) with a holistic philosophy of life (e.g., creating a unity with Heaven and Earth).[41] In other words, Confucius's *Analects* gives us a magisterial rendering of how a person can self-consciously try to integrate personal style (e.g., self-cultivation), a broadly conceived human relatedness to others (including nature and the Will of Heaven), and moral virtues (e.g., being ren and observing li) into a way of life that is meaningful and worth living on an everyday basis and also is communally and civically helpful.[42]

What I am suggesting is that psychoanalysis could possibly be enhanced by making the struggle for moral excellence, which Confucius regards as the key aspect of the human ideal, a bigger part of the analytic ideal. In particular, I am referring, for example, to the core Confucian concept that asserts that happiness for oneself and for others is mutually enabling. In other words, to the extent that one gives to others, acts responsibly toward others, and sacrifices for others, one is most likely to enhance oneself in terms of one's own humanity. For Confucius, the gentleman strives to always practice ren and act according to li. The individual's uprightness and decency are perfectly blended with the right amount of refinement, so that the gentleman neither insists on strict adherence to formal rules or literal meaning at the expense of the larger "for-the-Other" perspective nor is boorish. In relating to others, the gentleman is warm, caring and empathic. He has an iron will and tends to appear calm mainly because ren reduces the individual's likelihood of experiencing intense anxieties, especially those related to interpersonal relationships. The person's wisdom (i.e., the practical knowledge about how to navigate one's way through life to maximize one's own and others happiness) tends to protect him or her from confusion and perplexities just as courage reduces the fear of life. Above all perhaps, the gentleman is less concerned with personal advancement, success, and narcissistic gratification and more with what is right foremost on his mind; that is, he values and strives to live according to the Way.[43]

Thus, this quest for ultimate self-transformation, conceived mainly as living a life of moral excellence, fundamentally involves the individual transcending egoism and inordinate narcissism and also, by extension, nepotism, parochialism, ethnocentrism, chauvinistic nationalism, and of course, anthropocentrism. Psychoanalysis has a lot to say about the toxic effects of inordinate and malignant narcissism and the benefits of so-called healthy narcissism. However, what Confucianism adds to these concepts, or rather what it makes central to its theory of the self that is hardly central to mainstream psychoanalytic theories, is that it is the cultivation of compassion and empathy for others' suffering, including a cultivation of a greater sensitivity to nature and the cosmos as a whole, that is the most direct route to the good life as Confucians conceptualize it. As Tu Wei-ming wrote:

> To make ourselves deserving partners of Heaven . . . we [need] to go beyond the constraints of our own species, [otherwise] the most we can hope for is an exclusive, secular humanism advocating man as the measure of all things [e.g., as does psychoanalysis]. By contrast, Confucian human-

ism is inclusive; it is predicated on an "anthropocosmic" vision. Humanity in its all embracing fullness "forms one body with Heaven, Earth and the myriad of things." Self-realization, in the last analysis, is ultimate transformation, the process which enables us to embody the family, community, nation, world, and cosmos in our sensitivity.[44]

Such a view of the human condition greatly broadens what constitutes a successful analysis generally speaking. As Roth points out, Freud offers us the story of "the taming of the beast within" and Kohut narrates according to "the discovery of the self within." Moreover, Klein suggests "the mad person within raging about" and, finally, Schafer's version of psychoanalysis emphasizes the development of responsibility, from "self-as-victim of unknown psychic forces" to "master in one's own house."[45] However, the Confucian project, with its anthropocosmic vision, provides, not only a deeply humanistic outlook, but also one that maximizes one's likelihood of accomplishing self-transcendence. This is accomplished, in part, by self-mastery, in particular by reducing selfishness, egoism, and inordinate narcissism, and connecting oneself to a transcendent realm called Heaven, in which one strives at being ren and observing li. That is, more generally, it is by living and loving a life of kindness, compassion, righteousness, and goodness that the Confucian is able to truly do the Will of Heaven. Moreover, the Confucian sense of mission to create a more secure and hospitable world, to enhance the quality of life for as many people as possible, and to change society into a moral community is not merely a humanistic commitment but is profoundly spiritual.

While the Confucian view may sound like an unhelpful throwback to most psychoanalysts, who are uncomfortable with a spiritual/religious dimension to psychoanalysis, it should be noted that both Confucius and Freud had at least one important observation in common. Both Freud (and psychoanalysis in general) and Confucians emphasize feeling as the bedrock for knowing, willing, and judging. Human beings are mainly judged as self-actualized by their empathy, sensitivity, and capacity to love, and only secondarily by their rationality, volition, and intelligence.[46] As Confucius wrote, "the ability to take one's own feelings as a guide—that is the sort of thing that lies in the direction of Goodness [ren]."[47]

NOTES

1. Quoted from Burton Watson, *The Complete Works of Chuang Tzu* (New York: Columbia University Press, 1968), p. 358.
2. D. C. Lau and Roger T. Ames, "Confucius," in *Routledge Encyclopedia of Philosophy*, ed. Edward Craig (London: Routledge, 1998), p. 565.
3. See Tu Wei-ming, "Confucianism," in *Our Religions*, ed. Avrind Sharma (New York: Harper San Francisco, 1993), p. 141; and, by the same author,

Confucian Thought: Selfhood as Creative Transformation (Albany: State University of New York Press, 1985), pp. 19, 52. In this chapter I have liberally drawn from Tu Wei-ming's work.

4. Raymond Dawson, *The Analects* (New York: Oxford University Press, 2000), p. ix; A. S. Cua, "Confucian Philosophy, Chinese," in *Routledge Encyclopedia of Philosophy*, ed. Edward Craig (London: Routledge, 1998), 2: 538. It should be mentioned that although Confucius was concerned with human happiness, he said almost nothing about that experience that often decisively undermines one's happiness, namely, personal suffering, especially seemingly unjust personal suffering like the death of a child in an accident. This omission—or, rather, Confucius's weak and very subtle references to the problem of personal suffering—strikes me as a rather large gap for such a brilliant moral philosopher concerned with human happiness. However, some scholars believe that Confucius was aware of the problem of suffering (what person who lives 70 years in the world is not), but responded to it in a way more likely to be communicated among an educated elite than among ordinary people. As Irene Bloom further indicated (personal communication, March 3, 2002), living a good life, preserving one's moral integrity and autonomy, asserting one's dignity as a person, leaving behind a reputation for humaneness and concern for others, believing that over time (though not necessarily in one's own lifetime) Heaven's mandate will be realized in the world, these are the proper defenses against disappointment, bitterness, and grief.

5. Arthur Waley, trans., *Confucianism: The Analects of Confucius* (New York: Quality Paperback Book Club, 1992), 7:1, 2, 3, p. 123. Referred to as *The Analects* in all future notes. In this chapter I have mainly relied on Waley's translation. It should be noted that Confucius always viewed himself as part of an ongoing tradition called, in Chinese, the *ru* (literally, the "weaklings"), that is, the culturalists or ritualists. The ru were the antimilitarists who moved beyond an older martial code and were persuaded of the power of civility, morality, and, eventually, ritual over that of armed conflict (personal communication, Irene Bloom, March 3, 2002).

6. Lau and Ames, "Confucius," p. 566.

7. W. L. Reese, *Dictionary of Philosophy and Religion: Eastern and Western Thought* (Atlantic Highlands, N.J.: Humanities Press, 1980), p. 102.

8. Waley, *The Analects*, 12: 22, p. 169; A. C. Cua, "Confucian Philosophy, Chinese," p. 540. The Confucian Tao and the Tao of the mystical Taoists are quite differently conceptualized (see my chapter on Chuang Tzu, though some scholars do not view him as a mystic). Where the Taoists tended to view the Tao as a nameless reality to which we must relate ourselves, Confucius is conceptualizing the Tao of the ancient Sage Kings, which is equated with the Way to an ideal government and society, and the Tao of a virtuous man, equated with the right Way of being a man. It is also a term that he sometimes uses for righteousness and wisdom. See Kai-yu Hsu, "Confucius," In *World Philosophies and Their Works*, ed. John K. Roth (Pasadena, Calif.: Salem Press, 2000), p. 400.

9. Julia Ching, "Confucius," in *The Encyclopedia of Religion*, ed. Mircea Eliade (New York: Macmillan Publishing Company, 1987), 4: 41.

10. Huston Smith, *The World's Religions: Our Great Wisdom Traditions* (New York: Harper San Francisco, 1991), p. 172.

11. Waley, *The Analects*, 15: 23, 6: 28, pp. 198, 122. It should be noted that the Confucian Golden Rule is intentionally phrased in the negative form. This is based on the awareness that the ideal way for me is not inevitably the ideal way for my neighbor. This psychology is required for the harmonious coexistence of

different and conflicting beliefs in East Asian society. See Tu Wei-ming, *Confucian Thought*, p. 26.

12. Fung Yu-lan, *A History of Chinese Philosophy*, trans. Derk Bodde (Princeton, N.J.: Princeton University Press, 1983), 1: 69.

13. Wing-tsit Chan, *A Source Book in Chinese Philosophy* (Princeton, N.J.: Princeton University Press, 1963), p. 40.

14. Dawson, *The Analects*, p. xxiii.

15. Ibid., 12:1, p. 44. I prefer this translation of this sentence to Waley's ("He who can himself submit to ritual is Good," p. 162).

16. Waley, *The Analects*, 17:2, p. 209.

17. Herrlee G. Creel, *Chinese Thought* (Chicago: University of Chicago, 1953), p. 31.

18. Chan, *A Source Book in Chinese Philosophy*, p. 29.

19. Cua, "Confucian Philosophy, Chinese," pp. 542–543.

20. Tu Wei-ming, "Confucianism," pp. 154, 160.

21. Smith, *The World's Religions*, p. 175.

22. Wing-tsit Chan, "Confucian Thought," in *Encyclopedia of Religion*, ed. Mircea Eliade (New York: Macmillan Publishing Company, 1987), 4: 18.

23. Tu Wei-ming, "Confucianism," pp. 186–193 ("The Mencian Idea of the Five Relationships"). The idea of women being submissive is, of course, highly objectionable to the modern reader. As Robert Henricks points out, according to the Confucian ideal, woman should nurture the "three submissions." As a wife, she should submit to her husband; as a daughter, she should submit to her father; as a widow, she should submit to her eldest son. See *Great World Religions: Beliefs, Practices and Histories, Part 4* (Course Guidebook) (Chantilly, Va.: The Teaching Company, 1998), p. 12. Hendricks also discusses the virtues associated with each of the five relationships, virtues for which the "gentleman" strives (p. 12). The assumed superior social status of men and the danger of the authoritarian character of government, for example, are both limitations and potential dangers of certain teachings within the Confucian tradition; Smith, in *The World's Religions*, p. 176, further interprets the meaning for our time of the five relationships.

24. Waley, *The Analects*, 7:22, p. 127.

25. Fung Yu-lan, *A History of Chinese Philosophy*, p. 57; Lau and Ames, "Confucius," p. 567.

26. Creel, *Chinese Thought*, p. 36.

27. Waley, *The Analects*, 11:11, p. 155. See also Julia Ching, "Confucius," p. 41.

28. Ibid., *The Analects*, 3:13, p. 97.

29. Stephen Schuhmacher and Gert Woerner, eds., *The Encyclopedia of Eastern Philosophy and Religion* (Boston: Shambhala, 1994), p. 192.

30. Smith, *The World's Religions*, p. 186; Tu Wei-ming, "Confucianism," p. 159.

31. Tu Wei-ming, "Confucianism," pp. 143, 142.

32. Tu Wei-ming, *Confucian Thought*, p. 57; See also D. C. Lau's translation of *Mencius* (London: Penguin Books, 1970), 6A:14, p. 168.

33. Tu Wei-ming, "Confucianism," p. 205. See also Ruthellen Josselson, "Relationships as a Path to Integrity, Wisdom, and Meaning," in *The Psychology of Mature Spirituality*, ed. Polly Young-Eisendrath and Melvin E. Miller (London: Routledge, 2000), p. 92.

34. Tu Wei-ming, *Confucian Thought*, pp. 114, 124; Waley, *The Analects*, 6:28, p. 122.

35. Tu Wei-ming, *Confucian Thought*, p. 10.

36. Robert Bellah, "Father and Son in Christianity and Confucianism," in his *Beyond Belief: Essays in a Post-Traditional World* (New York: Harper and Row, 1976), p. 95. Quoted in Tu Wei-ming, *Confucian Thought*, p. 14.

37. Tu Wei-ming, *Confucian Thought*, p. 10.
38. Tu Wei-ming, "Confucianism," p. 145. See also Herbert Fingarette's *Confucius—The Secular as Sacred* (New York: Harper and Row, 1972).
39. Ibid., p. 145.
40. Ibid., p. 146. See also Waley, *The Analects*, 15:28, p. 199.
41. Ibid., p. 168.
42. Joel J. Kupperman, "Naturalness Revisited: Why Western Philosophers Should Study Confucius," in *Confucius and the Analects: New Essays*, ed. Bryan W. Van Norden (New York: Oxford University Press, 2002), p. 40.
43. Kai-yu Hsu, "Confucius," p. 402.
44. Tu Wei-ming, *Confucian Thought*, pp. 180–181.
45. Paul A. Roth, "The Cure of Stories: Self-deception, Danger Situations, and the Clinical Role of Narratives in Roy Schafer's Psychoanalytic Theory," in *Psychoanalytic Versions of the Human Condition: Philosophies of Life and Their Impact on Practice*, ed. Paul Marcus and Alan Rosenberg (New York: New York University Press, 1998), p. 327.
46. Tu Wei-ming, *Confucian Thought*, p. 174.
47. Waley, *The Analects*, 6:28, p. 122.

5

Taoism: The *Chuang Tzu*

> Just go along with things and let your mind move freely. Resign yourself to what cannot be avoided and nourish what is within you—this is best. What more do you have to do to fulfill your mission? Nothing is as good as . . . obeying fate [the spontaneous, universal process of change]—that's how difficult it is!
>
> Chuang Tzu[1]

Chuang Tzu (369?–286? B.C.E.), along with Lao Tzu, was one of the greatest teachers of Taoist thought.[2] As Columbia University professor William Theodore de Bary wrote in his foreword to Burton Watson's landmark translation of *The Complete Works of Chuang Tzu*, "The *Chuang Tzu* is one of the most justly celebrated texts of the Chinese tradition." It is a work that "any educated man should have read," including psychoanalysts, I would add.[3]

In this chapter, I draw from an ancient Chinese tradition in an attempt to gain insights into the human condition that can enhance psychoanalytic theory and practice. This effort is in part based on my conviction that comparative inquiry into different ways of conceptualizing the human condition forces us continually to re-evaluate our taken-for-granted habits of perceiving, thinking, and feeling, and thus to imagine alternative possibilities of being.[4] Such thought-provoking disruptiveness in the service of creative self-constitution speaks to the heart of the psychoanalytic enterprise, for both analysand and analyst.[5]

My claim in this chapter is that Chuang Tzu not only illuminates with startling clarity and poetic insight some of the central problematics of the human condition as modern people construe it, but also offers what is, in many ways, a reasonable and workable attitude toward our rapidly changing, highly pressured technological society. Psychoanalysis, which is also concerned with the "arts of living," can benefit from engaging with Chuang Tzu's philosophy of life, with its emphasis on personal autonomy, spiritual freedom, the life of the imagination, and cultivation of calmness and tranquillity. Much may be gained by taking a serious look at "one of the greatest poems of ancient China."[6]

WHO WAS CHUANG TZU?

Little is known about the life of Chuang Tzu except that he was a low-level governmental official early in his life and later refused a chief ministership in the state of Chou in order to maintain his independence. As Hinton has pointed out, he lived during the Warring States period (403–221 B.C.E.), a time when the Chou dynasty had fragmented into a number of independent states that were continually at war with one another. The old social order had shattered, and the Chinese were struggling to generate a new one. Although this was one of the most deadly and disordered phases in Chinese history, it was the golden age of Chinese philosophy, for there arose a "Hundred Schools of Thought" trying to imagine what the new social order should be like.[7] Chuang Tzu was a major contributor to this debate, though he was as much a poet as a social philosopher. In general, he had a critical attitude toward Confucianism, the then dominant social paradigm. Confucianism had the goal of achieving a good society through harmonious social relations. This, in part, would depend on rules of propriety that would cultivate good character. Over time, the Confucian Way became an inflexible, stifling and highly conservative system of thought and behavior. Conversely, Chuang Tzu's poetic "intraworldly" mysticism offered an escape from the social pressures and conformism of Confucianism, as well as some relief from the chaos and unhappiness that many Chinese felt.[8]

CHUANG TZU'S PHILOSOPHY OF SPIRITUAL FREEDOM AND INNER PEACE

As in Chinese philosophy and in psychoanalysis, broadly conceptualized, the central problem is: "how is man to live in a world dominated by chaos, suffering, and absurdity?"[9] Chuang Tzu's answer, like Freud's, is personal freedom, freedom from conventional thinking and being, including freedom from the neurotic worries and troubles that are rooted, in part, in our early conditioning and, especially, dualistic thinking. While some scholars have claimed that Freud's psychoanalysis has important mystical aspects to it,[10] Chuang Tzu's notion of freedom, unlike Freud's, has such a strong mystical thrust that spiritual transcendence becomes the primary goal: to escape chaos, suffering, and absurdity, you must "free yourself from the world."[11]

To achieve spiritual transcendence and inner peace requires ongoing work on oneself. However, according to Chuang Tzu there are different attitudes, ideas, and modes of conduct and a certain sensibility that one needs to cultivate and deeply internalize to facilitate the necessary self-transformation of consciousness that fosters a sense of spiritual transcendence. Following are a few key notions and practices from the book known as the *Chuang Tzu*. In the second part of this chapter I will connect these themes with psychoanalytic theory and practice and suggest their possible significance for our discipline.

THE TAO

Chuang Tzu developed a unique notion of the Tao (the Way), the impossible-to-define core concept in Taoist thought, which refers to "the unique source of the universe that determines all things," though it is actually a much more evocative, mysterious and powerful idea in Taoist thought.[12] Chuang Tzu's Tao is beautifully suggested when he writes:

> The Way has its reality and its signs but it is without action or form. You can hand it down but you cannot receive it; you can get it but you cannot see it. It is its own source, its own root. Before Heaven and earth existed it was there, firm from ancient times.[13]

For Chuang Tzu the Tao was equated with Nature, in both its spontaneity and its constant flux, each thing developing according to its own nature, in its own way and time. The Tao is not God, a prime mover, directing this process of constant change; it is rather the "totality of existence" that "embraces all forms of being, all life."[14] The Way, says Chuang Tzu, is even "in the piss and shit."[15] While things appear to develop from simple to higher life, and lastly to humans, ultimately we, too, return to simple stuff, thus concluding the cycle of change. By identifying with the vital rhythms of Nature, the individual participates in the infinity of the universe. His or her life is no longer strictly limited by biology and social context because he or she is now symbiotically related to the cosmos. He or she has fused with the Tao.[16] Thus, the individual resides in another dimension of the spirit, in the substance of the Tao, in emptiness, stillness, silence, and inaction. Such a person, according to Nivison,[17] tends to withdraw from the world, not so much in terms of egoist withdrawal or schizoid-like remoteness, but rather in the form of detachment and impartiality, while yet continuing to interact and function in the everyday world. Says Chuang Tzu, the goal is to "walk without touching the ground."[18] That is, the preferred modus vivendi is nondirectedness.[19] It is in this spirit that one may even have social, political, and familial commitments, though in a certain sense one is in, but not of, this world.

For Chuang Tzu, we can free ourselves from the chaos, suffering, and absurdity of life, not so much by reorganizing or remaking the external world, but rather by relinquishing the conventional values and modes of thought that distinguish pleasure from pain and good from evil and that designate one as desirable and the other as undesirable. In other words, the goal is to give up all either-or and dualistic modes of thinking, such as fact-value, self-object, mind-body, self-other, being-nonbeing, time-space, and life-death. In any universe of constant flux and continual self-transformation, things show up in consciousness as unlike, some small and some big, some unattractive, some beautiful, but Tao equalizes them as one. This is Chuang Tzu's famous doctrine of the "equality of all things."

According to this doctrine, as Wing-Tsit Chan describes it, reality and unreality, right and wrong, life and death, beauty and ugliness, and all opposites are reduced to an underlying unity. This occurs because all distinctions and oppositions are only relative: they are the consequence of a subjective perspective, they mutually cause each other, and opposites are resolved in Tao. That is, for Chuang Tzu, a thing necessarily produces its opposite. For example, life ends in death and construction requires destruction. Ultimately, however, opposites are synthesized by the Tao in a dialectical manner that foreshadows Georg Hegel.[20] The trick, so to speak, is for the individual to transcend the struggle between opposites as he or she stands in the center of the circle of conflict and to respond indifferently (actually impartially), though effectively. Put another way, it is a kind of "centered responsiveness" analogous to a hinge moving effortlessly and smoothly in its socket. "It does not stand for this and against that; rather it responds from a center to whatever occurs."[21] This is an important stage in transcending the empirical world and reaching the goal of merging with Tao.[22]

The more one can view the world as in constant, though rhythmic, flux and transformation, the more one will cultivate a mystical identification with existence and the world as a totality. This is Tao as a subjective experience and spiritual state. Chuang Tzu was well aware that to achieve this mystical identification with existence was no easy matter, in that one is firmly lodged in one's taken-for-granted way of thinking, feeling, and acting in the world. Chuang Tzu attempted to disrupt the reader by subverting the very values, beliefs, and modes of thinking that prevent him or her from creating the conditions of possibility for being free to achieve spiritual transcendence. Here are two well-known examples:

> Once Chuang Chou dreamt he was a butterfly, a butterfly flitting and fluttering around, happy with himself and doing as he pleased. He didn't know he was Chuang Chou. Suddenly he woke up and there he was, solid and unmistakable Chuang Chou. But he didn't know if he was Chuang Chou who had dreamt he was a butterfly, or a butterfly dreaming he was Chuang Chou.[23]

In this story, Chuang Tzu completely rejects the difference between subject and object and between reality and unreality, leaving his reader puzzled.[24] Moreover, as Hansen has noted, Chuang Tzu is suggesting that "the distinction between dreaming and waking, real and imaginary is part of a system of arbitrary conventional ways of discriminating." Chuang Tzu, he says, is trying to show "the dependence of such discriminatory judgments on a perspective, not the possibility that the senses present us with things that are not really there."[25] Such is Chuang Tzu's postmodern perspectivalism and relativism: judgments need to be made but always with awareness that things look different depending on your perspective.

In the second example, Chuang-Tzu forces his or her reader to question his confidence in an intellectual and philosophical approach to reality and in the rational character of language:

> There is a beginning. There is not yet a beginning to be a beginning. There is a not yet beginning to be a not yet beginning to be a beginning. There is being. There is nonbeing. There is not yet beginning to be nonbeing. There is not yet beginning to be a not yet beginning to be nonbeing. Suddenly there is nonbeing. But I do not know, when it comes to nonbeing, which is really being and which is nonbeing. Now I have just said something. But I don't know whether what I have said has really said something or whether it hasn't said something.[26]

By disrupting the reader's taken-for-granted way of thinking about the world, Chuang Tzu hopes to encourage him or her to be skeptical, and to rid his or her consciousness of the arbitrariness of culture. In these examples, it is the subject-object and reality-unreality distinctions, as well as the overall reliance on rational thought and language, that prevent the direct emotional experience of the unity of the Tao.

WU-WEI

The ideal man for Chuang Tzu tries to live his life according to the principle of "wu-wei," or inaction, one of Taoist thought's great contributions to Chinese philosophy. Wu-wei, says Watson, "is not a forced quietude, but rather the renunciation of any action that is occasioned by conventional concepts of purpose or achievement, or aimed at the realization of conventional goals."[27] Wu-wei, in other words, does not mean taking no action, but rather means doing nothing that is not natural or spontaneous. To the extent that one makes conscious striving and deliberate acting one's primary mode of being in the world, one is bound to come in conflict with the Tao, and as the following example shows, one's effectiveness in the world will be diminished:

> When you're betting for tiles in an archery contest, you shoot with skill. When you're betting for fancy belt buckles, you worry about your aim. And when you are betting for real gold, you're a nervous wreck. Your skill is the same in all three cases—but because one prize means more to you than another, you let outside considerations weigh on your mind. He who looks too hard at the outside gets clumsy on the inside.[28]

What Chuang Tzu is advocating is well known to psychoanalysts. The highest skill operates on an almost unconscious level and dwells in the more intuitive and spontaneous dimension of being. As the Taoists would say, there we are that much closer to union with the Tao. According to Liu, there are several gradations and meanings of wu-wei in Taoist thought: wu-wei as doing nothing; wu-wei as taking as little action as possible; wu-wei as a passive or flexible attitude toward culture; wu-wei as patiently waiting for the spontaneous transformation of things; and wu-wei as acting naturally. Perhaps most important for us in the West is wu-wei as a principle of restraint, of respect for limits,[29] especially on individual and collective narcissism, grandiosity, and omnipotence. In other words, wu-wei is an attitude of care and respect for the autonomy of other things; it is selfless action. Through nonaction the Taoist does nothing other than conform to the Tao. Moreover, says Lao Tzu, "Through nonaction, no action is left undone."[30] The result is a universalistic ethic that treats everyone and everything as part of and expressive of the Tao.[31] This is in part the basis for Chuang Tzu's compassionate approach to the disabled, the odd, the mentally ill, and the criminals that populate his stories.

CULTIVATING INNER PEACE

For Chuang Tzu, the Tao also represents a subjective experience and spiritual state. To the extent that one fuses with the Tao, through action modeled on Nature, one has inner peace. Tranquillity cultivation requires refashioning one's inner world (i.e, one's entire sensory, emotional, and cognitive experience) in a manner that is, in many ways, very different in method and outcome from the ways we in the West conceptualize it, for example, in psychoanalysis.

For Chuang Tzu detachment is the most desirable state of mind.[32] This is a state in which there is no differentiation between things, experiences, and feelings. Any distinctions, evaluative concepts, value judgments, or emotional preferences will damage the Tao, the most desirable state of consciousness. "No-mind and no-feeling" comprise the ideal state of mind for Chuang Tzu, for such an achievement implies union with the Tao of the universe, that is, an inclusive, universalist ethic.[33]

What Chuang Tzu advocates is using the mind as a mirror to reflect reality just as it is, without any distorting preconceptions and preferences. "The Perfect Man uses his mind like a mirror—going after nothing, welcoming nothing, responding but not storing. Therefore he can win out over things and not hurt himself."[34] As Chan points out, the mirror is a significant symbol for the mind both in Zen Buddhism and in Neo-Confucianism. The distinction is that in Buddhism, external reality is to be transcended, whereas for Chuang Tzu and the Neo-Confucianists, external reality is to be responded to naturally and faithfully, like a mirror objectively reflecting all.[35]

There are a number of ways to achieve "no-mind, no-feeling." For example, "fasting of the mind," which means emptying the mind,[36] so that the Tao will move into the emptiness. "Sitting and forgetting" indicates that with sitting down and forgetting everything, including one's preconceptions, body, perception and intellect, one makes oneself identical with the Tao.[37] Chuang Tzu and later Taoists created meditation practices for emptying the mind to facilitate union with the Tao. Some of these practices have been integrated into Buddhist meditation.

Cultivating emptiness is a central idea for Chuang Tzu. This is emptiness as a kind of thoughtlessness or mindlessness, a discarding of conscious and discursive knowledge. By having an empty mind, one can relate and communicate with the real world without distortion and more authentically.[38] Paradoxically, when emptiness is fully developed, it becomes vastness, which is a union with the universe, with the Tao. This is experienced as a fertile void, an openness to the world and a sense of integration and wholeness. Says Chuang Tzu, "Be like the great swamp, which finds accommodation for a hundred different timbers."[39] Such a person, says Watts, has achieved a way of being that Chuang Tzu describes in terms of floating life, drifting like a cloud, riding the wind, flowing like water,[40] or wandering on and on in a great forest without thought of return.[41] This floating metaphor calls to mind Winnicott's work that relates play to the creative process. That is, for Chuang Tzu, the floating person is playful in that he or she has the capacity to shift and roam, refuses to be pigeonholed by any given stereotype, is not aligned with any fixed system, and is not overly serious about anything. This is the psychological context for the floating person's ability to cope, survive, and flourish.[42]

Emptiness that has been inundated by the Tao also has a relational thrust to it. That is, it is also a way of protecting oneself from injury from others, as it promotes both detachment and flexible accommodation to the external world. Such a mode of being in the world tends to generate a greater calmness of the mind, as this well-known example from Chuang Tzu suggests:

> If a man, having lashed two hulls together, is crossing a river, and an empty boat happens along and bumps into him, no matter how hot-tempered the man may be, he will not get angry. But if there should be someone in the other boat, then he will shout out to haul this way or veer that. If his first shout is unheeded, he will shout again, and if that is not heard, he will shout a third time, this time with a torrent of curses following. In the first instance, he wasn't angry; now in the second he is. Earlier he faced emptiness, now he faces occupancy. If a man could succeed in making himself empty, and in that way wander through the world, then who could harm him?[43]

How did Chuang Tzu approach the ultimate issues of suffering and death? They were viewed as part of the natural sequence of events, appropriately timed, and reflective of the changing nature and unity of the universe. In other words, like Ecclesiastes, Chuang Tzu viewed suffering and death as constituent parts of the never-ceasing fundamental laws of the universe and reflective of the unity of the Tao. Moreover, both death and life are one step of the flow of *ch'i* (breath, vital spirit, force), the basic substance of nature and of all life.

> Chuang Tzu's wife died. When Hui Tzu went to convey his condolences, he found Chuang Tzu sitting with his legs sprawled out, pounding on a tub and singing. "You lived with her, she brought up your children and grew old," said Hui Tzu. "It should be enough simply not to weep at her death. But pounding on a tub and singing—this is going too far, isn't it?"
>
> Chuang Tzu said, "You're wrong. When she first died, do you think I didn't grieve like anyone else? But I looked back to her beginning and the time before she was born. Not only the time before she was born, but the time before she had a body. Not only the time before she had a body, but the time before she had a spirit. In the midst of the jumble of wonder and mystery a change took place and she had a spirit. Another change and she had a body. Another change and she was born. Now there's been another change and she's dead. It's just like the progression of the four seasons, spring, summer, fall, winter. Now she's going to lie down peacefully in a vast room. If I were to follow after her bawling and sobbing, it would show that I don't understand anything about fate. So I stopped."[44]

As Fung Yu-lan points out, given Chuang Tzu's belief in the equality of all things, there is no form of existence which is not good.[45] Death, in other words, is simply a change from one form of existence to another; it is a kind of energy transformation. "Hence, if we look upon our present form of existence as something to find happiness in, there is no reason why we should not also find happiness in the new form of existence which we assume after death." The idea here is not to think of life and death as a beginning and an end, but rather as never-ending transformations. In this way, life and death have been equalized and the terror of death has been diminished or removed.

Finally, I should emphasize that Chuang Tzu used an approach to suffering and death that is similar to psychoanalysis in at least one fundamental way. He attempted to use a particular form of reason and argumentation to transform his emotions of sorrow into something less painful. By fully internalizing the laws of Nature, by fusing with the Tao, and by synchronizing one's emotions with the shifts in the external world through wandering, one may hope to become more accepting of the pain and transience of life.[46] As Chuang Tzu wrote, sounding like Freud in his resignation without despair as it pertains to life and death, "Man's life between heaven and earth is like the passing of a white colt glimpsed through a crack in the wall—whoosh!—and that's the end."[47]

THE SIGNIFICANCE OF CHUANG TZU FOR PSYCHOANALYSIS

The psychoanalytic context is one of the few places in our rapidly changing, pressured society where individuals are able to reflect on their inner experience and longing to be free from the chaos, suffering, and absurdity that constitute so much of daily life. This is probably what Erik Erikson meant when he once described psychoanalysis as the Western form of Eastern meditation.[48] Chuang Tzu provides us with a way of looking at life and a mode of being in the world that may be especially useful to analysands, who frequently find themselves unable to be even minimally happy in a world that often feels overwhelming, unintelligible, and dehumanizing. It is this alternative mode of being— the floating life, with its lightness of being—that I want to evoke in the reader.

INTRAWORLDLY MYSTICISM

As Yearley pointed out, for the "radical" Chuang Tzu, as he calls him, the perfected person focuses intensely on the perception that is directly present before him, only moving on to another perception when a new perception enters consciousness or the old one wanes and disappears. This "hold and let go" approach, says Yearley, sees life as a movie, a series of changing frames. Unlike other forms of mysticism in which union with an absolute reality or higher being is sought, intraworldly mysticism mainly aims to see the world in a new way, to create "a way through the world." "One neither obtains union with some higher being, nor unification with the single reality. Rather, one goes through a discipline and has experiences that allow one to view the world in a new way."[49] Chuang Tzu was thus advocating a mysticism in which man aims to attain a oneness with the universe, but he was not, as some have claimed, a "true" mystic, in that he did not believe that the universe had a purpose and ultimate meaning.[50]

In other words, says Yearley, Chuang Tzu was suggesting that we ought to deal with everything the way we deal with esthetic objects. For example, when we look at a beautiful rose, we stare at it, note its loveliness, and, when satisfied, move on to the next perception without clinging to the memory of the rose or trying to interfere with it. We simply engage the rose on its own terms with the fullness of our whole being. We then move on and become temporarily attached to another beautiful object of perception. "Life, in other words, is a series of esthetically pleasing new beginnings, and all such beginnings should be grasped and then surrendered as change proceeds."[51]

Chuang Tzu is here emphasizing the need to heighten our sensitivity in order to experience reality more directly. We psychoanalysts, like our analysands, are often full of false intellectualizations, heavy discursive reasoning and defensive emotional reactivity, rather than being immediately present. As a result we are less likely to grasp reality in full conscious awareness, one of the important goals of any mode of psychoanalysis. Whereas psychoanalysis mainly uses abstraction and conceptualization as its mode of engaging the world, Chuang Tzu tells us that the best way to go through the world is to experience life as it is lived, on its own terms, and without trying to hold on to experience. With this kind of moment-to-moment awareness, which is a kind of mindfulness,[52] the mind is less likely to be ensnared by any experience, and instead can move effortlessly and continuously, seeing the world as a series of movie frames, some more pleasing than others but always changing, just as Nature does. The trick is to be able to become a person in whom the "Tao acts without impediment."[53]

Such a view offers a new way to understand, experience, and manage our emotions, a way that enhances our freedom to respond to situations very differently, with less reactivity, more realistically and reasonably, and hence in a more relaxed fashion. As Graham points out in another context, the psychoanalyst, like most Westerners, is accustomed to think in terms of a dichotomy: "either as a rational agent I detach myself from nature, study the objective facts about it, make my own choices, resist becoming the plaything of physical forces like an animal, or else I welcome the Romantic idea of spontaneity, as the free play of impulse, emotion, subjective imagination."[54]

In contrast, says Graham, for Chuang Tzu the dichotomy is not applicable. He wanted to stay embedded in nature, to behave as spontaneously and instinctually as an animal, to be caused rather than to choose. Chuang Tzu had a disdain for misplaced emotion and narcissistically driven subjectivity and a respect for things as they objectively are. Like Freud, Chuang Tzu did not recommend giving in to one's unrealistic, unreasonable, and distracting desires; rather, self-control and self-mastery of one's passions were the goal (just as the craftsperson knows that if he or she becomes distracted by emotions he or she will lose his or her skill, so the sage cannot permit the clear mirror of his or her mind to be interfered with by passion.) The Taoist ideal is thus "a spontaneity, disciplined by awareness of the objective. . . . 'Follow the Way' [means], 'Respond with awareness (of what is objectively so).' "[55]

Chuang Tzu was suggesting that only when we relinquish or reduce our greed, lust, envy, hatred, and delusions—our narcissistically driven strivings—which are the bases of our grasping, clinging, and rejecting, are we likely to tone down our active "monkey mind," become less reactive to our conflicts and emotions, and attain greater serenity. Moreover, we are also more likely to relate compassionately to others in that we have undermined the basis of our egoism and the ego's identification with its pain. We are therefore better able to focus on, and attend to, others. The link to psychoanalysis is obvious: one of the best preparatory ways of achieving this nonattachment is to be psychoanalyzed. Ideally, psychoanalysis helps one to understand, control, and, ultimately, neutralize the childhood passions, unfulfilled needs, and pain that tend to motivate our destructive narcissistic strivings and interfere in our mindfulness, or moment-to-moment awareness. It is through the resolving and mastering of past conflicts that one is better able to enter into a nonegoistic alertness in which one can observe what is there without distortion and preconceptions. As in Buddhist meditation, the goal is to give up grasping and clinging, especially to old, fixed, ineffectual modes of being and self-representation, and to cultivate a more provisional, flexible, and adaptive self, which is capable of nonattachment. Says Chuang Tzu, "When I talk about having no feelings, I mean that a man doesn't allow likes or dislikes to get in and do him harm. He just lets things be the way they are and doesn't try to help life along."[56] That is, while an individual may have a wide range of emotional states, the key task is not to get bogged down in any one of them, but rather to be like a butterfly, capable of free and easy wandering.

Such nonattachment and mindfulness comprise a powerful method for self-understanding, relaxation, healing, and improving our ability to engage the Other altruistically.

WU-WEI AS CALMNESS OF MIND

Wu-wei, nonaction, is one of the great multimeaning contributions of Taoism to philosophy. It also is a useful sensibility to foster in analysands, one that tends to move against the prevailing way in which most people in our culture approach life, the latter view being an outgrowth of ancient Greek thought. For the Greeks, we are self-determining, and our chosen, willful actions are necessary to realize our aspirations. In contrast, for Chuang Tzu, Nature is more powerful and determinative of our actions and destiny. In other words, for Chuang Tzu, we are surrounded by forces that are largely beyond our control. In this sense, like Freud, he is a fatalist.[57]

Wu-wei is an internalization of this view of the human condition in that it insinuates that we pay a high personal price in the form of worry and anxiety for trying to control that which cannot be controlled in an absolute sense, which includes almost everything really important (e.g., when and to whom we are born, our relationships, work, old age, illness and death, etc.). Wu-wei, in other words, means accepting our impotence in the world, not with sadness or despair, but with equanimity, because this is the way Nature has prescribed the parameters of existence. Therefore, as Watts says, wu-wei is better translated as "don't force it."[58] Wu-wei does not mean complete passivity, but rather developing a suitable sensibility for every situation. The idea is to feel intuitively the kind of action that is required in a particular context. This is done intuitively because, for Chuang Tzu, we are not capable of discovering the right response to a situation strictly analytically, conceptually, and consciously. Watts gives a simple example of this type of intuitive approach to life. Suppose you are opening a lock and the key does not turn. If you force it, you will bend or break the key. "So what you need to do is jiggle, pull back and forth, and jiggle again, until you find the place where the key turns."[59]

For the analysand who lives life at a nervous and feverish pitch rooted in part in inflated narcissism and grandiosity, a wu-wei based sensibility decisively moves against his or her anxiety-ridden life. This is because it works against giving in to selfish motives and excessive, unrealistic desires, including the attempt to control that which cannot be controlled. Analysands constantly complain about feeling out of control, wanting to be in control, and/or feeling controlled, whether it is of themselves, of others, or of situations. It is a well-known psychoanalytic observation that an individual's desperate efforts to control or eliminate a troubling behavior only maintain and magnify the symptom. For example, the insomniac who attempts to force him- or herself to sleep is rarely successful, and the phobic who obsesses about dodging an anxiety attack inadvertently brings it on.[60]

Internalizing wu-wei means that by giving up the need to control, we paradoxically gain greater control. We are in control of control. In the psychoanalytic context, this suggests, for example, that to bring about an emotional breakthrough involves "an unself-conscious self-surrender, a relinquishing of control to the unconscious," that is, to something greater than, and beyond, the consciously experienced self.[61] Moreover, Taoism teaches that to achieve a goal, it is frequently necessary to begin with the opposite of what is sought.[62]

Such a sensibility is, in part, developed by having an analysand's choices be compatible with circumstances and context, and not with his or her unreasonable narcissistic strivings. In this sense, knowing which choice is best means first giving up purely self-serving motives and unrealistic and unreasonable efforts against natural law. Responding (not reacting) spontaneously to all things as they come is the goal, that is, flowing with the natural currents of the world and with the Tao. This does not mean the suppression of feelings, but rather the harmonious use of one's emotions and an increased sensitivity to context and timeliness. Paradoxically, says Chuang Tzu, one becomes more effective in life as a result of "not forcing it," and in a certain sense doing less, because one is not struggling against these forces. Thus, for Chuang Tzu, vacuity, serenity, mellowness, quietude, and embracing nonaction characterize the things of the universe at peace and express the ultimate nature of Tao and virtue.[63] In my view, such an attitude toward life will help an analysand to live a more balanced life, one that allows him or her to relax in the realm of the infinite, in the Tao.

This conceptualization on the part of the psychoanalyst can facilitate and deepen the understanding of what psychoanalysis is trying to achieve. It may help analysts in that it offers them a positive view of aspects of relinquishing control, one that can be communicated to their patients. Furthemore, it can diminish the sense of hurt and suffering experienced by analysands when they see the actions and events that occur in their lives as being a personal affront or attack, rather than part of the impersonal, "natural" flow of life. In this way, they are less likely to see themselves as victims or to blame others for their problems. Rather, they are more likely to understand that they do not have to fight the world or others in order to maintain their autonomy and integration. Paradoxically, by letting go of our desperate and inordinate need for self-assertion, we strengthen our integrity.

A SUPPLE MIND

Before concluding, I want to point out one last aspect of Chuang Tzu's thought that is relevant to the psychoanalytic enterprise. It is epitomized in his famous parable "Three in the Morning":

> But to wear out your brain trying to make things into one without realizing that they are all the same—this is called "three in the morning." What do I mean by "three in the morning"? When the monkey trainer was handing out acorns, he said, "You get three in the morning and four at night." This made all the monkeys furious. "Well, then," he said, "you get four in the morning and three at night." The monkeys were all delighted. There was no change in the reality behind the words, and yet the monkeys responded with joy and anger. Let them, if they want to. So the sage harmonizes with both right and wrong and rests in Heaven the Equalizer. This is called walking two roads.[64]

The idea is that in life it is important to be able to follow at least two courses at the same time. In other words, Chuang Tzu is stressing the advantages of not becoming stuck in one's perspective or system so that one cannot move back and forth between various points of view, opinions, and attitudes without extreme emotional discomfort. Such intellectual free-spiritedness can best be achieved when there is no narcissistic obstruction, no "pompous subjective interference."[65] Chuang Tzu, like Freud at his best, was thus advocating a healthy skepticism when it comes to our taken-for-granted personal beliefs and convictions, including our attitudes toward authority and our theoretical framework. Although absolute judgments are not possible in that "there is no absolute, constant, guide to all behavior in all circumstances and times," yet judgments are unavoidable and necessary to live a humane and reasonable life.[66] The important point is to be able to derive some pragmatic usefulness from a perspective by examining it critically for its usable truths (as opposed to its absolute truths) in particular situations and contexts. This requires a supple mind, one that is open, flexible, accustomed to thinking outside one's usual framework, and willing to engage many points of view as potentially helpful, regardless of how objectionable they may first seem to be. Psychoanalysis, in both its clinical and organizational contexts, would become a more tolerant, pluralistic, democratic, and critical discourse if it better absorbed the point of "Three in the Morning."

THE SPIRIT OF TAOISM

My intention in this chapter is not to convert the reader to Taoist philosophy or religion, but rather to suggest that there are some fascinating ideas in Chuang Tzu's thought that may have some usefulness for the psychoanalytic project. In particular, it is the spirit of Taoism, that is, its human values and way of thinking, its mode of being in the world, that I have attempted to evoke in the reader. I have suggested that psychoanalysis can be enhanced by engaging the *Chuang Tzu* as a way of enlarging our understanding of what it means to see reality, how to be more creative and effective in the world, and how better to manage chaos, suffering and absurdity. In this way, we psychoanalysts may increase our ability to help our analysands to soften the ground of their everyday experience.

Like Spinoza, Chuang Tzu advocated that people view their psychic pain and troubles from the perspective of the whole universe, from the view of eternity. When unity is perceived and experienced, the distinctions between pain and pleasure, past and present, and even life and death are diminished, if not eliminated, and one may feel a kind of oneness with the universe (perhaps somewhat like Freud's oceanic feeling). Such a state of mind, or cosmic self-awareness, is rooted, in part, in an acceptance of the changing, impermanent, and transient character of life. This requires relinquishing the "I" that is construed as permanent, fixed, and real, the delusion that one is unique and separate from others, and the idea that one's pressing narcissistic needs, such as being in control, require immediate gratification—or gratification at all. Taoists I have spoken with have told me that the giving up of narcissistic needs and the experience of an "I" is not felt as a painful loss. Rather, as one comes to perceive the web of interconnectedness and interdependence in the universe, the loss of the "I" is paradoxically felt as a greater sense of inner abundance, wholeness, clarity of seeing, and freedom. Psychoanalytic theory and practice can certainly benefit by further studying the form of consciousness and the general mode of being in the world comprised in the ancient wisdom with which Chuang Tzu has graced us.

NOTES

1. Burton Watson, *The Complete Works of Chuang Tzu* (New York: Columbia University Press, 1968), p. 161.

2. Modern scholarship has questioned whether Lao Tzu was the founder of the Taoist school of philosophy and Chuang Tzu's senior. The dating of Lao Tzu, and even his existence as a historical figure, have also been seriously questioned. It is thus impossible to say just what relationship existed between Lao Tzu and Chuang Tzu, and which texts they actually wrote. Perhaps they were contemporaries expressing the thoughts of two different branches of the Taoist school. See Burton Watson, "Chuang Tzu," in *The Encyclopedia of Religion*, Mircea Eliade, editor in chief (New York: Macmillan Publishing Company, 1987), p. 467.

3. William Theodore de Bary, Foreword, in Watson, *The Complete Works of Chuang Tzu*, p. vii. The first six chapters of the *Chuang Tzu*, the "inner" chapters,

are regarded by most scholars as the most original and brilliant chapters laying out Chuang Tzu's main ideas. There are also fifteen "outer" chapters and eleven "miscellaneous" sections, which were probably written by other Taoist authors and commentators.

4. Shigehisa Kuriyama, *The Expressiveness of the Body and the Divergence of Greek and Chinese Medicine* (New York: Zone Books, 1999), p. 272.

5. Paul Marcus and Alan Rosenberg, eds., *Psychoanalytic Versions of the Human Condition: Philosophies of Life and Their Impact on Practice* (New York: New York University Press, 1998).

6. Watson, *The Complete Works of Chuang Tzu*, p. 19.

7. David Hinton, *Chuang Tzu: The Inner Chapters* (Washington, D.C.: Counterpoint, 1998), p. xi.

8. Lee Yearley, "The Perfected Person in the Radical Chuang-Tsu," in Victor H. Mair, ed., *Experimental Essays in Chuang Tzu* (Honolulu: University of Hawaii Press, 1983), p. 130.

9. Watson, *The Complete Works of Chuang Tzu*, p. 3.

10. David Bakan, *Sigmund Freud and the Jewish Mystical Tradition* (London: Free Association Books, 1990).

11. Watson, *The Complete Works of Chuang Tzu*, p. 3.

12. Liu Xiaogan, "Taoism," in *Our Religions*, ed. Arvind Sharma (San Francisco: Harper, 1993), p. 232.

13. Watson, *The Complete Works of Chuang Tzu*, p. 81.

14. Watson, "Chuang Tzu," p. 467.

15. Watson, *The Complete Works of Chuang Tzu*, p. 241.

16. Farzeen Baldrian, "Taoism: An Overview," in *The Encyclopedia of Religion*, p. 292.

17. David Nivison, "Chinese Philosophy," in *The Encyclopedia of Religion*, p. 248.

18. Watson, *The Complete Works of Chuang Tzu*, p. 58.

19. Michael Crandell, "On Walking without Touching the Ground: Play in the Inner Chapters of the Chuang Tzu," in Mair, ed., *Experimental Essays in Chuang Tzu*, p. 114.

20. Wing-Tsit Chan, "Chuang Tzu," in *The Encyclopedia of Philosophy*, Paul Edwards, editor in chief (New York: Macmillan Publishing Company/Free Press, 1967): 1: 110.

21. Yearley, "The Perfected Person in the Radical Chuang-Tsu," p. 132.

22. Liu, "Taoism," p. 249.

23. Watson, *The Complete Works of Chuang Tzu*, p. 49.

24. Chan, "Chuang Tzu," pp. 190–191.

25. Chad Hansen, "A Tao of Tao in Chuang Tzu," in Mair, ed., *Experimental Essays in Chuang Tzu*, p. 50.

26. Watson, *The Complete Works of Chuang Tzu*, p. 43.

27. Watson, "Chuang Tzu," p. 468.

28. Watson, *The Complete Works of Chuang Tzu*, p. 201.

29. Liu, "Taoism," pp. 243, 282. In Victor Mair's translation of Lao Tzu's *Tao Te Ching* (New York: Bantam Books, 1990), p. 138, Mair emphasizes in his Afterword that wu-wei does not mean absence of action, but rather means allowing things to follow their own natural course. For the ruler, this suggests reliance on effective officials and the avoidance of an authoritarian approach to leadership. For the individual, it suggests achieving what is necessary without an ulterior motive.

30. Lao Tzu, *Tao Te Ching*, p. 16.

31. Baldrian, "Taoism: An Overview," p. 291.
32. Chuang Tzu's philosophical Taoism has strongly influenced certain Zen and other Buddhist concepts and practices. See Alan Watts, *Taoism: Way beyond Seeing* (Boston: Charles E. Tuttle Co., 1997), pp. 26, 82.
33. Liu, "Taoism," p. 246.
34. Watson, *The Complete Works of Chuang Tzu*, p. 97.
35. Chan, "Chuang Tzu," pp. 207–208. Chuang Tzu assumes that there exists an objective, knowable and uncontestable "reality." This assumption, with its respect for the phenomenal world, as well as Chuang Tzu's realistic aesthetics, which finds beauty in things just as they are, may trouble those with a postmodern sensibility.
36. Ibid., p. 110.
37. Liu, "Taoism," p. 246.
38. Watts, *Taoism*, p. 45.
39. Watson, *The Complete Works of Chuang Tzu*, p. 291.
40. Water is an important symbol for the Taoists, as to some extent it embodies their ideal mode of being in the world. Says Lao Tzu, "Nothing under heaven is softer or weaker than water, and yet nothing is better for attacking what is hard and strong because of its immutability." See Lao Tzu, *Tao Te Ching*, p. 54.
41. Watts, *Taoism*, p. 37.
42. Victor H. Mair, "Chuang-Tzu and Erasmus: Kindred Wits," in Mair, *Experimental Essays in Chuang Tzu*, pp. 86, 98.
43. Watson, *The Complete Works of Chuang Tzu*, p. 212.
44. Ibid., pp. 191–192.
45. Fung Yu-lan, *A History of Chinese Philosophy*, trans. Derk Bodde (Princeton, N.J.: Princeton University Press, 1952), 1: 236.
46. Crandell, "On Walking without Touching the Ground," p. 119.
47. Watson, *The Complete Works of Chuang Tzu*, p. 240.
48. Murray Blimes, "Psychoanalysis and Morals," *Psychoanalytic Review*, 86, no. 4 (August, 1999): 641.
49. Yearley, "The Perfected Person in the Radical Chuang Tsu," p. 131. It is not clear how the Taoist goal of unification with the Tao is not "unification with the single reality." Yearley does not clarify this seeming contradiction, but his emphasis, in his reading of Chuang Tzu, on a mystical approach to everyday life makes good sense.
50. Ibid., pp. 130–131.
51. Ibid., p. 136.
52. Jon Kabat-Zinn, *Full Catastrophe Living* (New York: Delta, 1990), p. 2.
53. Thomas Merton, trans., *The Way of Chuang Tzu* (New York: New Directions, 1965), p. 25.
54. A. C. Graham, "Taoist Spontaneity and the Dichotomy of 'Is' and 'Ought,' " in Mair, ed., *Experimental Essays in Chuang Tzu*, p. 10.
55. Ibid., p. 11.
56. Watson, *The Complete Works of Chuang Tzu*, pp. 75–76.
57. Hideki Yukawa, "Chuang Tzu: The Happy Fish," in Mair, ed., *Experimental Essays*, p. 59.
58. Watts, *Taoism*, p. 77.
59. Ibid., p. 77.
60. John R. Suler, "Paradox," in *The Couch and the Tree: Dialogues in Psychoanalysis and Buddhism*, edited by Anthony Molino (New York: North Point Press, 1998), p. 326.
61. Ibid., pp. 326–327.

62. Liu, "Taoism," p. 242.
63. Chan, "Chuang Tzu," p. 208.
64. Watson, *The Complete Works of Chuang Tzu*, p. 41.
65. Crandell, "On Walking without Touching the Ground," p. 112.
66. Hansen, "A Tao of Tao in Chuang Tzu," p. 35.

III

Greco-Roman Interlude

6

Stoicism: Marcus Aurelius's *Meditations*

> Dig within. There lies the well-spring of good: ever dig, and it will ever flow.
>
> Marcus Aurelius[1]

Marcus Aurelius (121–180 C.E.), was an emperor of Rome, the last great Stoic author of antiquity, "and one of the noblest figures" of the Greco-Roman world.[2] As Maxwell Staniforth wrote, Marcus Aurelius's *Meditations*, which were written daily, in every situation including war, "has justly been called the highest ethical product of the ancient mind."[3]

My claim is that psychoanalysis can be enhanced by intellectually engaging the ancient wisdom of Aurelius, and Stoicism in general. Aurelius's emphasis on personal autonomy, self-reliance, and self-mastery and his relentless effort to live a virtuous and tranquil life are relevant to the psychoanalytic project, for both analysand and analyst. Moreover, Aurelius forces the readers of his *Meditations* to reflect on their own moral lives and on their worries and troubles and how best to manage them. Indeed, with a marked emotional intensity, Aurelius, like many analysands, is preoccupied with his internal daily experience. For example, he wrote about his fears and anxieties, his sorrow at the behavior of his fellow human beings, his own personal shortcomings, and his hopes and dreams. Similar to the analysand, Aurelius attempted to make sense of his complicated, conflicted and paradoxical life, to cope with adversity and to manage a wide range of troubling emotions. He did this by placing his experience within an overarching framework of meaning, understanding and practice, that of Stoic philosophy.[4] Like the analysand in psychoanalysis broadly conceived, Aurelius was trying to generate answers to some of the age-old compelling questions about human existence: What is the "good life"? What is the "right" way to live to minimize one's psychic pain and maximize one's happiness? How does one create such a transcendent life?

WHO WAS AURELIUS?

Aurelius was the Roman emperor from 161 to 180 C.E. This was a time when the empire was faced with multiple disasters, including floods, fire, plagues (especially the arrival of smallpox in the Roman Empire), rebellions, and repeated attacks from barbarians. During the latter part of his reign, Aurelius wrote his *Meditations*. The *Meditations* are twelve books of unsystematic personal reflections akin to free associations on life, death, conduct, and the cosmos. Though Aurelius contributed nothing original to Stoic philosophy, one of the extraordinary aspects of *Meditations* is that we get a glimpse of the private struggles of a man at the height of his power, fame, and success as he tries to live honorably, intentionally, and with tranquillity according to the worldview and ethical principles of Stoicism.[5]

As Pierre Hadot has pointed out, *Meditations*, like all Greek philosophy of antiquity, was not a dry, abstract, academic discipline. Rather, it was a "spiritual exercise," that is, a tool for living life correctly or, in effect, a "therapeutic of the passions." The goal of a spiritual exercise was "a profound transformation of the individual's mode of seeing and being," that is, a radical change of everyday living.[6] It is therefore no wonder that Stoicism had an overwhelming emphasis on ethics (as opposed to physics and logic), that was greatly influenced by the courageous death of Socrates. Socrates' rational control over his emotions, his steadfastness, and his serenity as he faced death served as a paradigm of behavior for all Stoics.

While some scholars have described the influence of certain Stoic ideas on Freud, my aim is different. I want to highlight and further develop some of the Stoic insights about the human condition that may animate psychoanalytic theory and practice more sharply, so as to make it more effective in helping analysands in the "art of living." I should stress that I am not a Stoic devotee, nor do I think analysts and analysands should become Stoics. Rather, I want to convey something of the Stoic mode of being because I believe that a Stoic sensibility is extremely useful as one tries to live a reasonable life in our rapidly shifting, stressful technological and bureaucratic society.

DIFFERENTIATING WHAT WE CAN AND CANNOT CONTROL

Aurelius, like the Epicureans (a competing school of practical philosophy in ancient Greece), viewed happiness as the main goal of his moral philosophy. While the Epicureans tried to find it in pleasure, Aurelius strove for happiness through wisdom. One of the crucial components of Stoic wisdom, as articulated by Aurelius's main intellectual influence, Epictetus, was the capacity to distinguish that which one could control through human means (e.g., beliefs, judgments, desires, and attitudes) and to accept with dignified resignation, without complaint and fear, that which is beyond our control (e.g., things external to us such as the actions and opinions of others, our partners, children, money, jobs, worldly power, death, etc.).

This distinction was based on the Stoic belief that the whole universe was a living, organic, intelligent entity animated by the Logos (which was equivalent to such entities as God, Zeus, reason, creative fire, nature, providence, destiny, order). All people were under the dominion of the ruling Logos. Since the Logos permeated everything, whatever happened in the universe was controlled by the universal law of nature or providence. All human beings were interrelated parts of this universal, living, intelligent entity. Thus, since everything that happens to individuals was determined, the only way in which individuals could control their fate was to control how they reacted to external events. In other words, human freedom was manifested in attitudinal freedom and, given the Stoic cosmology, this was the only way the Stoic could triumph over providence. (The Stoics never provided an adequate rationalization for the fact that if providence controls everything, does it not also control our attitudes?) As Aurelius writes, "If you are distressed by anything external, the pain is not due to the thing itself but to your own estimate of it; and this you have the power to revoke at any moment."[7] Epictetus made the same point in his famous saying: "What troubles people is not things, but their judgments about things."[8]

Aurelius is making a deceptively subtle point, one that is, to some extent, reflected in the psychoanalytic encounter. First, like Freud, he is stressing that happiness is based, in part, on the nature of one's inner discourse, that is, on one's opinions and judgments about one's experience. In other words, as Hadot further points out, moral life is a dialectical exercise, whereby we engage in a dialogue with events and attempt to satisfactorily answer the questions they generate in us. The aim within Stoicism is to correlate our inner discourse to objective reality and to generate a pure and simple description of an event, without any distorting subjective value judgments, conventional social considerations, and passionate interference (that is, inordinate impulses, wishes or desires that could override rationality and create distress).[9] In psychoanalytic language, we would perhaps say, without any neurotic coloring and overdetermination. To the extent that we can get our thinking to correspond to reality, we are acting according to universal Reason and Nature and are therefore more likely to be happy. While this objectivist and realistic view of reality has been questioned by postmodernists, among others, the main thrust of Stoicism has influenced most types of psychoanalysis in that one needs a degree of detachment and distance from one's desires and social conventions in order to see things "as they really are" and to respond reasonably to events in one's life.[10]

The idea that while we cannot control most events, we can control our attitude toward what happens is one that I think analysts need to be more mindful of. Some psychoanalytic thinkers have inadvertently drawn from this Stoic insight. For example, Bruno Bettelheim powerfully affirms this Stoic principle when describing psychic and spiritual survival in the Nazi concentration camps:

> However restrictive or oppressive an environment may be, even then the individual still retains the freedom to evaluate it. On the basis of this evaluation he is also free to decide on his inner approval or resistance to what is forced upon him. [Such an attitude helped inmates perceive] what they had not perceived before; that they still retained the last, if not the greatest, of the human freedoms; to choose their own attitude in any given circumstance. Prisoners who understood this fully, came to know that this, and only this, formed the crucial difference between retaining one's humanity (and often life itself) and accepting death as a human being (or perhaps physical death); whether one retained the freedom to choose autonomously one's attitude to extreme conditions even when they seemed totally beyond one's ability to influence them.[11]

Clinical analysts can extract a number of useful, stoic-like ideas from the above, ideas that can possibly be helpful to their analysands. For example, in my view, Stoicism emphasizes that decision-making capacity and attitudinal freedom are expressions of a vital aspect of mature personhood, namely agency. *Agency* refers to doing, the capacity to intervene in the world. Moreover, where there is agency, there is usually a greater sense of self-efficacy. For an analysand to generate or maintain a somewhat coherent narrative of self-identity and a greater sense of autonomy and integration, he or she has to be frequently reminded that he or she has decision-making capacity and attitudinal freedom, which is the linchpin of his or her personhood. In other words, at any time, at any phase within a given sequence of conduct, he or she could act differently if so choosing.[12] Such an outlook works against the passivity, immobilization, and blaming of others and/or circumstances for one's problems that is so characteristic of neurotics. Rather, the Stoic stress on decision-making capacity, on distinguishing what can and cannot be controlled, is usually felt to be empowering for analysands. Perhaps most important, it heightens their sense of being responsible for their own lives.

LIVING IN THE PRESENT

Aurelius, like all Stoics, had a particular notion of time that he kept reminding himself of in *Meditations*: "Letting go all else, cling to the following few truths. Remember that man lives only in the present, in this fleeting instant: all the rest of his life is either past and gone, or not yet revealed."[13]

We should live in the present and experience the moment. This is an important emphasis for analysts and analysands to be more mindful of, for there is a danger of becoming too lodged in a retrospective consciousness as a point of reference, with well-known detrimental ramifications. While this notion of living in the present is bandied around in various circles, thanks in part to Stoic insight, it has a more profound meaning that can increase the analyst's effectiveness in helping analysands to cope with suffering and adversity and also to live more intensely.

As Hadot points out, the Stoics insisted on concentration on the present moment for a number of reasons: "It allows us both to grasp the incomparable value of the present instant, and to diminish the intensity of pain, as we become conscious of the fact that we only feel and live pain within the present moment."[14]

The point Aurelius and Hadot[15] were making is that only the present is within our influence, because it is the only thing that we can live. Becoming more mindful of the present, as the Buddhists say, implies becoming more mindful of our agency, and this increases the sphere of our freedom of thought and action. In other words, by encouraging analysands to live in the present, we increase their awareness of the precious and transient nature of their life and their freedom and responsibility to live life well. Says Aurelius:

> All the blessings which you pray to obtain hereafter could be yours today, if you did not deny them to yourself. You have only to have done with the past altogether, commit the future to providence and simply seek to direct the present hours aright into the paths of holiness and justice: holiness by a loving acceptance of your apportioned lot, since Nature produced it for you and you for it [i.e., consenting to the divine will]; justice, in your speech by a frank and straightforward truthfulness; and in your acts by respect for a law and for every man's rights [i.e., to actively serve the human community].[16]

From my experience, most analysands tend to be somewhat estranged from themselves. They are, for example, passively pulled backward by a painful and burdening past and forward by a harsh and/or seductive present. In addition, they frequently live ahead of themselves, in the uncertain, fantasized future. Following Aurelius's advice, they would benefit from living more in the dimension of being where they are most free and probably most authentically themselves, and where the past and future can only be experienced in moment to moment awareness of the present. Moreover, as Aurelius believed, happiness could best be obtained by placing the present instant within the context of the cosmos, and to give infinite meaning to every fleeting moment of existence.[17] In other words, according to Stoic dogma, happiness is available to us right now, because in a sense, we possess the whole of reality in the present instant. The trick is to be more mindful of the present, to foster a greater seriousness and care in living, and to give greater value to every moment because death can come at any time.

Such mindfulness is, of course, compatible with a psychoanalytic calculus in many ways. It increases our attention to our ongoing internal and external world; it encourages us to be more conscious of, and to derive pleasure from simply being; it increases our ability to focus and concentrate on what we are doing with the fullness of our whole being, that is, to live more intensely; and, in general, mindfulness enlarges our consciousness, especially of our freedom to think, act, and feel differently, including when life becomes nasty.

The second aspect of living in the present that Aurelius highlights pertains to coping with suffering, adversity, and evil. In order to grasp the Stoic method of coping with suffering we need to remember that it is not viewed anthropomorphically, but rather is conceptualized as willed by a more or less impersonal destiny, and is regarded as a largely natural phenomenon. That is, suffering and evil do not depend on us, nor can we control them, but they are the necessary consequences of natural laws.[18] As noted, the wise person—the one who is best able to cope with suffering—is the one whose actions are consistently guided by a reason which is synchronized with the will of Nature or God.[19] This means that happiness is not a result of choice (as is the current popular conception); rather it is a quality of existence that follows from consenting to what has to be, to what is out of our control. Thus, for Aurelius, the extent to which we can accept our fate without emotional distress will determine our happiness.

Accepting one's fate without emotional distress sounds like an easy recipe for happiness but as we analysts know this is an enormously difficult task. However, if one believes that one's suffering and adversity are merely a series of fleeting moments, they become easier to bear. In other words, mindfulness of the present can make one's pain more endurable for one understands that the pain is a process, it is dynamic and not standing still, that it is not "ours" but is rather an emergent process that we are experiencing.[20] Moreover, in a certain sense, the pain has an end point, in part because reality is always changing. According to Hadot, the Stoic idea here is:

> Not to let ourselves become discouraged by the global representation of the whole of life—that is, of all the hardships and difficulties which await us. . . . Like a song or a dance, our lives are divisible into smaller units, and consist only of such units. In order to execute a song or a dance step, we need to perform each one of these units in succession. Life, too, consists only of a series of such instants which we live in succession, and the better we are able to isolate each one and define it precisely, the better we shall be able to gain control over the entire series.[21]

No doubt many will not be convinced by the Stoic model of the universe and its strategy for managing personal suffering, though I think that there are parts of this approach that can be useful to the analyst. In particular, Hadot and Aurelius stressed that to some extent, we have the freedom to blunt the impact of the pain and sorrows of existence by dividing the present into manageable parts and strengthening our conviction that all suffering is inevitably self-limiting. This is because, thankfully, the present always passes since change and transformation are fundamental to the movement of the universe. A greater awareness of these two points can help shore up the analysand's ego as he or she tries to generate solutions to problems. In addition, by viewing his suffering as part of the impersonal Nature, as part of the natural flow of a basically benign universe (i.e., the universe is not designed to work against you), it will help him or her view the ordeal less personally, that is, with less anger and narcissistic injury. Such a view will also reduce the analysand's tendency to neurotically exploit a painful situation by unreasonably blaming him- or herself and assuming the role of victim. Such an outlook can, in general, help the analysand live a more reasonable life, one that is, as the Stoics say, more rational, realistic, and objective. In psychoanalytic language, this is a life that is less interfered with and distorted by neurotic and irrational wishes and infantile needs.

SOCIAL DUTY AND STRIVING FOR THE MORAL GOOD

Aurelius, and all later Stoics such as Epictetus and Seneca, focused on achieving internal serenity mainly via internal self-control, that is, by maintaining indifference to circumstances that are beyond one's control. However, this was only one of two poles. The other was social duty, that is, "useful citizenship in the cosmopolis that is the universe."[22] As Aurelius noted, humans are fundamentally social animals meant to care for others: "Neither can I be angry with my brother or fall foul of him; for he and I were born to work together, like a man's two hands, feet or eyelids, or like the upper and lower rows of his teeth. To obstruct each other is against Nature's law—and what is irritation or aversion but a form of obstruction?"[23]

Social duty was based on perhaps the key notion in Stoic thought: "Moral choice is the only property of worth."[24] That is, the only goal in life that is worth striving for is moral good, or virtue, which is an absolute as it is based on the universality of reason.[25] The essence of living the moral and virtuous life is to be cognizant of the fact that all men and women are citizens of the same human community and therefore deserve respect and compassion. This idea was rooted in the Stoic dogma that human relationships have the greatest meaning for human beings for they were the vessels of the divine spark that was equated with reason and God. What connected a man to his fellow man was the fact that each person shared this common element, this internal divinity. As Stumpf further says, "It was as though the Logos were a main telephone line and each person had his own phone and the entire circuit was on a party line, thereby connecting God to all men and all men to each other."[26]

It was this commitment to universal brotherhood and a universal natural law of justice that was one of the Stoics' main contributions to Western ethical and religious thought, especially to Christianity and to such thinkers as Immanuel Kant and Baruch Spinoza, among others. However, I believe that there is more that psychoanalysis can appropriate beyond this Stoic emphasis on the importance of social duty, "social feeling," as Alfred Adler called it, and a generally humanistic outlook. I am referring to the fact that Aurelius affirms the absolute value of moral conscience and espouses a passionate devotion for the centrality of the moral good and virtue to the definition of what it means to live the good life, that is, a life that is in accord with nature.

Of course, one of the problems that arises is that what actually constitutes "moral conscience," the "moral good," and "virtue" is a matter of one's perspective. Moreover, how can one know for sure that one is living a life in accord with nature? Obviously, this is a very complex philosophical issue, one that would take us into the intricacies of Stoic metaphysics, logic, and ethical theory, subjects that are beyond my expertise and the focus of this chapter. Rather, my intent is to suggest which Stoic values constitute the notion of the moral good and thereby both the spirit of Stoicism and a psychoanalytic ethic. A greater awareness of these enduring Stoic values can possibly strengthen and enhance psychoanalysis as a theoretical-practical matrix for living, and a life- and identity-defining narrative. In the last part of this chapter I will suggest how some of the Stoic values and insights can be practically used in the clinical setting

STOIC VALUES

For Aurelius, the things that most of our analysands view as important in life—money, acquisitions, sex, power, and fame—have a value in everyday living, but their value is only relative to context and circumstances. However, for all Stoics, says Hadot, lasting happiness is obtained only by pursuing the morally good, which is guided by universal reason. The goal, in other words, is "to be rationally coherent with ourselves. . . . [T]he essence of Stoicism is thus the experience of the absolute nature of moral conscience and of the purity of intention."[27] That is, the moral status of any behavior is determined by the person's disposition. Goodness and happiness are internal states, a disposition of the Logos. Moreover, the four virtues of practical wisdom, justice, courage and self-control constitute one's rational disposition.[28] The truly good person is thus one whose behavior is consistently determined by a reason that is correlated with the will of nature or God. What does all this mean for our analysands who are struggling to live a contented, reasonable and decent life?

First, Aurelius's *Meditations*, when viewed as a spiritual exercise, emphasizes the centrality of working on oneself in order to improve, transform, and create oneself. That is, to achieve wisdom, or maturity/health in psychoanalytic language, requires assuming a certain kind of relationship to oneself: a critical, questioning attitude toward one's own thoughts, feelings, and actions as well as toward others. In addition, Aurelius insinuates, one must critically reflect on how one is shaped by the conformist, normalizing, and coercive aspects of our society. Only in this way will one be able to maintain one's autonomy and refashion oneself as one wants.

My point is that analysands could benefit from conceptualizing their analysis more broadly than they usually do, as more than simply a "therapy" for particular problems or symptoms. Rather, analysis can serve a similar function for analysands as writing did for Aurelius, as a space for creating alternative forms of being and new forms of subjectivity, that is, new forms of meaning, pleasure and experience. Viewing analysis as Aurelius viewed philosophy—as a way of life, as a mode of existing in the world that has to be practiced all the time, the goal of which is to transform one's entire life—makes analysis more than a therapeutic method to relieve symptoms or improve personality functioning. Analysis, in this view, has a much broader, creative, and more compelling practical moral focus: it is a training or apprenticeship for wisdom.[29] Living according to wisdom tends to foster greater peace of mind, inner freedom, and cosmic consciousness.[30] Moreover, conceptualizing psychoanalysis as an apprenticeship for wisdom situates our discipline where I think it belongs, and not as a hard or soft science or medical subspecialty as some have claimed it to be. Rather, as Adam Philips points out, psychoanalysis is most fruitfully conceptualized as an extremely interesting, compelling and useful narrative of the human condition: "One good story—among many others—about what we are and who we want to be."[31]

Aurelius stressed that wisdom is achieved only when one's life is lived in accordance with universal nature. Extrapolating from this claim, the general idea is that it is desirable for an individual being to be embedded in an all-embracing, coherent fabric of meaning that comprehends the individual and all of his experiences, that by its very nature entails a transcendence of individuality. By relating oneself to a transcendent reality one is better able to integrate the affectively discrepant experiences of life, including death, into a comprehensive explanation of reality and human destiny.[32] Put somewhat differently, by having the capacity to "lose oneself" in a "higher" meaning-giving, all-embracing symbolic world—whether it be Nature, Reason, God, or the Unconscious—one is more likely to live a life of harmony with the universe. Aurelius is thus stressing the benefits of apprehending the interlocking and interdependent relationships between the multiplicity of parts of the universe and between the individual and the rest of the universe. To live in accord with nature thus means to observe how it works—its growth, development and changes—and to derive a feeling of connectedness and contentment at viewing oneself as organically related to the world and as belonging to the whole. Says Aurelius:

> All things are interwoven with one another; a sacred bond unites them; there is scarcely one thing that is isolated from another. Everything is coordinated, everything works together in giving form to the one universe. The world-order is a unity made up of multiplicity: God is one, pervading all things; all being is one, all is one (namely, the common reason which all thinking creatures possess) and all truth is one—if, as we believe, there can be but one path to perfection for beings that are alike in kind and reason.[33]

From a psychoanalytic perspective, such an outlook implies reducing one's narcissism and egoism and modulating it with a consciousness of being part of the universe that goes beyond the boundaries of one's individuality. By anchoring one's identity in a cosmic perspective, one renews one's connectedness to the world. In my view, many analysands have lost connection with the world qua world. They tend to see it as only a means for gratifying their wishes and desires. Being mindful of one's place in the universe means thinking and acting differently, as being a part of belonging to the larger whole. It means, for instance, viewing one's life with more humility and gratitude, two of the most infrequently used words by analysands in my twenty years of clinical practice. Humility, for example, by being mindful of the smallness of one's existence compared to the eternally changing universe. This implies not feeling that one deserves more than one gets in life. Gratitude means a sense of thankfulness at the way the universe seems to fit so well together (at least most of the time). This awareness encourages one to be appreciative for what one has, as opposed to complaining and getting angry about what one does not have. When our life is cosmically contextualized, even briefly, it tends to give each of us a more reasonable perspective on our personal problems and thus loosens our unhelpful and often painful interpretive grip on how we experience and act in the world.

As noted, Aurelius emphasized the importance of social duty or social responsibility as a means to achieving wisdom and as an expression of virtue. This idea is, of course, compatible, at least in the general sense, with psychoanalysis, namely, at the end of one's analysis, ideally one should have a greater degree of social feeling, a greater sense of commonality with other people and, perhaps most important, a greater compassion for them. However, I think that Aurelius is actually going much further than this in his claims regarding what constitutes the good life as insinuated in the following quotations: "Life is short, and this earthly existence has but a single fruit to yield—holiness within, and selfless action without."[34] "For everything I do, whether by myself or with another, must have as its sole aim the service and harmony of all."[35]

Aurelius was thus strongly advocating for a particular kind of self-world relation, one that I think should more sharply inform the psychoanalytic project. That is, as the great French-Jewish philosopher Emmanuel Levinas boldly asserted: responsibility for, and obligation to, the Other is absolute. I think that Aurelius would concur with the spirit of Levinas's claim, that one's responsibility and obligation to the other are greater than the individual's responsibility to satisfy them; they always demand more and are never accomplished by the fulfillment of any deed. That is, as a moral subject, the individual is always found lacking, because ethics is not just a component of one's existence, it delimits the entire realm in which one resides.[36] Such a notion of the subject, constituted by its encounter with the Other and the basis of ethical relations founded on that encounter,[37] possibly suggests a reorientation for psychoanalysis, away from viewing the Other as primarily a source for the gratification of one's relational needs and desires. In this formulation, "responsibility is the essential, primary and fundamental structure of subjectivity." As Levinas says, "The very node of the subjective is knotted in ethics understood as responsibility."[38]

Whether one arrives at this conviction via a Stoic, Levinasian, or some other mode of reasoning, paradoxically, there are enormous psychological and spiritual benefits to living a life that is animated by such a conviction of responsibility for the Other. In the extreme situation of the concentration camp, for example, those inmates who were more likely to maintain their autonomy and integration and to remain human (e.g., Jehovah's Witnesses, Catholic priests, devout Jews) had the capacity to imagine a moral order beyond themselves, one that provided the psychological, moral, and communal context for putting moral duty and responsibility for the Other above self-interest.[39] Analysands can derive greater satisfaction and meaning in their lives, and improved mental and even physical health as the coping research tends to suggest,[40] when they make service to others central, as opposed to tangential (or nonexistent), in their everyday lives. Deepening one's capacity for feeling and acting responsibly and compassionately towards others is often given short shrift in psychoanalytic discussions about what constitutes the postanalytic ideal. Striving to foster such a sensibility in analytic work, critics say, is too "super-egoish." In my view, psychoanalysis could be enhanced if it made transforming the analysand's moral life in this way a more central and integrated part of its theory and practice.

STOIC SPIRITUAL EXERCISES AND PSYCHOANALYTIC TECHNIQUE

Before closing this chapter, I want to offer some suggestions on how some specific Stoic spiritual exercises can perhaps make psychoanalysis a more robust technology of the self and a more effective practice for helping analysands in their training for wisdom. I present these exercises as simply food for thought, as brief illustrations that are meant to insinuate how ancient wisdom, in this case Stoic wisdom, can possibly strengthen our clinical effectiveness.

As one reads *Meditations* one notes that Aurelius frequently repeats himself. At first one thinks that this is not on purpose in that repetition in a diary is quite common. Later, however, one recognizes that Aurelius is intentionally repeating himself. Most important, he often repeats himself by trying to make the same point in a more compelling and striking manner.[41] This was a well-known Stoic technique, namely,

Stoics believed that in order to make an insight stick it was necessary to repeat it in an impressive, evocative manner.

Obviously, this technique has significance for psychoanalysts in that it reminds us that for an interpretation to make an emotional difference to an analysand, it should be presented in a striking manner. I am not suggesting that we shock our analysands into living a reasonable life, but rather that we become more mindful of how important and useful it can be to gently "disrupt" our analysands. By destabilizing, deconstructing and defamiliarizing[42] their currently accepted, taken-for-granted notions of themselves and the world, we encourage our analysands to think differently. Moreover, using a striking formulation, as Aurelius does in his diary, can help analysands move beyond logical and conceptual thinking and discursive understanding, often a form of resistance, and to make an intuitive leap into another level of comprehension, that of the unconscious. Similar to Freud, for Aurelius living one's life in unconsciousness was regarded as a sign of a flawed and truncated existence. Rather, total consciousness and clarity were an important Stoic goal. This meant confronting one's unconscious wishes and beliefs, the social biases and false and conventional value judgments that have unconsciously conditioned our existence and limited our consciousness of our freedom.

Throughout Aurelius's diary, he made a distinction between the inner dialogue that is "objective," that is a "pure" description of reality and the "subjective" inner dialogue that includes conventional social notions and emotional considerations.[43] For Aurelius, the aim was to see reality more objectively and realistically without the distortion of subjective factors. To operate this way is to be in sync with Reason. While this Stoic model may be unacceptable to some, the idea of trying to view reality scientifically and physically can be useful to analysands especially when they are faced with adversity. Aurelius refers to this approach as giving "physical" definition to reality. The aim is to train one's mind not to add anything to reality, to define reality in its nakedness by separating it from the value judgments that are rooted in our habitual way of construing the world and our interfering and distorting social and emotional biases,[44] including neurotic fears and wishes. Here are two simple examples of this technique.

Imagine telling the following to a male analysand who is afraid of having sexual intercourse with a woman because her vagina is viewed as dangerous, as a seductive vehicle for his castration. All the usual interpretations have not been successful in significantly reducing his sexual performance anxiety; therefore you tell him to try to see copulation as simply "the rubbing together of abdomens, accompanied by the spasmodic ejaculation of a sticky liquid."[45]

In the second example, imagine a female analysand who is furious because she heard from her work colleague that another colleague was talking negatively about her behind her back: "Never go beyond the sense of our original impressions. These tell you that such and such a person is speaking ill of you; that was their message; they did not go on to say it had done you any harm."[46] Adding "I have been harmed" to one's inner dialogue would be an instance of the self-destructive value judgment that goes beyond the "objective" internal dialogue, which makes the situation worse for the analysand.

Both these examples, says Aurelius, are reflections that

> go to the bottom of things, penetrating into them and exposing their real nature. The same process should be applied to the whole of life. When a thing's credentials look most plausible [or threatening], lay it bare, observe its triviality, and strip it of the cloak of verbiage that dignifies it.[47]

In psychoanalytic language, such an approach, especially when it is said in a striking and evocative manner, can make an analysand's anxiety and anger more manageable because it strengthens the ego's ability to discriminate external and internal reality and to become more aware of itself. That is, such an approach makes the analysand more mindful of how internal elaborations and neurotic fears are self-inhibiting and self-destructive. By training the analysand's ego to cut through the mental patterns separating him or her from a more direct experience of what is happening in the present, he or she will be more likely to recognize the difference between constructive and reasonable thinking and getting lost and trapped in unhelpful thoughts, feelings, and narratives. In other words, through this technique of physical description, we expand the analysand's freedom to think, feel, and act differently and, hopefully, more reasonably.

CLOSING COMMENT

I have tried to suggest that there is much to be gained by psychoanalysis intellectually engaging ancient Stoic wisdom as depicted in Marcus Aurelius's *Meditations*. In particular, I discussed the importance of helping analysands to differentiate that which they can and cannot control, of living in the present, of cultivating greater humility and gratitude in their self-world relation and making responsibility to the Other a central concern in their lives. I have further suggested that conceptualizing analysis as a training for wisdom can broaden its domain and make it a more robust life and identity-defining narrative. I have also offered some tentative examples of how practical Stoic wisdom can possibly benefit psychoanalytic technique. Perhaps most important, my aim throughout this chapter has been to convince the reader that it is the spirit of Stoicism, with its emphasis on the dignity, freedom, and autonomy of the person, that ought to more sharply animate psychoanalysis and thereby further humanize it.

NOTES

1. Marcus Aurelius, *Meditations*, trans. Maxwell Stanforth (Middlesex, England: Penguin Books, 1964), 7:59, p. 115.
2. Maxwell Staniforth, "Marcus Aurelius," in *The Encyclopedia of Philosophy*, ed. Paul Edwards (New York: Macmillan and Free Press, 1967), 5: 156. Many scholars do not regard Aurelius as a major philosopher, though he has received considerable attention because most of the writings of the best of Stoic philosophers have been lost. The major exception to this is Epictetus (Professor W. V. Harris, personal communication, September 7, 2001).
3. Ibid. While Staniforth's high regard for Aurelius illustrates the received view, I do not fully agree with his statement. For example, though ironically Aurelius was in general a gentle, tolerant and decent man, and a devout follower of the Roman religion, he viewed the Christians as guilty of profanation. While he was emperor, Christians were subject to systematic oppression. See Patrick J. Healy, "Marcus Aurelius Antoninus," in *The Catholic Encyclopedia* (online edition) (New York: Robert Appleton Company, 1999), 2: 1–6. The Prophets of Israel, Jesus, the Buddha, Confucius, Lao Tzu, and Socrates, all ancient ethical thinkers, did not have an equivalent moral lapse in their ethical practice.
4. Stoicism was founded by Zeno (334–262 B.C.E.). He convened his school on the *Stoa*, the Greek word for "porch," hence the term *Stoic*.
5. In particular, it was Stoicism as interpreted through the freed Roman slave and Greek philosopher Epictetus (60–100 A.D.). Epictetus developed the religious and moral side of Stoicism.
6. Pierre Hadot, *Philosophy as a Way of Life* (Oxford: Blackwell Publishers, 1997), p. 83.
7. Aurelius, *Meditations*, 8:47, p. 131.
8. Pierre Hadot, *The Inner Citadel: The Meditations of Marcus Auerelius*, trans. Michael Chase (Cambridge, Mass.: Harvard University Press, 1998), p. 107.
9. Ibid., pp. 85, 104.
10. In my view, the best study to date on the philosophy of Aurelius is Pierre Hadot's *The Inner Citadel*. I have, therefore, extensively drawn from his superb study as well as his earlier book on ancient philosophy, *Philosophy as a Way of Life*.
11. Bruno Bettelheim, *The Informed Heart: Autonomy in a Mass Age* (Glencoe, Ill.: Free Press, 1960), pp. 158–159.
12. Paul Marcus, *Autonomy in the Extreme Situation: Bruno Bettelheim, the Nazi Concentration Camps and the Mass Society* (Westport, Conn.: Praeger, 1999), p. 91.
13. Aurelius, *Meditations*, 3:10, p. 59.
14. Hadot, *The Inner Citadel*, p. 59.
15. Ibid., p. 132.
16. Aurelius, *Meditations*, 12:1, p. 179.
17. Hadot, *The Inner Citadel*, p. 222.
18. Ibid., p. 207.
19. Phillip W. Long, "Ethics of Stoicism," in *Dictionary of the History of Ideas*, Philip W. Wiener, editor in chief (New York: Charles Scribner's Sons, 1973), 4: 321.

20. Jon Kabat-Zinn, *Full Catastrophe Living* (New York: Dell Publishing, 1990), p. 282.
21. Hadot, *The Inner Citadel*, pp. 134–135.
22. Philip P. Hallie, "Stoicism," in *Encyclopedia of Philosophy*, ed. Paul Edwards (New York: Macmillan and Free Press, 1967), p. 20.
23. Aurelius, *Meditations*, 2:2, p. 45.
24. Long, "Ethics of Stoicism." p. 321.
25. Mark Forstater, *The Spiritual Teachings of Marcus Aurelius* (New York: HarperCollins, 2000), p. 37.
26. Samuel Enoch Stumpf, *Socrates to Sartre: A History of Philosophy* (New York: McGraw-Hill, 1975), p. 124.
27. Hadot, *The Inner Citadel*, pp. 308, 309.
28. Long, "Ethics of Stoicism," p. 320.
29. Hadot, *Philosophy as a Way of Life*, pp. 265, 264.
30. Ibid., p. 265.
31. Adam Philips, "Paging Dr. Freud," *New York Times Book Review*, June 7, 1998, p. 24.
32. Peter Berger and Brigette Berger, *Sociology: A Biographical Approach* (New York: Basic Books, 1972), p. 352.
33. Aurelius, *Meditations*, 7:9, p. 106.
34. Ibid., 6:30, p. 97.
35. Ibid., 7:5, p. 106.
36. Colin Davis, *Levinas: An Introduction* (Cambridge, U.K.: Polity Press, 1996), p. 54.
37. Ibid, p. 79.
38. Emmanuel Levinas, *Ethics and Infinity*, trans. Richard A. Cohen (Pittsburgh: Duquesne University Press, 1985), p. 95.
39. Marcus, *Autonomy in the Extreme Situation*, pp. 175–181, 192–195.
40. Kenneth I. Pergament, *The Psychology of Religion and Coping: Theory, Research, Practice* (New York: Guilford Press, 1997).
41. Hadot, *The Inner Citadel*, p. 166.
42. Roy Schafer, *Retelling a Life* (New York: Basic Books, 1992), p. 156.
43. Hadot, *The Inner Citadel*, p. 102.
44. Ibid., p. 103.
45. Aurelius, *Meditations*, 6:13, p. 92. Quoted from Hadot's translation in *The Inner Citadel*, p. 105.
46. Aurelius, *Meditations*, 8:49, p. 132.
47. Ibid., 6:13, p. 92.

IV

Western

7

Judaism: Ecclesiastes

> Everything has its appointed time, and there is a season for every event under the sky.
>
> Ecclesiastes[1]

This chapter looks at one of the most profound, subversive, and beautiful books in the Hebrew Bible, Ecclesiastes, known as Koheleth ("member of the assembly") in Hebrew. Ecclesiastes does not present a consistently thought-out system or logical structure in his reflections; rather, in his brief talks, parables, maxims, and proverbs, we are presented with a series of free associations on the meaning of existence, the good that man can achieve in life and the problematics of attaining or creating an enduring sense of personal happiness. Specifically, Ecclesiastes contains the melancholy, skeptical, ironic, and rationalist reflections of a philosopher-poet at the sunset of his life rather than a straightforward, unambivalent pious affirmation of faith and the virtues of living a religious life. Not only does Ecclesiastes strongly question some of the core beliefs in Jewish tradition and its worldview, but most important for this chapter, he raises many of the most profound questions about human experience and conduct for life that have been of concern to most serious thinkers for thousands of years, including in our time, to psychoanalysts.

My argument in this chapter is that, as one of the most illustrious of the "Wisdom" writers, those ancient professional teacher-sages who were committed to developing "a realistic approach to the problems of life, including the practical skills and the technical arts of civilization,"[2] Ecclesiastes not only identifies, with dazzling brilliance and poetic perceptiveness, some of the most profound and compelling problematics of the human condition as modern humanity conceives it, but also offers what I believe is in many ways a sensible and feasible attitude toward contemporary life. Moreover, Ecclesiastes' way of looking at life is not only similar to certain life attitudes and values embodied implicitly in the Freudian worldview, but also possibly suggests what psychoanalysis might in part appropriate or further explore and develop as it tries to enhance itself as a narrative of the human condition and a compelling "technology of the self." In other words, Ecclesiastes provides us with some of the most illuminating and insightful reflections on modern existence and our sense of what, for many, ultimately matters in life. Psychoanalysis, as it is concerned with self-transformation and creative and reasonable life-conduct, can only benefit from an engagement with this at times angst-ridden, but always courageous, truth seeker and lover of life from Jerusalem.

WHO WAS ECCLESIASTES?

There is a vast and divergent scholarly literature on Ecclesiastes. Both the more skeptical and pious have found support for their preferred interpretation.[3] Briefly, as noted by Robert Gordis, in my view the seminal scholar on Ecclesiastes, the Book of Ecclesiastes was written in Hebrew by a Jew residing in Jerusalem, who knew Aramaic but no Greek, though he was knowledgeable about certain Greek ideas such as the "golden mean."[4] The book was written towards the end of Ecclesiastes' life, about 250 B.C.E., which correlated with the experience of national defeat, humiliation, and subjugation, between about the fifth to the second centuries. Scholars have inferred that Ecclesiastes was probably something of a country gentleman, a bachelor with no children who probably came from a comfortable upper-middle-class background with a socially and politically conservative outlook. The tradition of the Synagogue, however, assumes, incorrectly according to most scholars, that it was none other than Solomon, the son of David, who wrote the Book of Ecclesiastes.[5]

Ecclesiastes was one of the professional teachers of Hebrew Wisdom, one manifestation of the literary genre that was part of the social world of the Fertile Crescent, which existed in Egypt, Babylonia, Syria, and Palestine during the second and first millennia B.C.E.[6] Ecclesiastes probably taught in one of the well-to-do local academies that educated upper-class Jewish youth. Wisdom literature is the most secular branch of ancient Hebrew literature, compared to Torah (with its focus on the practical and exacting obligations of living a pious and God-fearing life) and Prophecy (which focused on the ethical perfection of the Jewish nation and social justice). Wisdom, as R. B. Y. Scott has pointed out, in general "taught a practical philosophy through which good men might find satisfaction in life, in a moral order which had established itself through experience."[7]

While Hebrew Wisdom had its antecedents in more ancient cultures (e.g., Egypt, Phoenicia, and Mesopotamia) and neighboring groups (e.g., Edomites), there are basically two main kinds of Wisdom literature, which embodied the contrasting attitudes among the Jewish sages.[8] The first is exemplified in the Bible by the Book of Proverbs. It tends to be conservative, pragmatic, didactic, optimistic, and worldly wise. The second type is highly critical, almost rebellious, in its attitude toward traditional beliefs. This second type of Wisdom literature tends to be theoretical, individualistic and pessimistic. Ecclesiastes, like Job, is in this second group. The former sought a rational comprehension of human existence and a foundation for ethics, through the use of reason to observable data and experience.[9]

While Ecclesiastes believed in God, for it was inconceivable at that time for a Jew to do otherwise (though not exactly the conventional God of his time), his focus as a Wisdom teacher was on the problems of individual existence and experience. That is, on the difficulties of creating an existentially tolerable if not meaningful life and attaining a degree of personal happiness—all within the context of certain deeply troubling "facts" of human existence. For example, the transitory nature of life, the certainty of death, and man's sense of helplessness before an ultimately unfathomable and uncontrollable universe. Ecclesiastes, like Freud, is characterized by his unshakable intellectual integrity, his courageous use of reason in facing the most agonizing problems of life, his absolute refusal to sureness where he saw ambiguity and uncertainty, and his relentless devotion to truth, regardless of the uncomfortable ramifications in one's personal life.[10] Moreover, like Freud, Ecclesiastes was attempting to reconfigure his subjectivity, to fashion a self as an autonomous and self-governing being, both within the context of the parameters of the society in which he lived and in terms of what he took to be the limitations inherent in being (and in Eccelesiastes' case, in terms of the seeming limitations and enigmas in God's relationship to humanity). Finally, as I will attempt to suggest, like Freud at his best, Ecclesiastes was committed to a relentless critique of himself and his world as his main mode of self-fashioning. Ecclesiastes questioned nearly all of the taken-for-granted social paradigms and interpretations of self that were operative at his time, and in this sense he was, to some extent, attempting to fashion a new form of life that departed from the coercive normalizing institutions of the priestly scribes and orthodox theologians within his community. Finally, as I will suggest, like Freud, Ecclesiastes ended up, in part, advocating an attitude toward life characterized by resignation without despair, combined with an unwavering commitment to striving after joy in life, fleeting as these joyful experiences may be.

The Book of Ecclesiastes is overflowing with provocative ideas about life, love, suffering, growing old, and death, and it is impossible in this essay to discuss all of them. I therefore will focus on a few of the major themes that embody his "philosophy of life," as it were, and seem to be most relevant to psychoanalysis. In the final section, I will discuss the implications for psychoanalysis of Ecclesiastes' insights into the human condition and the ethical wisdom that emanates from it.

"VANITY OF VANITIES, ALL IS VANITY" (OR "CHASING AFTER WIND")

From beginning to end, Ecclesiastes bluntly asserts one of his recurring claims, that from his wide-ranging experience of life, he knows the entire human enterprise is fundamentally empty and ultimately meaningless:

> Vanities of vanities, says Koheleth, vanities of vanities, all is vanity [in Hebrew *hebel*, translated as "vanity," means "vapor" or "breath"]. What profit has a man of all his toil beneath the sun [i.e., the earthly context of man's activities and vicissitudes]? One generation goes and another comes, but the earth is forever unchanged. The sun rises and the sun sets, breathlessly rushing towards the place where it is to rise again. Going to the south and circling to the north, the wind goes round and round, and then returns its tracks. All the rivers flow into the sea, but the sea is never full; to the place where the rivers flow, there they continue to flow. All things are tiresome, one cannot put them into words, and so the eye is never satisfied with seeing nor the ear filled with hearing. What has been will be, and what has been done will be done again; there is nothing new under the sun. There may be something of which man says, "Look, this is new!" It has already occurred in the ages before us [including the musings of Koheleth]. For there is no recollection left of the earliest generations, and even the later ones will not be remembered who come at the very end.[11]

Ecclesiastes is here declaring his key conviction about life, that our existence, our experience of our life's struggles and all that we attempt to achieve, is like a vapor or a breath. Like nature, we are part of a repetitive and eternal cycle, without an end point or inherent purpose. Nothing really new ever happens, our experience of our life is of an endless movement without change. What appears to be new is actually a function of our truncated memory, that is, we forget the past. Thus, as the famous quotation goes, "there is nothing new under the sun." From this perspective of the universe, concludes Ecclesiastes, all human efforts are pointless. That we can neither fully comprehend nor modify the predetermined pattern of life is most beautifully expressed in the famous "Catalogue of the Times," once popularized by the rock group The Byrds:

> Everything has its appointed time, and there is a season for every event under the sky.
> There is a time to be born, and a time to die,
> A time to plant and a time to uproot,
> A time to kill and a time to heal,
> A time to wreck and a time to build.
> A time to weep and a time to laugh,
> A time to mourn and a time to dance,
> A time to scatter stones and a time to gather them,
> A time to embrace and a time to hold off embraces.
> A time to seek and a time to give up,
> A time to keep and a time to cast off,
> A time to tear and a time to repair,
> A time to be silent and a time to speak.
> A time to love and a time to hate,
> A time of war and a time of peace.
> What profit then has the worker in his toil?[12]

In Ecclesiastes' view, all that happens to man seems to be predetermined, and correlated to its uniquely apt time. However, why it occurs this way and not in some different way, and what it all means (if anything) is an unfathomable enigma.[13]

In this interpretation of Ecclesiastes, the analogy between the processes of nature and human experience concludes that life proceeds in an endless repetition, which is always a negative force. Some scholars, however, have interpreted this passage differently, which is worth pointing out since it suggests a less pessimistic side to Ecclesiastes. Perry, for example, notes that while it appears that we are part of nature and thus subject to its causality, and that the direction of life is irreversible, from positive to negative (e.g., "the sun rises and the sun sets," "a time to be born, a time to die"), Ecclesiastes also is aware of the counterpoint, and here perhaps lies a tepid optimism.[14] That is, the alternative to natural determinism and pessimism, says Perry, is a concept of cyclicality such that following decline and death, there is a new start. For example, despite its previous setting, the sun always rises again. In other words, continues Perry, while Ecclesiastes seems to be saying, on one hand, that endless repetition is negative, the notion of cyclicality, which can be negative or positive, opens the possibility of trying again. Moreover, says Perry, in the human context, many of the verses in the "Catalogue of Times" actually insinuate hopefulness and optimism, for example, "A time to weep but also a time to be happy." While I agree with Perry that both pessimism and, to some extent, a restrained optimism are woven into Ecclesiastes' reflections, I believe the pessimism is the much stronger voice, and for good reason, based on how Ecclesiastes construes the workings of the harsh world.

How does Ecclesiastes know that life is fundamentally futile, that is, what does he base his assertion on? He bases it on two forms of personal experimentation to give meaning to existence, one broadly philosophical-intellectual and the other sensual, both of which are entirely contemporary, but which, says Ecclesiastes, have failed him as a satisfying justification for his existence:

> I, Koheleth, was king over Israel in Jerusalem. I applied my mind to search out and explore in my wisdom all that happens beneath the sky—a sorry business it is that God has given men to be afflicted with. . . . Said I to myself, "Here I have greatly increased my wisdom, beyond all those who were before me over Jerusalem, for my heart has attained much wisdom and knowledge." But as I applied my mind, I learnt that wisdom [equivalent to "perfect goodness" for the Wisdom writers, says Gordis[15]] and knowledge are madness [unrestrained and unprincipled behavior rooted in the belief that life is meaningless and there is no moral law operating in the world[16]] and folly. Yes, I perceived that this, too, is chasing after wind. For the more wisdom, the more grief, and increasing one's knowledge means increasing one's pain.
>
> Then I said to myself, "Come let me try you out in joy and enjoy pleasure," but this, too, was vanity. Of laughter I said, "It is folly," and of joy, "What good is it?" For I had explored the matter with my mind, by stimulating my body with wine (while my mind was acting with wisdom) and by taking hold of frivolity, so that I might see what course is best for men under the sky during the brief span of their lives.[17]

Ecclesiastes is here noting that God has lodged in humanity an irrepressible desire to find the Truth, to make some ultimate sense out of life by imposing an all-embracing, comprehensive order and a system on his experience. That is, Ecclesiastes is making the profound deconstructionist point that any attempt to frame a complete philosophic system can be achieved only by doing violence to an ultimately unfathomable reality. In other words, in religious language, "What God is doing is his own secret and whether He is well-disposed or ill-disposed toward man is unknown."[18] While humanity's desire to find the Truth is compelling, according to Ecclesiastes, this is impossible, and the humbler search for usable truths is the best we can do. Moreover, Ecclesiastes ironically notes, in a certain sense the quest for and attainment of knowledge and wisdom (or "insight" as psychoanalysts call it) can lead to more psychic pain. In a sense, ignorance is bliss although

Ecclesiastes clearly values knowledge and wisdom above ignorance, foolishness, and madness, but not by much.

Ecclesiastes also says that he tried to derive enduring meaning in his life largely through the attainment of sensual pleasure, for example, in the form of wine, women, song, wealth, and possessions. That this gratification of the appetites, pleasure for its own sake, ultimately left him feeling unsatisfied is not surprising since, as he himself notes, these acquisitions are even more transient and ephemeral in the long run than knowledge and wisdom. This is especially the case as one gets older, when one's bodily responsiveness to pleasurable stimulation is diminished and when one tends to quickly habituate to once novel pleasures.

Thus, Ecclesiastes's main claim is that experience—including its intellectual and sensual aspects—is as fleeting and insubstantial as a vapor. The evidence, in part, for this he says is that generations come and go and nature is in endless motion, yet nothing new results. Human effort and so-called achievement are pointless, whether to change the world (e.g., to fight for social justice as the Prophets did was pointless since nothing changes and there is nothing new under the sun), to reach understanding (i.e., we are forever ignorant of the "real" meaning of events, life is an insolvable enigma since God chooses not to reveal Himself), or to attain happiness (i.e., we have a God-given "design fault," and so we are never really satisfied no matter how much we acquire).[19]

If this is not a grim enough characterization of the human condition, Ecclesiastes adds other observations from his experience to support his pessimistic outlook:

> Furthermore, I saw under the sun that in the place of judgment there was wickedness, and in the place of righteousness, wrong.... Again I saw all the acts of oppression that are done under the sun. Here are the tears of the oppressed, with none to comfort them; and power in the hands of their oppressors, with none to comfort them. So I praise the dead who already have died, more than the creatures who still are alive. And more fortunate than both is he who has not yet been born and so has never seen the evil deeds that are being done under the sun.[20]

Ecclesiastes' sense of the fundamental meaninglessness and inscrutability of life is further elaborated through his pained observation that there appears to be no divine or human justice in the world (in contrast for example, to what the Prophets believed). Ecclesiastes was struck by the fact that time and again, according to his experience, it is as if man lives in an ethically indifferent universe. In Ecclesiastes' language, this meant that while he believed that there was a God who had creative and boundless power, He often did not wish to intervene in human history at the appropriate time, or if He did intervene, it was usually too little too late. Ecclesiastes thus passionately protests against a world in which the powerful are evil and the weak vulnerable to victimization. He sees no evidence for, nor comfort in, a belief in the Hereafter where the wicked will be punished and everything will be put right (a commonly held view in his day).

Perhaps even more outrageous to Ecclesiastes is that our character, behavior, and achievements appear to make no difference to our everyday or ultimate fate in this world. The righteous and the wicked, the wise person and the fool end up about the same, and both meet the same inevitable end, death. In fact, he somewhat sardonically notes that it is all too common for the righteous and wise to suffer and the wicked and foolish to prosper. Moreover, he claims that it is impossible for a person to know whether God will act kindly toward him or her, thus emphasizing a most tragic aspect to life, that we are uncertain of our fate. In fact, Ecclesiastes even sarcastically questions whether we are superior to the animals since it is uncertain whether our spirit ascends to Heaven and the animal's descends to the earth.[21]

It is in his final reflection, in his magisterial "Allegory on Old Age," that Ecclesiastes describes the fact that we must grow old; we gradually but decisively physically deteriorate and die, putting into sharp focus the brevity and tragic limitations to existence. For this reason and because it suggests what he thought was the most workable attitude toward life, given his stark and pessimistic view (discussed in the next section), it is worth quoting the Allegory in its entirety:

> Sweet is the light [read: "life"]
> And it is good for the eyes
> To see the sun! [read: "life"[22]]
> For if a man lives many years,
> Let him rejoice in them all,
> And remember that the days of darkness will be many,
> And that everything thereafter is nothingness.
>
> Rejoice, young man, in your youth,
> And let your heart cheer you in your youthful days.
> Follow the impulses of your heart
> And the desires of your eyes,
> And know that for all this,
> God will call you to account.
>
> Banish sadness from your heart,
> And remove sorrow from your flesh,
> For childhood and youth are a fleeting breath.

Remember your Creator in the days of your youth,
Before the evil days come and the years draw near,
Of which you will say, 'I have no pleasure in them.'
Before the sun [the forehead[23]] grows dark,
And the light [the nose] of the moon [the soul] and the stars, [the cheeks]
And the clouds return after the rain. [enfeebled eyesight due to trouble and sickness]

In the day when the watchmen of the house [the flanks, ribs, arms] tremble,
And the strong men [the legs] are bent.
The grinding maidens [the teeth] cease, for they are few,
And the ladies peering through the lattices [the eyes] grow dim.

When the doubled doors on the street [the ears] are shut,
And the voice of the mill [a failing stomach] becomes low.
One wakes at the sound of a bird,
And all the daughters of song are laid low.

When one fears to climb a height,
And terrors lurk in a walk,
When the almond-tree blossoms, [the whitening of the hair]
The grasshopper becomes a burden, [the decline of sexual vitality]
And the caperberry [a sensual fruit] can no longer stimulate desire.
So man goes to his eternal home,
While the hired mourners walk about in the street. . .

Before the silver cord [the tongue or the spine] is severed,
And the golden bowl [the marrow or the head] is shattered,
The pitcher [the gall or the stomach] is broken at the spring,
And the wheel [the skull] is shattered at the pit.
The dust returns to the earth as it was,
And the spirit returns to God, who gave it.
Vanities of vanities, says Koheleth, all is vanity.[24]

For Ecclesiastes, while we are aware that the time and context of our death is unknown, this awareness only adds to our sense of uncertainty and helplessness in a fundamentally unintelligible universe. Ecclesiastes ironically notes that as our life draws to its absolute conclusion after a long and decisive period of deterioration, this tragedy is but a professional routine for the hired mourners, thus emphasizing that the vanity of life is mirrored and climaxed in the vanity of death.[25] Death for Ecclesiastes means that all activity is ended, although, as Gordis notes, he "does not deny that life comes from God." However, while Ecclesiastes' God is conceived as real and transcendent, as the creator of the physical universe and of humanity, and as ruling over the course of events over the world, divine intervention in nature or human affairs is impossible since nothing new happens under the sun. Thus, the doctrine of divine Providence, a core belief in traditional Judaism, has become, for Ecclesiastes, an arbitrary and absolute determinism.[26] Says Gordis, "Before the mystery of death, only the language of religion proves adequate. But Koheleth does not conceive of God as Comforter or Redeemer," unlike the ancient Hebrews of his time.[27] (Nor did Ecclesiastes view God as a punisher as the Prophets did.)

Last, says Ecclesiastes, while life is depleted of its meaning by death, so all values are undermined if not blotted out by their opposites. So, for example, wisdom and knowledge often cause more psychic pain, things of surpassing merit or quality are frequently destroyed by some seemingly preordained yet inexplicable bad happening or disaster, frequently people do not acknowledge or affirm good deeds or wisdom, rendering them ineffective, capricious power is often in the hands of wicked people causing much anguish to others and social instability, a famous or good man is frequently forgotten, and the hard-earned achievements and acquisitions of a lifetime may be destroyed or lost through one crucial mistake in judgment.[28] All values and the reality that they reflect are here dialectically conceived, implying that there is no absolute ethical foundation in which one can anchor one's life.

This, then, is a summary of the way the world looked to Ecclesiastes. It is a rather grim view of life; in fact, as one commentator noted, all this sounds like advocacy for suicide.[29] Yet this is absolutely not Ecclesiastes' conclusion as we shall soon see. In the rest of this chapter I show what the worldview and ethical wisdom of Ecclesiastes have to do with psychoanalysis and specifically in what ways his "Freud friendly" form of life and technology of the self can possibly enhance the psychoanalytic one.

THE SIGNIFICANCE OF ECCLESIASTES' ETHICAL WISDOM FOR PSYCHOANALYSIS

Ecclesiastes' philosophy of life is in part rooted in the conviction that it is unwise, if not impossible, to impose a comprehensive order and system, a "worldview," on experience (e.g., the philosophical-intellectual- and sensual-based approaches described earlier). For to do so, is to do violence to experience by, for example, reducing it to comfortable and banal formulas that do not do justice to the complexity, ambiguity, and contradictory character of experience. For Ecclesiastes, the experience of life cannot be reduced to a system by means of moral principles since they collapse amid the anomalies of experience just as the attempt to reduce life to a system by means of theoretical ideas collapses as it tries to resolve the antinomies and paradoxes of existence.[30] In other words, as Emmanuel Levinas has suggested, we seem to have a basic tendency to totalize individual experience by assuming either that the world is entirely for us, or that the infinite (i.e., for Levinas, something-outside-everything, the Other, or God) can actually be captured and encapsulated by individual experience and concepts. Ecclesiastes was thus brought to reincorporate such pseudototalities into the infinite by the conclusion that God is to be feared,[31] that is, God operates according to what appears to humans as an arbitrary and absolute determinism. In this sense, the person of faith is more open-minded than the classical secular person of experience since the former, unlike the latter, is unwilling to foreclose on God's nature or to infer the nature of things in general from particular human experiences. The person of faith thus relinquishes the urge to pin things down and put them firmly in their place.

Such a view, which is against imposing an all-embracing system and order on experience, is congruent with the best of psychoanalysis. For example, as Alan Bass has pointed out, Freud was against the idea of a psychoanalytic worldview (Weltanschauung), in part because it was antipsychoanalytic, that is, it went against the basic thrust of psychoanalysis, which, for Bass, following Freud, is that "it cannot be systematic."[32] Philosophers, theologians, and psychotics, according to Freud, strive for systematicity, but psychoanalysis should not, in part, because it fundamentally concerns itself, says Bass, with "unconscious energic processes" that by definition are contradictory, paradoxical, and ambiguous, and therefore must challenge our habitual conscious patterns of organizing data (in Ecclesiastes' time this meant, for example, challenging the received wisdom of the priestly scribes and orthodox theologians).

In other words, for Bass, like Freud (and Ecclesiastes), to seek out or create a worldview is to succumb to an "illusory wish fulfillment" (says Ecclesiastes, we "cannot discover the meaning of God's work which is done under the sun, for the sake of which a man may search hard, but he will not find it, and though a wise man may think he is about to learn it, he will be unable to find it"). A commitment to such systematization is not only a form of imprisonment, but also misses some of the essential things about psychoanalysis that suggest what Freud (and Ecclesiastes) thought constituted aspects of the human condition: for example, that human consciousness is inescapably ambiguous, contradictory, paradoxical, and fluid.

It is thus impossible, and perhaps misguided, to attempt to systematize Freudian psychoanalysis, whether as a theoretician or practitioner. Rather, Bass suggests, psychoanalysis (and, Ecclesiastes would say, one's attitude toward life) must push against the tendency to mold itself into the habitual patterns of conscious perception and against worldviews; it should strive to be more like an endless movement that perpetually undoes itself (says Ecclesiastes, "all the rivers flow into the sea, but the sea is never full; to the place where the rivers flow, there they continue to flow").

While maintaining an antisystematicity assumption Ecclesiastes does nevertheless suggest that some attitudes toward life tend to be more useful than others. He thus offers some helpful, practical, experientially based attitudes toward existence that are strikingly compatible with a Freudian perspective. Both theoretical and clinical psychoanalysis can possibly benefit from being more cognizant of these attitudes as it both articulates its interesting and illuminating psychoanalytic narrative of the human condition and strives to help people achieve a greater degree of happiness amid their predicaments.[33] In the spirit of Ecclesiastes' dialogic, open, pluralistic, and non-authoritarian intellectual and spiritual approach to truth and reality,[34] these attitudinal suggestions I describe represent some of the usable truths, as opposed to absolute Truths, that may be food for thought.

Throughout his experience-guided discourse, Ecclesiastes asserts or implies that one must face the painful and distressing facts of life, that is, one must not continue to assert or accept as true that which does not hold up to critical evaluation, to the evidence, and most important, to one's experience.[35] Ecclesiastes notes, for instance, that to the orthodox theologians and priestly scribes of his day, it was believed that the righteous will be rewarded in this life and the wicked will be punished. However, experience indicated to him that this is frequently not the case. Moreover, Ecclesiastes says that it is simply false that a commitment to wisdom and goodness, the striving after pleasure, or the hoarding of wealth and material possessions adds up to sustained, solid, let alone permanent, happiness.

For the psychoanalyst, the idea that one must face facts and act accordingly is roughly similar to Freud's commitment to, and advocacy of, facing up to the hard truths about one's life even if the consequences are deeply disturbing. This idea speaks to what I believe is at the heart of psychoanalysis. Continuing to assert so-called irrational and unreasonable convictions, to allow them to have a strong interpretive grip on one's life, is to succumb to neurosis. For example, the analysand who insists that his compulsive rituals and obsessive thinking actually protect him from external, real-life catastrophe is plainly not facing up to the evidence concerning the workings of the world. And the analysand who claims that having three consecutive marriages to men who turn out to be alcoholic is a sign of how defective contemporary men are in general, rather than accepting that it is she who unconsciously seeks out and chooses this type of man, is not facing up to the psychological evidence of her life. While no amount of so-called evidence and critical evaluation is a guarantee that one has the Truth (since, for example, philosophically speaking, all evidence and facts are discourse specific, contestable, and can never be absolutely adjudicated), nevertheless, what Ecclesiastes is pointing to is the importance of testing one's core convictions about one's life in terms of one's hard-earned experience and having the courage and good sense to abandon claims that seem to go against the way the world hangs together.

A second attitude toward living that Ecclesiastes articulates and that is fundamental to the psychoanalytic project is that one must learn to live with what cannot be altered and to submit to the inevitable.[36] As Ecclesiastes repeatedly notes, in a certain sense, what is cannot be changed by human efforts and we do not now, and will never, know why God acts the way He does. In other words, the world keeps moving, regardless of our wishes and our feeble efforts (relatively speaking) to intervene, and to understand why it moves in one way and not another is an eternal mystery. Whether we call it Providence, Fate, Luck, or the Reality principle, the point is the same, the need to accept life on its own terms since we are not in control of most things, let alone the really important things (e.g., "a time to be born and a time to die"—in both instances we have no choice in the matter).

In a similar way, the analysand who was abused or neglected as a child, or for that matter any patient who has suffered at the hands of his or her parents or from life's circumstances, needs to be able to accept that that which occurred is a harsh fact of their existence, an event that was out of their control and, in a certain sense, an affirmation of the irreversibility of lived time. For after all of the talking and working through of the personal meaning of the traumatic experiences, at the end of the day, the analysand has to accept that what was, was; it was a quirk of fate that he or she ended up in the circumstances they did (e.g., being born to abusive parents). We know that analysands tend to hold on to their pain and rage as they believe, usually insist, that it should have been otherwise and that they could have (should have) made it different. One way of understanding this is that they do not "fear God," as Ecclesiastes calls it. That is, they are not conscious of His boundless and incomprehensible power,[37] they have not fully embraced their helplessness in the context of the arbitrary and absolute determinism of life. Without having internalized the notion that the world and its happenings remain fundamentally unknowable and uncontrollable, one will continue to hold on to one's pain and rage. That we cannot change what was means in a sense that we should avoid being fixed in a permanently intense retrospective consciousness, one that is in part driven by the angry claim that life is unfair. Moreover, as we do not know what awaits us in the future, good or bad, we should surrender to our fate. That is, it is prudent for us to make the most of the good times while we can and not be excessively troubled when things turn bad.[38]

THE SUPREME DUTY: CARPE DIEM, ENJOY LIFE (EVEN IF LIVING IS A "SORRY BUSINESS")

As I have indicated, the logic of Ecclesiastes' philosophy of life could well lead one to conclude that chronic despair is the only option. That is, as Ecclesiastes describes it, given the fragility and impermanence of human accomplishments; the uncertainty and lack of control of our destiny; the impossibility of achieving true knowledge, understanding, and insight into the world; and, of course, the inevitability of death, why bother living? And yet, Ecclesiastes never advocates suicide nor despair, but rather insists that we are Divinely obligated to make joy, including engaging in sensual pleasures, the goal of all our activities.[39] Says Ecclesiastes: "Therefore I praise joy, for there is no other good for man under the sun but to eat, drink, and be joyful and have this accompany him in his toil, during the days of his life, which God has given him beneath the sun."[40]

As Gordis notes, Ecclesiastes "sets up the attainment of happiness as the goal of human striving, not merely because he loves life, but because he can not have justice and wisdom [i.e., Truth]. Joy is the only purpose that he can find in a monotonous and meaningless world, in which all human values, such as wealth, piety, and ability, are vanity, where all men encounter the same fate and no progress is possible."[41] In other words, for Ecclesiastes, the only certainty that he has is that we have an intrinsic desire for happiness. Since God created humanity, He also created this desire and therefore, Ecclesiastes claims, that God's fundamental purpose for us is the deepening and expansion of our pleasures and the striving after happiness. To fail to obey this divine commandment is to be a sinner.[42] I would add that it is also foolish. For as Ecclesiastes eloquently notes, it is the most sensible goal to enjoy life with all the relish one can muster, especially in one's youth, since we are vulnerable to the sudden and often cruel twists of fate; physical decline and, of course, death, the end of all activity, await us soon enough.

Like in Freudian psychoanalysis, a degree of Stoic fatalism and Epicurean hedonism have their expression in Ecclesiastes' philosophy of life. Putting aside his religious language and categories, his conclusion that the striving after pleasure and joy is a fundamental human motivation and goal is, of course, entirely compatible with the Freudian project. The questions that remain to be answered are what exactly constitutes joy and pleasure for Ecclesiastes, how is it best attained, and what, beyond what we have already said, tends to work against experiencing it? It is impossible in this chapter to detail all of this, but a hint of what Ecclesiastes has in mind may be helpful.

For Ecclesiastes, like Freud, joy and pleasure are palpable, sensual, and concrete experiences. For example, Ecclesiastes says:

> Enjoy life with the woman whom you love
> Throughout all the vain days of your life,
> Which God has given you under the sun.
> Throughout your brief days,
> For that is your reward in life
> For your toil under the sun.
> Whatever you are able to do, do with all your might, for there is neither action nor thought nor knowledge nor wisdom in the grave towards which you are moving.[43]

Ecclesiastes is here advocating the importance of a love relationship (of any persuasion) and zestful and purposeful activity to attaining a degree of happiness. No psychoanalyst would disagree with this. However, what Ecclesiastes adds here is rarely emphasized in the psychoanalytic narrative yet is an insight that can only heighten the satisfaction associated with love and purposeful activity. I am referring to the fact that the enjoyment of these experiences is enhanced by a greater mindfulness of the transitoriness of life. Moreover, it is this sense of resignation in the face of the brevity of life, in the face of life's all-too-frequent frustration and harshness, that makes these experiences that much more enjoyable and lasting. Such an attitude also fosters one of the most underrated sensibilities in the modern secular world, a sensibility that religious traditions have emphasized as fundamental to attaining a degree of happiness, a sense of gratitude for what one has. For Ecclesiastes, a certain "downsizing" of one's narcissism is a prerequisite for even episodic and praiseworthy pleasure, let alone a more solid and lasting sense of happiness.

In contrast, Ecclesiastes mocks the masses of people who choose to live their lives in a way that is not mindful of its tragic character as described throughout this chapter. These are the narcissists and those, for example, who are driven by envy and greed, who do not embrace with melancholic resignation (though without despair) the absolute limitations on existence, and who have not cultivated a sense of gratitude for that which they do have. Such people insist that they are masters of their own destiny, that through seeking and attaining more and more acquisitions they will be forever safe and happy.

In other words, in a number of different contexts, Ecclesiastes criticizes as vanity those who fetishize their existence. Fetishization, as I mean it, is "the organization of perception and action, by the personality, around a very striking and compelling—but narrow—theme," such as money.[44] Such a person builds him- or herself firmly into his or her cultural world such that he or she is imprisoned in his or her own narrow behavioral mold. The reason a person artificially inflates a small area of the world and overvalues it, insinuates Ecclesiastes, is that it represents an area that he or she can firmly hold on to, skillfully manipulate, and easily use to justify him- or herself: his or her actions, sense of self, and options in the world. In psychoanalytic parlance, such a person is neurotic in that he or she demonstrates, for example, an extreme conceptual and behavioral poverty, the blocking of the forward momentum of action and the restriction of experience.

Ecclesiastes is particularly hard on those who lust after wealth: "He who loves money will never have enough of it and he who loves wealth will never attain it—this is indeed vanity. For as wealth increases, so those who would spend it, hence what value is there in the owner's superior ability, except that he has more to look upon?"[45] Ecclesiastes is here critiquing those who make money, or symbolically any acquisition, the primary focus of self-value, the center of his or her universe. Whether it is classical greed, diligence and thrift (which, for Ecclesiastes, are subspecies of greed), or the quest after fame and power (which, he says, is frequently rooted in envy and the desire to compete and outdo others), Ecclesiastes is making an insightful observation from which psychoanalysis could benefit: that the attempt to generate an absolute, closed, narrow, and concrete foundation to base and guide one's existence is misguided.

That is, in Ecclesiastes' religious language, for example through festishization, the individual denies his or her creatureliness, denies God's transcendence and infinitude, and makes him- or herself the Creator as he or she worships earthly things. In the psychoanalytic lexicon, such a person is perhaps best described as a malignant narcissist, as one who has developed a primary, self-centered, and driven hedonism that becomes an unhindered and toxic egoism. Such a person forecloses any contact with a source of meaning which remains open, available and untotalized, whether that meaning is called God or the Other (the latter may be a significant other, says Ecclesiastes, "enjoy life with a woman you love.")[46] In other words, the enjoyment and pleasure of, say, money, fame, power, and sex are ultimately empty and meaningless when they becomes fetishized, that is, become a neurotic fixation. However, following Levinas, enjoyment and pleasure can be more; they can be a basis for individuation when it is sanctioned by the consciousness of the Other.[47] And, says Levinas, to be conscious of the Other mainly means to be responsible to the Other.[48] As Ecclesiastes cautions us, "Remember your Creator in the days of your youth"; that is, when pleasure and joy are most intense and motivating, as in youth, be mindful of the fact—and this is probably true even more so in middle and especially old age—that it is the rooting of joy and pleasure in responsibility and care for the Other that is likely to make them the most satisfying and meaningful. In other words, the striving after and attainment of money, fame, power, and sex are most likely to be sources of joy, and not sources of malevolent self-transformation, when they are knotted to the ethical relation. Moreover, it is the sense of gratitude, in religious language—a consciousness that God has provided us with the means of enjoyment—that encourages the prudent enjoyment of one's acquisitions and pleasures rather than degrading oneself or the other by the abuse of them.[49]

A FINAL WORD

I have tried to illustrate some of the brilliant and profound insights about the human condition that are embodied in the ethical wisdom of Ecclesiastes and may, in some form, enhance theoretical and clinical psychoanalysis, conceived in this chapter as a "practice of the self." Most important, Ecclesiastes advocates resignation without despair, that is, cultivating an inner attitude toward life that strives to transcend the tragic limitations and pangs and sorrows of existence through a frank and courageous acceptance that they cannot be transformed. Ecclesiastes thus promotes dedicating oneself to striving after joy in life, not so much for the reasons the idealistic pious believe, because it is a gift from God to be treasured, but because the search for joy is the only sensible goal, considering the frustrating, tragic, and fundamentally futile nature of existence. Freud probably saw life in a similar way when he wrote that the purpose of psychoanalysis was to transform neurotic misery into common unhappiness![50]

I want to close by reminding the reader that the last six verses of the Book of Ecclesiastes was, most scholars believe, written by an orthodox editor who probably was a friend or colleague of Ecclesiastes but was distressed by his skepticism. While these verses were an attempt at damage control, I think the editor unconsciously actually wrote verses that capture the very core of what Ecclesiastes believed and advocated and they should be regarded as integral and consistent with the rest of the book, at least in my reading of the book of Ecclesiastes: "In sum, having heard everything, fear God and keep His commandments, for that is man's whole duty. For God will bring every deed to judgment, even everything hidden whether it be good or evil."[51]

Despite all his uncertainty, ignorance, conflicts, and angst, Ecclesiastes believed that practice should not wait for theory just as life so often does not wait for understanding and insight.[52] What really matters, what perhaps makes life the most meaningful, is the ethical relation, which means as Ecclesiastes has taught us, creating joy that is rooted and expressed in responsibility to the Other.

NOTES

An earlier verson of this chapter was published in the *Psychoanalytic Review*, 87, no. 2 (April 2000): 227–250.

1. Robert Gordis, trans. and commentator, *Koheleth—The Man and His World* (New York: Jewish Theological Seminary of America, 1951), p. 141.
2. Gordis, *Koheleth*, p. 16–17.
3. Gordis, *Koheleth*; Elias Bickerman, *Four Strange Books of the Bible* (New York: Schocken Books, 1967); H. L. Ginsberg, *The Five Megillot and Jonah* (Philadelphia: Jewish Publication Society of America, 1969); James L. Crenshaw, *Ecclesiastes: A Commentary* (Old Testament Library) (Philadelphia: Westminster, 1987); T. A. Perry, *Dialogues with Kohelet: The Book of Ecclesiastes* (University Park: The Pennsylvania State University Press, 1993); Meir Zlotowitz, *Koheles: Ecclesiastes: A New Translation with a Commentary Anthologized from Talmudic, Midrashic and Rabbinic Sources* (The ArtScroll Tanach Series) (New York: Mesorah Publications, 1996).
4. Gordis, *Koheleth*, pp. 68, 22, 78.
5. Zlotowitz, *Koheles: Ecclesiastes: A New Translation with a Commentary Anthologized from Talmudic, Midrashic and Rabbinic Sources* (representing the tradition of the synagogue); Ginsberg, *The Five Megillot and Jonah*. This view is, in part, based on the opening verse in which Ecclesiastes introduces himself as Solomon: "The Words of Koheleth, son of David, King in Jerusalem." However, most scholars believe that Koheleth is using a literary convention. That is, says Gordis, he is impersonating Solomon because he wants to demonstrate that both wisdom and pleasure are meaningless as goals in life and Solomon was well known to have had an abundance of both. To further complicate matters, the name Koheleth, translated as *convener* or *gatherer*, is in the Hebrew feminine form, thereby implying (assuming that Solomon was not a transvestite) a female author (Rabbi Dr. Martin S. Cohen, personal communication, January 25, 2002).
6. Gordis, *Koheleth*, p. 9.
7. R. B. Y. Scott, ed., *The Anchor Bible: Proverbs: Ecclesiastes* (Garden City, N.Y.: Doubleday and Company, 1965), p. xvii.
8. Ibid., pp. xviii, xix.
9. Ibid., p. 196.
10. Gordis, *Koheleth*, pp. 37–38.
11. Ibid., 1:2–11, p. 136.
12. Ibid., 3:1–15, p. 144.
13. Scott, *The Anchor Bible*, pp. 202–203. Ecclesiastes never resolves the contradiction to which all determinists are vulnerable. That is, Ecclesiastes was assuming human freedom of choice in terms of the practical attitudes and conduct he was recommending, yet he claims that all is predetermined by God. See Gordis, *Koheleth*, p. 55. I think that Ecclesiastes was both advocating resigned submission to the order of the world yet also encouraging us not to be passive. In other words, in a limited sense, we have freedom of action as well as a choice between courses of action. See A. Cohen, ed., *The Five Megilloth* (London: Soncino Press, 1970), p. 154.
14. Perry, *Dialogues with Kohelet*, pp. 14–21.

15. Gordis, *Koheleth*, p. 268.
16. Ibid., p. 291.
17. Ibid., 1:12–2:3, pp. 138–140.
18. Scott, *The Anchor Bible*, p. 198.
19. Herbert G. May and Bruce M. Metzger, "Ecclesiastes," in *The New Oxford Annotated Bible with the Apocrypha: Revised Standard Version* (New York: Oxford University Press, 1973), p. 805.
20. Gordis, *Koheleth*, 3:16, 4:1–3, p. 148.
21. Scott, *The Anchor Bible*, p. 203.
22. For the references to light and the sun, see ibid., p. 183.
23. There have been many interpretations of this allegory, based on Talmudic and other sources. I have mainly drawn from Cohen's *The Five Megilloth* and Ginsberg's *The Five Megillot and Jonah* for my parenthetical entries.
24. Gordis, *Koheleth*, 11:9–12:8, pp. 186–188.
25. Ibid., p. 337.
26. Scott, *The Anchor Bible*, p. 198.
27. Gordis, *Koheleth*, p. 339.
28. Scott, *The Anchor Bible*, p. 203.
29. Ibid.
30. D. Guthrie and J. A. Motyer, eds., *The New Bible Commentary, Revised* (Grand Rapids, Mich.: Eerdmans Publishing Company, 1970), p. 575.
31. Perry, *Dialogues with Kohelet*, pp. 27–28, 35.
32. Alan Bass, "The Question of a Weltanschauung and of Defense," in Paul Marcus and Alan Rosenberg, eds., *Psychoanalytic Version of the Human Condition: Philosophies of Life and Their Impact on Practice* (New York: New York University Press, 1998), pp. 412–413.
33. Adam Phillips, "Paging Dr. Freud," *New York Times Book Review*, June 7, 1998, p. 24, and in Marcus and Rosenberg.
34. Perry, *Dialogues with Kohelet*, pp. 6–7.
35. Scott, *The Anchor Bible*, p. 204.
36. Ibid., p. 205.
37. Gordis, *Koheleth*, p. 237.
38. Cohen, *The Five Megilloth*, p. 153.
39. Gordis, *Koheleth*, p. 252.
40. Ibid., 8:15, p. 174.
41. Ibid., p. 83.
42. Ibid., p. 115.
43. Ibid., 9:7–10, p. 178.
44. Ernest Becker, *Angel in Armor: A Post-Freudian Perspective on the Nature of Man* (New York: Braziller, 1969), p. 85.
45. Gordis, *Koheleth*, 5:9–10, p. 158.
46. Perry, *Dialogues with Kohelet*, p. 27.
47. Ibid.
48. Emmanuel Levinas, *Ethics and Infinity*, trans., Richard A. Cohen (Pittsburgh: Duquesne University Press), pp. 95–101.
49. Cohen, *The Five Megilloth*, p. 165.
50. Joseph Breuer and Sigmund Freud, *Studies on Hysteria*, in *Standard Edition of the Complete Psychological Works of Sigmund Freud*, ed. James Strachey (London: Hogarth Press and the Institute of Psycho-Analysis, 1953–1974), 2: 393. (Original work published in 1895.)
51. Gordis, *Koheleth*, 12:14, p. 190.
52. Guthrie and Motyer, *The New Bible Commentary*, p. 578.

8

Christianity: Saint Augustine's *Confessions*

> What then do you want to know? [asks Reason]. I want to know God and the soul. Nothing more? Nothing at all.
>
> Saint Augustine[1]

Saint Augustine (354–430), a brilliantly original synthesizer of Greek and Christian philosophy, was born in Thagaste, North Africa. He became the Bishop of Hippo in 396 and was one of the great Church Fathers (an early Christian theologian who fashioned orthodox Christian doctrines and Biblical interpretation). Augustine is regarded by scholars as "the most influential Christian writer outside of the Bible"[2] and is credited with writing, among other great books, the masterpiece I will periodically draw from, the *Confessions*, called "the most influential autobiography of all time."[3] Augustine, one of the most profound ancient spiritual introspectionists, provides the modern reader with a broad range of psychological insights into the human striving for religious meaning in existence. His reflections on love, grace, and sin, for example, show him to be, like Freud, capable of astutely probing the deepest recesses of the human soul.

In this chapter we will focus on the main problem that Augustine thought faced all humans and that captivated him throughout his life, namely, the problem of the human moral condition. That is, Augustine's life's work was devoted to a study of morality, to delineating the certain road to happiness, which, he believed, was the aim of human behavior. For Augustine, we are made by God such that we strive for happiness, though we get waylaid from reaching our goal for a variety of complex and deeply psychological reasons. While Aristotle thought that happiness is achieved through a harmony of reason and desire, through an individual fulfilling natural functions through a well-ordered and well-balanced life, Augustine maintained that happiness demanded that the individual go beyond the natural order to the supernatural or transcendent realm. Hence, it was the journey of the soul to God, best expressed through his doctrine of love, that was Augustine's main metaphor for finding and creating happiness.

AUGUSTINE'S VERSION OF THE INNER SELF

Augustine is widely regarded as the creator of the Western tradition of interiority, a tradition of inwardness to which psychoanalysis is heir.[4] In particular, it is his concept of the self as private inner space that I believe psychoanalysis has embraced. Moreover, Augustine's radical reflexivity—his brutally honest self-searching—is an important forerunner of psychoanalytic self-exploration. It should be emphasized that Augustine's self-exploration is more than superficial, disengaged, intellectual introspection by an isolated Cartesian ego in search of demonstrable knowledge using human reason. Augustine's inward turn, as reflected in his *Confessions*, does not reveal an absolute faith in the human ability to know or in human reason's capacity for understanding, nor a radical subjectivism. Rather, Augustine explores the highly conflicted, ambiguous, conscious, and unconscious levels of existence. He does this largely because he does not proceed simply from "I think," but also from "I will, I seek."[5] It is only in the inner self that one can discover transcendence. The way inward is the way upward, and this double move is the royal road to wisdom and to ultimate happiness.

As Cary points out, Augustine conceptualizes the inner self as a kind of space proper to the soul, though this is not meant to be taken literally because the soul, it was believed, does not have a spatial mode of being like a body. Rather, Augustine's self is more akin to an "inner world of representations."[6] So, for instance, memory does not only contain images and temporal realities but includes eternal and intelligible realities.[7] That is, Augustine's inner space is more than the isolated, individualistic, private internal world as we analysts tend to conceive it. The inner world is the domain in which the self finds intelligible truth and, above all, that one eternal Truth that is called God. Thus, Augustine's psychology of the inner self always includes a transcendent yearning and significance to it, an inward turn away from the sensible toward investigating the soul, and a turn upward toward contemplating God and achieving mystical union with Him.

For Augustine, knowing ourselves and knowing God are indivisible. There are few ancient thinkers who took self-analysis, the Delphic command "know thyself," as seriously as Augustine. He strongly believed that self-analysis is the process or context in which the relation to all else occurs. What Augustine discovered in his soul-searching was the following path-breaking insight: Self-analysis "is not to lead to narcissistic self-contemplation that ends in a small, closed insularity, but to the vast sea of being and goodness, to the Other in us, who is found in the intimacy of self-presence."[8] In other words, self-analysis that does not enhance our capacity to love others, that does not strengthen our commitment to an ever-widening sense of fellowship and community, and that does not encourage us to put the common good before individual gain is incomplete, if not deeply flawed. Such truncated self-analysis and self-knowledge will not foster the enduring happiness that we long for. That is to say, for Augustine the ultimate goal of self-analysis is godliness in our actions and intentions, a godliness that is rooted in the pledge of Christ and the faithful and exacting obedience to the eternal law, this being the only true and lasting basis for happiness. Most important, the motivational power of godliness is love, of God and neighbor. It was Jesus, in his role as mediator, teacher, redeemer, and sacrifice, that personified the purest form of selfless love.

THE ROLE OF LOVE IN ATTAINING HAPPINESS

Like Freud, Augustine regards love and its vicissitudes as central to the human condition and to our attainment of what they both thought was at best possible in this distress-filled existence, namely, a modicum of happiness. Both Augustine and Freud viewed love as basically the force or the soul of life—comprising life's motivational power. Given that we are incomplete and insufficient—in psychoanalytic language, neurotic—we therefore, says Augustine, inevitably attach our self, desires, and affections to an object of love. An individual can decide to love from a wide range of objects largely depending on the particular form of incompleteness that predominates in his or her personality. We may mainly love physical objects (e.g., money, possessions, power), other persons (e.g., family, friends, a group), or ourselves (e.g., our body or intellectual or artistic creations). Augustine recognized that from any of these objects of love a person can gain considerable satisfaction. This is because all things emanate from God who, Augustine claims, personifies goodness itself. That is, for Augustine, nothing is evil in itself since evil in not a positive thing in the universe but the absence of something (to be discussed shortly).

The crucial point for Augustine's psychology of love is that there is nothing intrinsically wrong with any of these types of love, nor even in the object a person loves. Rather, the problem is the way in which we relate ourselves to our objects of love and in what we expect regarding the outcome of our love. This problem, which is the same problem that Freud grappled with, can be put as a question: If everyone expects to attain satisfaction and happiness from love, why are most people miserable? Augustine's answer is his concept of "disordered" love.

DISORDERED AND RIGHTLY ORDERED LOVE

Augustine observed that every object of love is different, the needs and wishes (i.e., the form of incompleteness) that drive an individual towards the particular object are different, and the consequences of loving the object are different. Moreover, Augustine believed that there was some sort of ideal psychological fit between various human needs and wishes and the objects that can gratify them. Love, he felt, was the act that harmonizes these needs and wishes and their objects. What Augustine adds to his discussion of love that is uniquely Christian is that fundamentally, we not only love objects, other persons, and ourself, but also, and more than anything else, we love God. For Augustine this love of God, conceived as a yearning to connect with the infinite and for mystical union with God, is an irreversible aspect of the human condition.

I realize that at this point in my discussion, such "God talk" puts me perilously close to losing most of my secular psychoanalytic readers. Therefore, let me try and make this notion of love of God as intrinsic to the human condition a bit more serviceable to those who may not have the religious sensibility that makes Augustine's assertion seem intelligible, if not reasonable.

For Augustine, each recipient of love—objects, other persons and oneself—can provide an individual with only so much fulfillment and happiness, depending in part on the magnitude and nature of the needs and wishes of the lover. While Augustine does not devalue the love of objects and of oneself, he clearly believes that the love of others is the "higher" form of love, that such a love relation provides not only more, but a higher quality of lasting fulfillment and happiness than say hoarding money and possessions (love of objects) or exercising to make one's body beautiful or even creating an artistic work (loving oneself).[9] The idea here is that each object of love fits with the inner disposition and expectations of the lover and it is a mistake to expect more from a particular object of love than its unique nature can provide. So, for example, in general, for most people the need for affiliation and nurturance can not be adequately fulfilled by hoarding physical objects. Most important for Augustine, the human spiritual need to connect with the infinite and to attain the more or less enduring happiness that comes with such a transcendent connection can only be satisfied by loving an object whose nature fits with such a spiritual need, namely, God. As I have said, for Augustine we are hardwired to love God, we are passionately driven to connect with the infinite, to connect with the source of being, truth and goodness, the one eternal reality, which is the basis of ultimate happiness. Indeed, there is not a culture in the world that does not have some form of religion that includes a notion of a superordinate transcendent reality or God that one strives to make intimate contact with.

However, according to Augustine, there are a number of obstructions that impair our ability to correctly love and be happy. In particular, we make a series of category mistakes. We forget or choose to disregard the fact that objects of love are not interchangeable. A physical object, say money, or a thing like power, cannot, in the long run, adequately substitute for the nurturance and care that a person can provide. Similarly, a finite thing or person can not substitute for the infinite God. For example, loving one's wife as if she were the source of being, truth, goodness, and eternal reality (an extreme form of idealization) will almost always turn into infantile dependency and disappointment. Moreover, and this needs to be stressed, the loss of the loved other, one's wife in my example, is always feared. That is, to love another human being as though he or she will never die, as if he or she were God, is unreasonable and is the source of much relational pain. In fact, it is perhaps the essence of disordered love.

Nevertheless, it is very common in our society that individuals have the strong conviction that they can obtain ultimate happiness by loving objects, other persons, and themselves. Augustine was well aware that these are reasonable objects of love, but the category mistake is to believe that these objects of love are the basis of ultimate, eternal happiness. Only God can guarantee true and lasting happiness for only in this relation, says Augustine, the human being does not have to fear the loss of the beloved. Disordered love is Augustine's term for expecting more from an object of love than it is capable of providing. Such disordered love is often anxiety ridden, frightened, greedy, and clinging. It generates the wide range of psychopathology, especially relational psychopathology, with which psychoanalysts are familiar. In contrast, "rightly ordered love" allows us to evaluate things according to their proper value and priority; it helps us to generate reasonable and appropriate goals, desires, and actions for the pursuit of, and relationship to, what we love. Perhaps the main reason for disordered love is our pride, or, more generally, our sinfulness, Augustine's key term for narcissistic pathology and one that we shall discuss shortly.

Why does Augustine focus on love as the medium to achieve happiness? The main reason, says Bavel,[10] is that every "virtue," every good mode of behavior that fosters a person's capacity to live according to right reason animated by faith, is a form of "rightly ordered love," Augustine's favorite definition of virtue.[11] For example, temperance, the virtue that modulates the desire for natural pleasures such as for sexual intercourse, is love that knows how to guard its integrity while at the same time being completely devoted to the other who is loved. Fortitude, the virtue that entails a steadiness of will in doing good regardless of the difficulties involved in the performance of one's responsibility, is love that is capable of shouldering much for the sake of the beloved. Justice, the continual and permanent commitment to give everyone his or her rightful share, is love that does not desire to keep for itself the good things of life but knows how to share them equally with others. Prudence, the virtue of discerning those things to be done and to be avoided, is love that knows how to choose what will enhance love and what will damage it. Even the basic virtues of everyday social life can be viewed as a form of love: good-heartedness, gentleness, honesty, patience, faithfulness, and joy, for example, are based on love because there is no one who can live these qualities if there is no will to do good to the Other. The point is that for Augustine, love is viewed as the dynamic, motivational reality that gives man direction in life and is the measure of his humanity: "My weight [motivational power] is my love," Augustine says in a famous quotation from his *Confessions*.[12]

I have indicated that for Augustine, the love of God and the love of neighbor go hand in hand. Deeds of love such as righteousness, justice, and peace are an expression of one's love of God. In other words, while Augustine was advocating being otherworldly, he clearly meant "being otherworldly in the world."[13] That is, he clearly recognized that loving God meant doing His will by performing the well-known ethical commandments that personify Christian conscience and charity at its best. However, Augustine adds another fascinating element to his analysis of love, one that has relevance for psychoanalysis. He says that our love, especially in its purest, strongest, and most sustained form, must be driven by divine love and mirror it; that is, love is ultimately a gift from God and an act of divine grace.

Grace, the totally gratuitous gift from God, on which we have absolutely no claim, is Augustine's term for a number of interrelated Christian doctrines, such as "the illumination of the mind by divine Truth, the Word of God, and the movement of the will by divine Love, the Holy Spirit."[14] While Augustine's doctrines of grace are of great originality and insight, the relevance of his psychology of grace to understanding the dynamics of love and the enhancement of our capacity to love is what mainly interests us at this point in our discussion. In this context, Augustine's concept of grace can be recast in more general terms. Grace, says Harvey Cox, is "the means [by which] God—who is love and power—enables human beings to do what they cannot do entirely on their own." Moreover, Cox continues, grace need not be viewed as something foreign or shadowy. Rather, it encompasses all the ways in which God, who animates all of life, nurtures and sustains, that is, loves that which is life giving and life affirming and that which is striving toward justice and human community. Grace, in other words, "is what makes righteousness—full human life in community—possible."[15] Grace, as Augustine says, is ultimately what makes love of one's neighbor, that is, the concrete Other, ultimately possible.

Augustine's notion of grace, at least as I interpret it, is perceptively pointing to the following psychological insight: that while loving requires inner readiness, commitment, hard work, and a sense of responsibility to the other, it ultimately comes about through the operation of a mysterious power, a power that Augustine and other theologians call God. Martin Buber, the great German-Jewish philosopher, for example, points out that the event of relation, the love relation involving one's whole being, "I-Thou," can not be coerced, planned or chosen to happen. Rather, such a transformational encounter is experienced by the person as a kind of miraculous gift, as grace. Moreover, for Augustine, nothing bad can result from such authentic, rightly ordered love, for it is an undeserved goodness from God who is goodness itself. That is, for Augustine, rightly ordered love is always associated with goodness; it always strives to make things better and more beautiful.

Augustine's notion of grace has significance for the psychoanalytic project. By helping our analysands to become more mindful of the fact that the love relation is in a certain sense beyond our being, powers, and claims, we are supporting a psychological insight that is frequently underappreciated by analysands and analysts, namely, that love can not be demanded, coerced, or controlled; it requires absolute respect both of the other's otherness and for the unpredictability of human freedom. Most important, by developing this sensibility, analysands inevitably foster one of the most desirable states of mind, which is hardly ever spoken about in the psychoanalytic literature, let alone mindfully cultivated by analysts in their work. I am referring to what Christians call a grateful heart. That is, for an analysand to have the capacity for a deep and abiding sense of gratefulness for the love he or she is privileged to give and to receive is, in a certain sense, to have achieved an outlook on life that is as close to a guarantee of enduring happiness as probably exists. For a deep sense of gratitude usually leads to a deep feeling of contentment with one's life. As the ancient rabbis remarked in the *Ethics of the Fathers*, "Who is rich? He who is happy with his portion."[16]

AUGUSTINE'S PSYCHOLOGY OF SIN

As I have said, Augustine was troubled by the fact that while we are hardwired to love God, and by extension our neighbor, there were psychological forces that obstructed and derailed this natural tendency. That is, Augustine was well aware that there was an awful lot of mean-spiritedness and downright evil in the world. In particular, we seemed inclined to selfishness, egoistic love, phoniness, self-aggrandizement, and seeking advancement at others' expense. In other words, Augustine thought that while most people gave lip service to love of God and neighbor, they were a macabre parody on love and human decency. Our fallen nature, he concluded, was to sin.

This double vision of the human condition in which existence is seen in terms of conflicting desires for salvation (i.e., via love of God/humanity) and the irresistible urge to sin is the basis for describing Augustine as perhaps the first psychologist of inner conflict and the divided self. In particular, it was Augustine who divided the human condition in terms of two conflicting elements, the conscious, rational mind or reason, and sexual desire. As Brown points out, Augustine developed "a highly-sophisticated view of the psychological tension between reason and instinct in sexuality."[17] Freud, of course, inadvertently appropriated aspects of this view of the human condition in his characterization of existence as a conflict between Eros and Thanatos, between so-called mature, healthy sexual desire and infantile sexuality, between ego and id, and between super-ego and id.

Augustine's psychology of sin is best understood within the context of his notion of original sin, a concept that makes most psychoanalysts and others shudder, in my view for good reason. For there are few concepts that have caused more pain for more people in human history. However, I believe that the concept of original sin has its usefulness for psychoanalysis once the notion is reinterpreted within a modern idiom (and renamed), that is, once it is taken metaphorically and not literally. For the notion of original sin highlights an important insight about the human condition that analysands and analysts often overlook and would benefit from thinking about and possibly internalizing.

Augustine's controversial concept of original sin is very complex and its details are quite beyond the scope of this chapter. However, briefly, Augustine's main claims are as follows according to one Augustine scholar, Paul Rigby: (1) The sin and punishment of Adam and Eve are inherited. That is, it was Adam and Eve's sin which inflicted the chaos, suffering and death that characterize the human condition. (2) The infant soul comes into this world guilty. (3) Infant sins are not metaphorical, they are real, severe, and inherited from generation to generation. (4) Baptism is the mandatory means of salvation for all, including infants.[18]

In other words, humans continue to bear the painful consequences of Adam and Eve's sin, the original fall. Most important, while a decisive change in moral outlook and acts of repentence can help reinstate man to his original happiness, it is only through the grace of God that it can occur. Augustine "proves" the truthfulness of his original sin notion in part by pointing to the amount of suffering in the world and to the intrinsic painfulness of the human condition. It is not by chance, Augustine insinuated, but rather prophetic, that we come into this world in tears rather than laughing.

This original sin notion is rough stuff for the contemporary analysand and analyst to imagine as enhancing to the psychoanalytic project. However, embedded in these objectionable literal claims is a kernel of wisdom, which a few psychoanalytic scholars have noted.

Pattison, for example, points out that the concept of original sin is not perilous and far-fetched if we view it as meaning that all people "are born with limited capacities to pursue the good, and left to our own devices all of us will betray ourselves and our fellow man."[19] That is, analysands and analysts would benefit from the almost inevitable reduction in their narcissism that comes about through a greater mindfulness of the fact that we are all fundamentally flawed creatures. We are frequently selfish, impatient, dishonest, envious, mean-spirited and sometimes downright cruel. Most important, we are limited and flawed in our capacity to love and in our relations with others, the main area of interest in psychoanalysis. In other words, the concept of original sin teaches us that unless checked by moral force, by conscience and moral action, we are all prone to the everyday "inhumanity" towards others, especially to those dear to us, which is often the basis for our own subversion in terms of guilt and other forms of unhappiness. Freud memorialized a similar insight in his concept of the death instinct, that innate instinct to destroy or dissolve oneself, a view that Melanie Klein more fully developed in her claim that aggression was a projection of the individual's inherent self-destructive drive. Most later analysts have preferred to speak about the general innate tendency toward aggression toward others. Both formulations, however, speak to Freud's awareness of our flawed nature, to our inherent sinfulness, as Augustine would say.

Augustine's psychology of individual sin was often discussed in terms of the mother of all sins, which, in a sense, is reenacted in every specific act of sin, namely, the "tumor" of pride. Pride is the desire to replace God with oneself; it is the betrayal and abandonment of God. In other words, pride characterizes those people who put their faith not necessarily in themselves per se, but in the range of human projects, societies, and groups that stand over and against God.[20]

As Augustine views it, pride is a particular malignant form of self-love or narcissism. Augustine realized that not all self-love is sinful, and in fact he often praises certain forms of self-love as natural and compliant with what God wants from us. However, what Augustine was criticizing was a certain destructive attitude that he observed in his religious community and society in general, one that is still extremely common today, namely, viewing self-love as the main source of gratification and as the final and ultimate good, rather than the love of God.

The main thrust of the prideful being is that he or she is not satisfied with the universe as fashioned, but seeks more, to reconfigure it, and thus to establish him- or herself as God, as the Creator. Such a reconfiguring or reordering is based on a false claim to self-sufficiency, to falsely believing that one is self-created, self-sustained, and self-dependent. However, as I have pointed out, for Augustine we are not self-sufficient, neither physically, psychologically, nor spiritually. Rather, we need to be connected to the infinite God, the source of being, goodness, justice, and absolute reality. It is precisely this prideful turning away from God that leads us to a state of narcissistic entitlement, to the seeking of various forms of self-destructive overindulgence, and ultimately, to unhappiness. By attempting to fulfill an infinite need, to connect with God and receive His love and salvation, with finite entities, we love things more than we should in relation to what they can provide for us. Thus, the narcissist demands more from our relationships than they can possibly give. Our craving for love or its symbolic extensions, praise, money, knowledge and power, becomes inordinate and "disordered," and we desperately attempt to achieve peace of mind by satisfying our inordinate, misplaced, impossible-to-gratify desires. Such a prideful mode of being ultimately tends to foster the qualities that analysts associate with narcissistic pathology, such as self-hatred, envy, greed, jealousy, panic, emptiness, manipulativeness, and restlessness.

What Augustine is saying is that we can love ourselves in a reasonable manner—that is, we can have a "normal" amount of narcissism—only if we subordinate ourselves to God, the source of being, truth, goodness, and the one eternal reality, which is ironically, ultimately outside our total grasp and is ineffable. To subordinate ourselves to God in part means, to paraphrase the Jewish theologian Yeshayahu Leibowitz, to view oneself as having value and significance only insofar as one stands before God. That is, to subordinate oneself to God means being mindful of our ultimate fraility and dependence in the cosmos and our lack of ultimate control over our fate; it means being mindful of the transience of earthly pursuits and pleasures and of our creaturely equality with others. Most important, it means, to parapharase Emmanuel Levinas, embracing being-for-the-Other as an ethical and psychological necessity for living the good life, the kind of life that is most likely to give one lasting happiness.

I believe that analysands would greatly benefit from a psychoanalysis whose theory and practice was infused with just such an overarching sensibility, what the Christian calls humility. For it is the moral virtue of humility, a human quality that is rarely discussed in psychoanalytic circles, that prevents an analysand from seeking gratification of unreasonable and unrealistic desires for self-aggrandizement and self-affirmation, those prideful desires being the basis for much unhappiness. By having a sense both of God's infinite love and power and of one's ultimate lack of self-sufficiency and powerlessness in the universe, we are more likely to have reasonable expectations for our lives. Moreover, it is a well-known observation that the greater the congruence between one's expectations and one's fate, the greater the sense of experienced happiness.

THE *GIFT OF PERSEVERANCE* IN THE FACE OF SUFFERING

In one of Augustine's last books, the *Gift of Perseverance*, he is preoccupied with a problem that is crucial to his central doctrine of the salvational nature of love of God, and one that has relevance to the suffering analysand. Says Peter Brown, his preeminent biographer, what consumed Augustine toward the end of his life "was no longer the mobilization of love that caused man to act," as in the *Confessions*, but rather "the mysterious resilience that would enable some men to maintain this love" of God "for the full course of their lives."[21]

In other words, Augustine was preoccupied with how individuals could maintain their faith in an omnipotent, loving and just God and thereby sustain their humanity and Christian decency, amidst their pain-filled existence and obviously imperfect world. Says an elderly Augustine in a letter, "Everyone should realize the misery which is part of human life extends from the tears of the newly born to the last breath of the soon to die."[22] This somber statement calls to mind Freud's famous, rather pessimistic comment that the purpose of analysis is to transform neurotic misery into common unhappiness.

I wish to comment on the two important questions that these quotations point toward, which speak to the heart of the psychoanalytic project. The first question is theological and I will not say much about it for it is beyond the scope of this chapter and my expertise, namely, "Why does an all-powerful, all-loving, just God allow evil to occur in His created world?" The second question, the one I will focus on, though briefly, is decidedly psychological, "How does one cope with suffering?"

Augustine realized that in order for him and his faith community to sustain their love of God amid suffering and to have a philosophically and intellectually honest and firm basis for this love, they needed a coherent theodicy, a way of justifying God's goodness and justice in view of the evil in the world. Augustine's inconclusive and not entirely satisfactory explanation for evil claimed that "evil had no independent, substantial existence in its own right, it existed as privation, as a distortion or damage within the good."[23] Evil is analogous to hole in a shirt or blindness in an eye.[24] In other words, says Cary, evil is "anything that is not as it should be, a defect in being, or corruption of something's natural goodness." This includes, he says, sin (evil of will), error and ignorance (evil of the mind), illness and disease (evil of the body), disorder (evil in the universe), and death (evil of the soul).[25]

What Augustine has done in effect is to deny any positive evil in the world and thereby preserve a view of God as the All-Good Creator of the world. This formulation allows Augustine and his community to maintain the basis of their faith, namely their love of the just and merciful God, and the religious world of meaning that supports this faith. While there is corruption in the world—evil viewed as a rupture of the right relation of parts within a whole, like the rot in a tree—God cannot be viewed as the cause of it. For the mature Augustine, evil must therefore be accounted for mainly in terms of the corruption of the human will which is God-given as free, a corruption for which we must take responsibility. Evil is thus our creation, not God's.

While Augustine's theology got God off the hook so to speak, how was one supposed to deal with suffering that was personal, say, for example, the sudden, premature, and grotesque death of a loved one in a robbery? That is, how was the survivor supposed to maintain their love of God in the face of seemingly undeserved and unfair suffering? Augustine's views on this subject are also inconclusive and are, in my view, no more inadequate than are other psychological/theological accounts of how best to "manage" suffering. Still, what interests us is how in Augustine's view one's love of God, one's religious world of meaning, and one's humanity are sustained in the face of suffering.

Augustine maintains that while suffering in life is unavoidable, mainly due to our original fall from grace, it should be transformed to whatever extent possible into a life-affirming experience. For instance, the pain of the loss of a loved one can be viewed as an indication of the depth, goodness and truth of the love one felt and lived with the deceased. Moreover, such a painful loss can remind one that clinging to material earthly things and not fully appreciating and cherishing them while you have them, rather than looking upward and striving to connect with the infinite God, is unwise. In other words, the death of a loved one can encourage the survivor to hope, the best response to tragedy according to Christian theologian Gabriel Marcel. That is, to look ahead to heaven, a life beyond death where all loves will be eternal[26] and one will rejoin those whom one loved.

Most important, perhaps, for Augustine, suffering only becomes sustainable and ultimately transfigured when one's life imitates and is fused with Christ, especially in his crucifixion. For it is the crucifixion that powerfully shows, not only the transient nature of earthly existence, but the magnificent love that God has for his human creation. It is this passionate internal connection with Christ that constitutes grace, that transformational indwelling of the Holy Spirit, the gift of divine love that for the believing Christian ultimately makes one's suffering "sufferable."[27]

What does all of this have to do with psychoanalysis? First, Augustine's capacity to generate a theodicy that allows him to sustain his love of God and his religious world of meaning points to the importance of helping analsyands, especially secular analysands, to develop a comparable symbolic world that can make their suffering more "sufferable." That is, a symbolic world is "a system of meaning or metaphor by which a person can organize their individual experience into a patterned whole."[28] Analysts need to help analysands develop the conceptual/affective resources, whether in religious or secular terms, for managing the marginal and anomic experiences that constantly threaten a person's existence. Sickness, injury, and death, for example, in Augustine's way of seeing the world, are interpreted as events in a larger cosmic history and as such are given an ultimate significance, a "higher" meaning that makes these facts of existence more endurable. His theodicy, like all theodicies, provides "ultimate meaning for human life in its ability to integrate the painful and terrifying experiences of life, and even death itself, into a comprehensive explanation of reality and human destiny."[29] As I have pointed out elsewhere,[30] psychoanalytic theory lacks just such symbolic resources in its current theorizing, especially when compared to the religious worldview: it does not provide what religion provides at its best, namely, an overarching, though extremely practical, supportive and transforming connection to a meaning-giving, affect-integrating universal matrix,[31] what Berger beautifully described as a "sacred canopy."[32] This limitation in psychoanalytic theory and praxis has blunted the potency of psychoanalysis as a compelling and socially relevant life and identity-defining narrative of the human condition and a method for coping and self-improvement.[33]

Augustine's views on coping with suffering also point to the benefits of cultivating a quality of mind and heart that is rarely noted in psychoanalytic literature, one that, at first glance, seems to go against the active, mastery-oriented approach to coping with personal problems that psychoanalysts tend to advocate. That is, for Augustine, while attempts to give positive meaning to one's suffering are an admirable and necessary act of the will, for one to ultimately go beyond one's suffering and to be able to live, love, and affirm God again, one needs to have grace, that mysterious divine power that Augustine felt operates in the world and on which humans are totally dependent.

In psychological and secular terms, what this concept of grace is hinting at is the need for analysands to have a greater awareness of their radical contingency. That is, they are advised to interiorize the fact that in a certain sense, they are not autonomous, self-determining, and self-sufficient nor in ultimate control of their fate. Moreover, to narcissistically insist otherwise is to set themselves up for more frequent, intense, and to some extent, avoidable suffering. In other words, in Augustine's view, by an analysand dispossessing his or her self, that is, by becoming less self-referential and narcissistic, including decentering his or her human reason in the sense of admitting his or her ultimate incomprehension about the reasons for and the meaning of his or her suffering, he or she is most likely to create the psychological conditions of possibility for overcoming that suffering. While suffering is by definition highly narcissistic and self-absorbing, such self-dispossession and decentering of reason are the necessary condition for the development of the humility that is needed as one faces the ultimate mystery of why one suffers, and perhaps the most important question to the sufferer, when will the suffering end? Such an awareness of our ultimate ignorance in the face of convincingly explaining or justifying one's suffering, of our radical dependence on a mysterious, healing power Augustine calls grace, actually paradoxically frequently opens up the opportunity for the individual's most creative and liberating responses to his suffering. Such creative responses to loss, often preceded by this terrible sense of ignorance, unintelligibility, and a loss of meaning and purpose in life, have been described by psychoanalysts in terms of a healthy mourning process, sublimation, and reintegration and self-healing following traumatic loss.

DISORDERED AND ORDERED LOVE AND THE EARTHLY AND HEAVENLY CITIES

As I have said, Augustine viewed the problem of ultimate human happiness in terms of choosing the "correct" object to love (i.e., God and others), and then having the inner qualities for loving them properly, that is, with the care, devotion and passion that they require and deserve. Moreover, when one loves wisely and well, when one's love is "rightly ordered," one is inclined to goodness, to virtuous behavior, and to living according to what Augustine would describe as right reason animated by faith, faith in the loved and loving God. In psychoanalytic language such virtuous behavior, such a move towards goodness, requires a high degree of autonomy and personal integration. Most important, it requires a capacity for discerning moral process and respectful, generous, for-the-Other relatedness. In contrast, "disordered" love is mainly "for oneself," it is avaricious, selfish and prideful, the personification of sin, or what analysts call narcissistic pathology.

It was within the context of the demise of Roman hegemony to barbarian invasions, causing many to blame Christianity for Rome's decline, that Augustine wrote his most important and magisterial book, the *City of God*, his refutation of the accusations against Christianity and the place in which he detailed his understanding of the two forms of love.[34] In the *City of God*, written between 413 and 427, Augustine argued that humanity can be divided between, on the one hand, those who mainly love God, and on the other, those who mainly love themselves and the world. Each group forms in their own way a society, since they are, Augustine claims, a group of rational people united by an agreement upon the things they love. The city of God, the "Heavenly City," is symbolized by Jerusalem and is equated with the Church and its sacred values. The "earthly city" is symbolized by the evil biblical city of Babylon (and, to some extent, Rome), and is equated with civic society and secular values. The main difference between the two cities is the object of one's love and the aim to which all of one's energies and efforts are focused. Says Augustine in this often quoted passage, "the earthly city was created by self-love reaching the point of contempt for God, the Heavenly City by the love of God carried as far as contempt of self. In fact, the earthly city glories in itself, the Heavenly City glorifies in the Lord."[35]

It should be pointed out that for Augustine, these two contrasting life orientations, symbolized by the two cities, are not necessarily separate; they are often "interwoven" and "mingled" with one another, in individuals and in communities.[36] Moreover, Augustine does not characterize the earthly city strictly negatively; he understands that the things and goods that the earthly city desires are not inherently evil, but rather, what is sinful is making the love of these things the ultimate good and the absolute basis for one's happiness. Augustine brilliantly and provocatively develops his philosophy of history in the *City of God*, and he ultimately argues for a third alternative to Jerusalem or Babylon, an alternative that has bearing on the analysand's struggle to live a reasonably fulfilling and happy life: Babylon as shaped and infused by Jerusalem, civic society secular values, and the secular mind-set animated with the "higher" (in his view), more humanizing, and life-affirming sacred values and worldview of the Heavenly City.

What Augustine is getting at seems to be this: The surest road to happiness is to live a life that is morally praiseworthy in God's eyes, in essence, one that is rooted in rightly ordered love, "in Christ's twofold command to love God with all your heart, mind, and soul, and to love your neighbor as yourself." This is in contrast to the surest road to unhappiness, that of disordered love, "the love of created things as if they were God, that is, as if they could make you ultimately happy."[37] As Smith points out in another context, this is the gist of Jesus's revolutionary message about what constitutes living the good life. It is also what I think Augustine was trying to focus human awareness on, namely: "God's overwhelming love of humanity, and the need for people to accept that love and let it flow through them to others."[38]

This notion of happiness goes beyond classical moral psychology, including Freud's version of it, which, in part, asserts that happiness, or mental health (or integration, adaptation, adjustment, etc.), as Freudian analysts call it, is mainly a question of achieving a rational mastery of the passions or drives. Where id was, ego shall be. Augustine's notion also goes beyond what object relations theorists like W. R. D. Fairbairn conceive of as the main therapeutic goal, roughly equated with happiness, that is, reconstituting the individual's capacity to form and maintain authentic, real relationships with others.[39] And while Heinz Kohut's self-psychology probably most resonates with Augustine's approach to attaining happiness, especially in Kohut's postanalytic goal of "belated structure building" and developing the "capacity to find an empathically responsive selfobject milieu,"[40] which could include God, self-psychology can also be enhanced by an Augustinian gloss.

My point is that Augustine adds a uniquely spiritual dimension to psychoanalysis, including a notion of happiness that I believe analysands who are so inclined can benefit from reflecting on, if not embracing, as they struggle for a modicum of personal fulfillment and peace of mind. That is, to the extent that one can experience God as infinite love who is absolutely devoted to one's personal salvation; that one can perceive God's infinite love, not only for oneself, but for all others; and that one is to able to allow God's love to enter into, dwell, and transform one's very being, one may attain the conversion of heart, the radical and permanent self-transfiguration that makes deep and abiding happiness and peace of mind a real possibility, if not a reality. For it is just such an interior conversion that gives one that "profound and total gratitude for the wonders of God's grace" which as I have claimed, is one of the most solid and reliable internal bases for achieving a sense of enduring, fulfillment, happiness and tranquillity of spirit.[41] This formulation may take us beyond psychoanalysis as conventionally construed, but this is precisely my point: that psychoanalysis, like all things human, should be open to a dimension of experience that is beyond itself.

It is this notion and its related insights that I believe constitute the best of the Augustinian experience: that pride, selfishness, and avarice (i.e., narcissistic pathology), with the inordinate love of temporal goods and earthly things, are the main psychological reasons for human misery. The antidote to this doomed approach to life, the sure road to happiness as Augustine calls it, is an inward turn, with the fullness of one's whole being, toward the infinite, merciful, and loving God.

Such an inward turn, at its best, is characterized by a profound awareness that grasping and clinging to earthly things in whatever form—possessions, people, fame or power, for instance—is as unreasonable as trying to hold on to smoke. Those who have obtained this illuminating, heart-felt, intuitive knowledge of God, who have experienced His transforming love, are noticeable by their humility and humanity, that is, by their quiet submission to a power beyond themselves, a power that fills them with gratitude, a generosity of spirit, an openness of heart, and an ever-inquiring mind, which is aimed at fathoming the eternal, unchangeable, and, at times, unintelligible and mysterious God. Most important in my view, those who have this heartfelt, intuitive knowledge of God are characterized by their passionate commitment to a for-the-Other orientation in the world.

Finally, for Augustine it is ultimately only through the grace-infused, healing love of God (and of Other), that we can achieve what Augustine (and Freud, though using secular language) believed we perhaps most yearn for, namely, a unity with the infinite Good, that which the Christian equates with God, and which, in psychoanalytic parlance, is equated with the cosmic breast, that "oceanic feeling" that Romain Rolland referred to in his famous letter to Freud. It is this mystical, cosmic, passionate feeling and source of bountiful life energy and hope that Rolland thought, and Augustine insinuated, is the source of the religious impulse and sensibility.

Freud could not locate in himself the oceanic feeling, a feeling that, he theorized, was rooted in the experience of the infant at the breast before learning to differentiate the self from the outside world.[42] Augustine, however, has blessed us with an extraordinary narrative that beautifully, brilliantly, and boldly conveys the exquisite merging and timelessness that is probably the ultimate unconscious psychological basis, not only for the inward turn toward God, but for any kind of lasting peace of mind. It is perhaps this desire for fusion and eternity, personified in what Augustine thought was the ultimate happiness, namely, an uninterrupted enjoyment of God coupled with the guarantee that it would not end,[43] which, in part, drove his search for religious meaning in existence. Says a lamenting and yearning Augustine on the first page of his *Confessions*: "To praise you is the desire of man, a little piece of your creation. You stir man to take pleasure in praising you, because you have made us for yourself, and our heart is restless until it rests in you."[44]

NOTES

1. Saint Augustine, *Soliloquies and Immortality of the Soul*, trans. by Gerald Watson (London: Aris and Phillips, 1990), p. 31.
2. Philip Cary, "Augustine: Philosopher and Saint," in *The Great Courses on Tape* (Course Outline) (Chantilly, Va.: The Teaching Company, 1997), p. 5.
3. William L. Reese, "Saint Augustine," in *Dictionary of Philosophy and Religion: Eastern and Western Thought* (Atlantic Highlands, N.J.: Humanities Press, 1980), pp. 39–41.
4. Philip Cary, "Interiority," in *Augustine through the Ages: An Encyclopedia*, ed. Allan D. Fitzgerald (Grand Rapids, Mich.: Erdman's Publishing Company, 1999), pp. 454–456.
5. Stephen J. Duffy, "Anthropology," in Fitzgerald, ed., *Augustine through the Ages, An Encyclopedia*, pp. 24–31.
6. Cary, "Interiority," p. 454.
7. Saint Augustine, *Confessions*, trans. Henry Chadwick (Oxford: Oxford University Press, 1991), pp. 179–220.
8. Duffy, "Anthropology," p. 27.
9. As Philip Cary pointed out, for Augustine, friendship, the deepest form of love of the other, is literally the best thing on earth (personal communication, March 12, 2001).
10. Tarsicius J. van Bavel, "Love," in Fitzgerald, *Augustine through the Ages*, p. 509.
11. Saint Augustine, *City of God*, trans. Henry Battenson (London: Penguin Classics, 1984), p. 637.
12. Saint Augustine, *Confessions*, p. 278.
13. Peter Brown, *Augustine of Hippo* (Berkeley: University of California Press, 1969), p. 324.
14. J. Patourt Burns, "Grace," in Fitzgerald, ed., *Augustine through the Ages*, p. 398.
15. Harvey Cox, "Christianity," in *Our Religions*, ed. by Arvind Sharma (New York: HarperCollins Publishers, 1993), p. 374.
16. *The Prayer Book: Weekday, Sabbath and Festival*, trans. and ed., Ben Zion Bokser (New York: Hebrew Publishing Co., 1995), p. 242.
17. Brown, *Augustine of Hippo*, p. 390.
18. Paul Rigby, "Original Sin," in Fitzgerald, ed., *Augustine through the Ages*, p. 608.
19. E. Mansell Pattison, "The Holocaust as Sin: Requirements in Psychoanalytic Theory for Human Evil and Mature Morality," in *Psychoanalytic Reflections on the Holocaust: Selected Essays*, eds. Steven A. Luel and Paul Marcus (New York: University of Denver and KTAV Publishers, 1988), p. 89. Augustine may well be wrong about original sin, and perhaps it makes more sense to believe that we are born innocent. Yet, apparently, to most people, it *feels* the other way, as if for as long as one can remember one has been sinning and impure. Moreover, from

Christianity: Saint Augustine's *Confessions* 157

a psychological perspective, it seems good to take account of that feeling (Cary, personal communication, March 21, 2001).

20. John C. Cavadini, "Pride," in Fitzgerald, ed., *Augustine through the Ages*, p. 679.

21. Brown, *Augustine of Hippo*, p. 405.

22. Donald X. Burt, "Health, Sickness," in Fitzgerald, ed., *Augustine through the Ages*, p. 417.

23. R. A. Markus, "Saint Augustine," in *The Encyclopedia of Philosophy*, ed. Paul Edward (New York: Macmillan Publishing Company and the Free Press, 1967), 1: 203.

24. Cary, "Augustine," p. 32.

25. Ibid., p. 37.

26. Burt, "Health, Sickness," p. 417.

27. Clifford Geertz, "Religion as a Cultural System," in his *The Interpretation of Cultures* (New York: Basic Books, 1973), p. 105. As Cary points out, while Augustine dealt with the problem of suffering as a pastoral issue, he did not deal with the theoretical problem of why God allows bad things to happen to good people. In part, this is because of his philosophical assumption that every person is born in original sin and therefore not innocent before God. More important, no one asked Augustine, and he did not ask himself, the theoretical question of why there is seemingly undeserved suffering. That is, such a question was not part of the sociointellectual reality in which Augustine lived. Though the Psalms, the Prophets, and Job dealt with the problem of undeserved suffering in a profound and searching way, this problem did not get serious attention in the Western philosophical and theological tradition until the eighteenth century. It is, in other words, a characteristically modern question (Cary, personal communication, March 21, 2001).

28. Barry Magid, "The Evil Self," *Dynamic Psychotherapy*, 6, no. 2 (1988): 111.

29. Peter Berger and Brigette Berger, *Sociology: A Biographical Approach* (New York: Basic Books, 1972), p. 352.

30. Paul Marcus, "The Religious Believer, the Psychoanalytic Intellectual, and the Challenge of Sustaining the Self in the Concentration Camps," *Journal for the Psychoanalysis of Culture and Society*, 3, no. 1 (Spring 1998): 61–75.

31. James W. Jones, *Contemporary Psychoanalysis and Religion* (New Haven: Yale University Press, 1991).

32. Peter Berger, *The Sacred Canopy* (Garden City, N.Y.: Doubleday, 1967).

33. Marcus, "The Religious Believer, the Psychoanalytic Intellectual, and the Challenge of Sustaining the Self in the Concentration Camps."

34. Augustine, *City of God*. This translation, by Henry Battenson, is one of the most reliable available in paperback.

35. Ibid., p. 593.

36. Ibid., p. 430.

37. Cary, "Augustine," pp. 55, 56.

38. Huston Smith, *The World's Religions: Our Great Wisdom Traditions* (New York: Harper San Francisco, 1991), pp. 326–327.

39. Paul Marcus and Alan Rosenberg, *Psychoanalytic Versions of the Human Condition: Philosophies of Life and Their Impact on Practice* (New York: New York University Press, 1998), p. 163.

40. Paul H. Ornstein, "Heinz Kohut's Vision of the Essence of Humanness," in Marcus and Rosenberg, eds., *Psychoanalytic Versions of the Human Condition*, p. 225.

41. Smith, *The World's Religions*, p. 327.

42. Sigmund Freud, *Civilization and Its Discontents*, in *Standard Edition of the Complete Works of Sigmund Freud*, ed. James Strachey (London: Hogarth Press and the Institute of Psycho-Analysis, 1953–1974), 21: 57–146. (Original work published 1930).

43. Augustine, *The City of God*, p. 444.

44. Saint Augustine, *Confessions*, p. 3.

9

Islam: The Koran

> We have returned from the Lesser Holy War [with the external enemy] to the Greater Holy War [with the selfish passions].
> Muhammad the Prophet[1]

There is probably no religion on earth in which one sacred book, namely, the Koran, has achieved such scriptural saturation of the daily life of its adherents, 900 million Muslims in a world population of 5 billion! And yet, of the three Abrahamic-based religions discussed in this book, it is Islam that is by far the most misunderstood by Westerners. Islam is also the least written about in terms of its connection to, and possible enhancement of, Western psychotherapy and psychoanalysis. In a certain sense this is a pity since the goals of Islam as described in the Koran, at least in terms of what constitutes the "good life," are to some extent similar to psychoanalysis. That is, while Islam's modality to reach the Koranic goal of perfecting one's soul as one moves nearer to God, a total spiritualization of one's thoughts and actions as the believer might put it, is very different from the goals and practices of secular psychoanalysis as conventionally articulated, Islam, like psychoanalysis, is a powerful way to achieve a state of integration and wholeness, happiness and peace of mind.

A CORE BELIEF OF ISLAM

With a few notable exceptions, the basic theological concepts of Islam are nearly identical to those of its precursors, Judaism and Christianity.[2] Moreover, as Seyyed Hossein Nasr has pointed out, Islam's fundamental character is reflected, in part, in its essentiality, universality and majestic simplicity, this being one of the reasons it has such wide appeal.[3]

It is the Koran (Recital), that is the most powerful organizing force within Islam and the main text on which Islamic spirituality is based.[4] As a whole, it is an extremely deep and compelling collection of reflections upon God, the cosmos, and the human condition. According to tradition, the earthly Koran (the original is believed to be in heaven and is therefore literally eternal and uncreated), was revealed by God to His Prophet Muhammad over a twenty-two-year period (610–632) in the form of a recital. This recitation was delivered orally to Muhammad in Arabic via the angel Gabriel. Each verse was delivered gradually in stages, at the most opportune moment, in order to increase the likelihood that its message would be absorbed by the Muslim community. Most important, to the believer, the Koran reflects the literal will of God: it is the presence of God on earth. Thus, Islam means surrender to God and a Muslim is one who surrenders to the will of God.

Of the "Five Pillars of Islam," bearing of witness, prayer, alms, the fast of Ramadan, and pilgrimage to Mecca, the first, the *Shahaada*, is by far the most important to the believing Muslim, as it is the one pillar that is mandatory at all times and in all contexts. The *Shahaada* reflects the main thrust of Islam as it asserts the following: "There is no god but the God [Allah] and Muhammad is the messenger of God."[5]

In the first part of the *Shahaada* the Muslim is required to uncompromisingly declare the oneness, unity, uniqueness and the transcendence of God. This assertion reflects Islam's powerful, unshakable commitment to monotheism—One God, One Book, One Prophet as Muslims say. There is absolutely no place for any form of polytheism or idolatry in Islam, including the more subtle forms of idolatry that are commonplace in our culture, the worship of money, power, pleasure seeking, etc. The Koran makes it absolutely clear that perhaps the greatest sin is to substitute some other power for God for this is tantamount to denying God's revelations or inventing a falsehood about Him.

It should be mentioned that the Koran views its form of monotheism as perfected compared to that of the "People of the Book," Jews and Christians, who in a certain sense have betrayed God and Moses. Jews, according to the Koran, have diminished the universal ethical monotheism of the prophet Abraham to the "God of our Fathers, Abraham, Isaac and Jacob" and to the "chosenness" of the Jewish people, while Christian trinitarianism is regarded as a form of polytheism. Thus, while the Koran views the messages of Judaism and Christianity to be corrupt and incomplete (e.g., their scriptures were misinterpreted and mistranslated from the original Hebrew and Greek), they have a degree of validity and efficacy and therefore demand respect. In other words, the Koran counsels Muslims to leave it to God to judge Jews and Christians who have rejected the Koran and its Prophet, the Koran being regarded as the perfection and completion of Jewish and Christian revelations. Thus, religious persecution and forced conversions of the People of the Book are forbidden in the Koran.

The second part of the *Shahaada* expresses the Muslim's recognition that humans require guidance in living in accordance with God's will. God has graciously provided assistance through a succession of prophets (e.g., Adam, Noah, Abraham, Moses, Jesus, etc.), Muhammad being the most perfect, and the final messenger that God has sent to guide mankind to live a God-infused life, one that will contribute to mankind's redemption. Muhammad is thus the paradigm of piety for the Muslim community, the person whose character and lifestyle one should emulate in every way. The other four pillars of Islam are ways of helping the believer remember, strengthen and actualize the word of God and the exemplar of Muhammad in their lives.

The exordium that begins the Koran, and whose first sentence precedes all but one of the 114 of the *suras* (chapters), further suggests how the Muslim view God and the human condition as well as what man should strive for in his life, namely, to live in accordance with God's will, to live the "straight path":

> In The Name Of God The Compassionate The Merciful. Praise be to God, Lord of the Universe, the Compassionate, the Merciful, Sovereign of the Day of Judgment! You alone we worship, and to You alone we turn for help. Guide us to the straight path, The path of those whom You have favored, Not of those who have incurred Your wrath, Nor of those who have gone astray.[6]

According to the Koran, for the Muslim the human situation is characterized by an internal struggle between the forces of knowledge and goodness and ignorance and evil.[7] The main purpose of the Koran is to teach men and women how to "please God," and by doing so, to achieve God's grace which is in part, experienced as peace of mind.[8] *Tawhid*, unity, is the Arabic word for bringing about this sense of serene oneness, this integration of mind, body and spirit as one lives according to the will of the One, indivisible, omnipotent, omniscient, just, merciful and forgiving God. How then does one attain this interiorization of God, the goal of human existence for the Muslim, that by God's grace, according to the Koran, gives one the peace of mind that Muslim's and secular analysands long for? In other words, what constitutes this "straight path" that the Muslim believes will liberate him from the restrictive limitations of the material world and ego consciousness to the illimitable luminous realm of the Infinite? As the great Sufi poet

Rumi wrote, "the house without a window is Hell, the function of religion is to make a window."⁹

SURRENDER (*ISLAM*), FAITH (*IMAN*), VIRTUE (*IHSAN*)

There are three interrelated stages of spiritual development for the Muslim that I want to briefly describe for they will serve as context for the remainder of the chapter. These stages of spiritual development are greatly influenced by Sufi interpretations of Islam's message, especially in terms of the centrality of emotions. Some scholars might view this to be technically problematic. However, as I will later suggest, each stage points to important insights about the human condition that have bearing on psychoanalysis, at least in terms of helping the analysand to eliminate the hindrances in his psyche that prevent him from becoming, what I regard as a praiseworthy analytic goal, namely, becoming more open to the spiritual realm. As will become obvious, from a psychoanalytic point of view, each stage represents a deeper internalization of God, that is, an ever-widening apprehension of God's presence and a spiritual consciousness.

In its most literal form, the first stage, that of *islam*, absolute surrender or resignation to God's will, refers to the Muslim's obligation to live his life according to the exterior requirements of Islam, for example, to the Five Pillars and to the dos and don'ts of the *Shariah*, Islamic law. This is known as the exoteric requirements of Islam. However, psychologically speaking, the call to surrender to God means much more than knowledge of, and obedience and conformity to sacred law. In religious language it is a call to ontological and moral surrender by the created to the Creator. In secular terms, what surrender is demanding of the individual is to be mindful of the contingent nature of existence and our total dependence on the universe, whether conceptualized as Nature, Necessity, Fate, or God. In other words, surrender means coming to terms with the weak, fragmentary, and fleeting nature of existence and most important, with our lack of control in life, especially as it pertains to ultimate concerns. Such an awareness of our vulnerable and dependent nature tends to generate a sense of both humility and gratitude, especially to God as the Muslim would describe it.

As Smith points out, *surrender* is a term that rubs Westerners the wrong way, for it has military connotations that suggests defeat. However, surrender can also have a positive meaning and this is what the Koran is really getting at. Surrender, says Smith, can be thought of as a form of unrestrained giving of oneself, as intense commitment or dedication to say a spouse, child or cause. In this sense, the Koranic call to be a "slave" to Allah (God) is to be liberated from the many forms of slavery that analysands manifest, such as selfishness, the lust for power, greedy materialism and the inordinate wish for self-aggrandizement. Surrender, in other words, does not have to mean relinquishing but can be viewed as a form of existential engagement. In the case of Islam, this engagement means having a total commitment and dedication to God such that one's entire life is focused on God and nothing is kept back from Him.[10] Most important, perhaps, for Muslims, surrender to the will of God (or to Nature, etc., as the secular analysand might describe it) encourages them to transcend the confinement of their own ego consciousness and enslavement to their selfish desires and infantile wishes, toward what might be called an infinite sublimation in God, one that fosters a sense of self-transcendence, security and inner peace. This religious teaching is, of course, in many ways in sync with those of all major religious teachings.

While all those who have fully accepted Koranic revelation are said to be Muslims who have internalized islam, surrender to God, as manifested in living according to the Five Pillars and the *Shariah*, there are those believers who have acquired a more profound form of spiritual development, a form of internalization that is characterized by a stronger faith in God and the hereafter. This second spiritual stage of iman, faith, refers to an intensification of one's connection to God, as manifested in a more fervent and passionate faith in Allah, in His angels (Muslims have an elaborate angelology), His holy Books, in Muhammad and his previous messengers (e.g., Abraham, Jesus), the Day of Reckoning or Judgment, and predestination of evil and good.[11]

Finally, we come to the highest stage of spiritual development, ihsan, virtue, morality or beauty, the stage that is best associated with the esoteric branch of Islam, Sufism, Islamic mysticism. In this mode of being, the Muslim lives always mindful of being in God's presence. Ihsan not only entails obedience and conformity to the external rules of Islam, nor simply inner faith. Rather, in addition, it entails a complete detachment at all times from worldly interests and passions and a receptiveness to that which God wills. Such a believer has lost his ego consciousness and selfish desires and has become a viceregent of God on earth. That is, this mode of being is characterized by *dhikr*, remembrance of God, as manifested by the forgetting or transcendence of the self in God, and a recapturing of the experience of loving intimacy with Allah, religion being viewed as the sine qua non of human existence for all Muslims, especially the Sufi. That is, Islam asserts that religion is hardwired, it is our nature to strive towards transcendence since God created us in His own image. The sublime mysticism of Rabiah al-Adawiyah and the extraordinarily beautiful poetry of Jalal al-din Rumi personify this spiritual stage of *ihsan*, especially the exhilaration and peace of mind that goes along with a spirit that is open to the Infinite and a life lovingly devoted to God. As the great Islamic jurist, theologian, and mystical thinker Al-Ghazali wrote, the greatest joy, the one that all Muslims should strive for, is the seeing of God in the spiritual or intellectual sense of the beatific vision. Like Saint Augustine, the highest stage of religious experience is the unmediated, direct visualization of the beauty and splendor of God.

GOD

As one reads the Koran one is struck by the awesome power of God. Indeed there is probably no other scripture or religious tradition that reiterates as often as does the Koran that God is one, indivisible, and omnipotent, the single divine power in the universe: "To God belongs all that the heavens and the earth contain. Whether you reveal your thoughts or hide them, God will bring you to account for them. He will forgive whom He will and punish whom He pleases; God has power over all things."[12]

There is little doubt in my mind that the average Muslim fears God's punitive capability in a way that is probably more palpable than most of the other major religions discussed in this book. Indeed there are many passages in the Koran that are pure fire and brimstone in character and convey in stark terms the hellish fate of the sinner. In other words, the Koranic universe is in a certain sense, a morally black-and-white one. If you stay on the straight path, God will be merciful and forgiving and paradise awaits you and if you unrepentantly veer off this path, punishment and hell fire are your fate. Says the Koran:

> But the true servants of God shall be well provided for, feasting on fruit, and honored in the gardens of delight. Reclining face to face upon soft couches, they shall be served with a goblet filled at a gushing fountain, white, and delicious to those who drink it. It will neither dull their sense nor befuddle them. They shall sit with bashful, dark-eyed virgins, as chaste as the sheltered eggs of ostriches. . . .
> But he that defies God and His apostle and transgresses His bounds, shall be cast into a Fire wherein he will abide for ever. Shameful punishment awaits him. [And elsewhere it is written] Truly, those that commit evil and become engrossed in sin shall be the inmates of the Fire; there shall they abide forever.[13]

Needless to say this simplistic view of reward and punishment and the version of the human condition that undergirds it is not one that psychoanalysis would endorse as plausible nor desirable to embrace. However, there are aspects of Islam's conception of God that I think can sensitize analysands to something that they often lose sight of in how they live their lives. That is, implicit in the Islamic notion of God is the important point that choices and decisions, especially in the ethical and moral realm, really matter. In other words, the Koran is suggesting that life is a very risky, uncertain and at times, dangerous enterprise, one that requires constant critical self-reflection, especially about the consequences of one's decisions and actions on others and for that matter, on all of creation. The Koranic message foreshadows Friedrich Nietzsche's notion of eternal reoccurrence, the idea that one should mindfully live one's life, that is, with passion and commitment, as if one was condemned to repeat it over and over again. What the Koran adds to Nietzsche's notion is the idea that if one lives a life without moral passion, commitment, and most importantly a clear sense of right and wrong (as delineated by the Koran and its other holy texts), then one is going to suffer. To the Muslim this may be conceptualized as literal punishment by Allah, but taken less literally punishment refers to the guilt, anxiety and the other forms of self-loathing and self-punishment that are often the consequences of living a life of selfish desire and bad conscience.

This internal struggle between the lower and higher self as the Koran calls it, between selfish desire and the proclivity to doing evil on one hand, and a for-the-Other orientation and a striving to realize the Good in accordance with God's will on the other, forms the dialectical context for the Islamic notion of *jihad*, meaning struggle or effort. Like psychoanalysis, Islamic tradition emphasizes that in order to live in accordance with God's will and achieve loving intimacy with Him—in secular terms this is roughly equated with achieving integration, wholeness, and ethical maturity—one requires self-knowledge, which demands relentless soul searching and critical self-analysis. As Muhammad famously said after returning from one of his final military battles, "We have returned from the Lesser Holy War [*jihad*] to the Greater Holy War," the latter being "the war against the soul." The great philosopher al-Ghazali further elaborates, "The real *jihad* is the warfare against the passions," the evil in one's heart that prevents one from achieving greater proximity to God.[14] As in psychoanalysis it is self-mastery, especially of one's narcissistic cravings and selfish desires that is the pre-condition to God-consciousness, personal happiness, and building a just, harmonious, and compassionate society. What Muhammad was getting at is thus entirely in sync with the psychoanalytic enterprise. That is, only when one brutally confronts one's personal failures, especially one's moral flaws in our dealings with others, and most important perhaps, our failures towards those we love the most and feel responsible for, can one attain the contemplativity that is in part the basis for breaching the divide that separates man from God. As Muhammad said,

"He who knows himself knows his Lord."[15] Islamic tradition, especially Sufism, provides a systematic theory and set of practices to achieve and sustain a high degree of self-knowledge, self-control, and a for-the-Other, God-animated outlook.

While I have been stressing Islam's view of God in terms of God's omnipotence and transcendence, it should be emphasized that the Muslim does not only fear Allah but views him as profoundly merciful, compassionate, just, and immanent. In fact, according to a well-known *hadith*, a saying of Muhammad, on the Divine Throne is written, "Verily My mercy precedes My Wrath."[16] Most important, the fact that God gave mankind the holy Koran, a clear guide to His will, is the evidence par excellence that He is merciful. God is also conceptualized as present in the everyday world; in fact his presence is felt in one's innermost life, says the Koran: "We know the promptings of his soul, and are closer to him than his jugular vein." And again, "He has knowledge of all your thoughts and actions."[17] For the Muslim, God is not only the All-seeing, punitive though just Judge, he also is merciful, compassionate, long-suffering, gracious and eager to forgive. Salvation, success in paradise as the Muslim would describe it and the peace of mind that goes with it, is possible if one tries with utter sincerity and honesty to live according to God's will, despite episodic failures in one's conduct. A famous *hadith* beautifully makes this point:

> He who approaches to Me one span, I will approach to him one cubit: and he who approaches near to Me one cubit, I will approach near to him one fathom, and whoever approaches Me walking, I will come to him running, and he who meets Me with sins equivalent to the whole world, I will greet him with forgiveness equal to it.[18]

There is an important point in the Muslim's view of God that has bearing on psychoanalysis, in particular as it relates to the all-too-common problem of how one copes with adversity and undeserved suffering such as the accidental death of a loved one.

First, it should remembered that for the Muslim God's nature is inherently unknowable. We only sense God's nature through His acts of creation, a subject I will take up in the next section. Moreover, while the problem of predestination, how to reconcile human responsibility with God's omniscience and omnipotence, has been debated without consensus by Islamic philosophers and theologians, for the average Muslim this problem is viewed as largely irrelevant in that God's ways, as is his nature, are unknowable and often unintelligible. The crucial challenge is not so much to try and discern God's motivation and the cosmic meaning of His actions but rather, to be ever mindful of the fact that one will be judged according to one's behavior. In other words, even amidst tough situations, the Muslim is engaged in *jihad*, the struggle to rise to God's challenge to what He expects as articulated in the Koran and its accompanying sacred writings.[19]

Thus, when life gets rough, the Muslim draws from his self-transcending spiritual resources for comfort, support and hope. First he knows that God never inflicts more pain on man than what he can endure, says the Koran: "We never charge a soul with more than it can bear."[20] Such a view makes one's suffering "sufferable" in that one feels that ultimately, with God's gracious help, one will be able to prevail though this will at times require incredible patience and trust in God's mercy. Sometimes, says the Koran, God makes one suffer in order to test one's faith: "We created man to try him with afflictions." Abraham, in his willingness to kill his son as God commanded him, is one of the Koranic examples of the perfect faith. Second, the Muslim draws on prayer as a way of coping; in particular he is mindful of the fact that if he is humble, shows fortitude, and obeys the sacred law, he will ultimately meet God and return to him, this being the concept of recompense in the hereafter.[21] In other words, things will ultimately be put right in this or the next world for God is always just. Finally, the Muslim fervently believes in a kind of fatalism, that nothing occurs that is not God's will, though the positive meaning of a happening may not be perceived by finite man, says the Koran: "It is He who ordains life and death"; "God governs the destiny of all things."[22]

What can the secular analysand draw from the Muslims' view of God as it pertains to the problem of coping with adversity and undeserved suffering? I think there is at least one important insight: the Muslim teaches us to face up to the brute, often painful facts of existence as beyond his ultimate control and understanding. Put succinctly, the Muslim confronts with utter honesty and acceptance the fact that we are weak, helpless and alone before God, or in the universe as the secularist would describe it. Rather than burn with anger or be frazzled by anxiety at what appears at times to be the workings of an ethically indifferent universe, one is better off surrendering to the will of God, to the operation of a mysterious force in the universe called Absolute Being or, as the secularist might call it, Necessity. It is this attitude of acceptance, of grateful surrender to God, resignation without despair in the face of the contingent nature of life and to our particular fate, that paradoxically allows one a degree of self-transcendence of one's suffering. This Koranic message is fundamentally the same one advocated by all of the great religions discussed in this book, namely that to be human, and I would add to be wisely human, means to graciously accept that we and all of the natural world for that matter, are dependent, contingent, relative and finite.

CREATION

For the Muslim, God is the transcendent, sovereign creator of man and the material world. While God and man are irrevocably qualitatively different, in a certain sense God's divine imprint can be intuited through the created order for as God says, "I have fashioned him and breathed of My spirit into him." Elsewhere in the Koran we read:

> To God belongs the East and West. Whichever way you turn there is the face of God. [Elsewhere it is written:] Do you not see how God causes the night to pass into the day and the day to pass into the night? He has pressed the sun and the moon into His service, each running for an appointed term.[23]

As Huston Smith has pointed out, there are at least two implications of viewing the material world as willfully created by an omnipotent and All-Good God. First, it implies that the created order is both real and significant, this probably being one of the reasons for the amazing development of Islamic science while Europe was in its Dark Ages. Second, given the fact that the created order was created by the All-Good and omnipotent God, it too must be good. Like Jews and Christians, says Smith, the Muslim has a favorable view of the material aspects of existence.[24] Such a view of the material world is basically compatible with a psychoanalytic calculus; the world is best approached according to Freud as real and significant, as something to be realistically reckoned with, the Reality Principle, and the world is good, that is, it is capable of giving one pleasure, sustenance and meaning as long as one is free enough from neurosis to be able to embrace life without reserve.

Such a God-emanating and God-animated Islamic view of the world has other positive ramifications on how one experiences the cosmos and relates to the natural order, a self-world relation that some analysands may find life enhancing.

The main function of the Koran is to help man to become sensitive to the Divine Presence in the created order. That is, in the Koranic universe there is a spiritual significance to nature, it is one of the royal roads to God, it is a foretaste of the beatitude of Islamic Paradise as Muslims conceive it. The Muslim lives in a self-sustaining matrix that aims to strengthen the unity between the Koranic Revelation (the word of God), our inner world, and the cosmos, specifically God's disclosures in nature. The goal of life for the Muslim is to reveal unity as reflected in the multiplicity of the world so as to assist us in realizing unity.[25] That is, the unity of God is reflected in the unity of His creation (especially the unity of the "family" of humanity), and the order of the world, and to the extent that one has internalized this notion one has achieved God-realization in one's outlook and life.

In order to achieve this unity according to the Koran it is essential to be mindful of how God discloses his divinity through the created order, in both nature and in the individual being. The Koran speaks of "signs" that are evident in the created world and in the "self," at least to those who are open to the world of the Spirit:

> Surely in the heavens and the earth there are signs for the faithful; in your own creations and in the beasts He scatters far and near, signs for true believers; in the alternation of night and day, in the sustenance God sends down from heaven with which He resurrects the earth after its death, and in the marshaling of the winds, signs for men of understanding. [And elsewhere it is written] On earth, and in yourselves, there are signs for firm believers. Can you not see.[26]

What such an outlook may suggest to the analysand is the following: Because God created all things, one can theoretically discern an order and purpose in the universe. In fact, more than miracles, it is the extraordinary order and regularity in the universe, for example, that the sun rises in the morning and sets in the evening, that is most striking to the Muslim. Being appreciative in the abode of inwardness of the melody and rhythm of the universe counters the amorphous blunting of feeling and leveling of everyday experience that is so common these days to those who are lodged strictly in the secular outlook. It is this "creation consciousness" that can act in some sense as an antidote to the secular analysand's sense of ennui depicted so astutely by existential writers.[27]

Moreover, according to the Muslim, because human beings and the natural order are not here by serendipity, that is, they were created by a willful act of the sovereign God, human existence is inherently meaningful. This is a view that moves against the hard to pin down alienation and meaninglessness that analysands so often complain about in one form or another. As the Koran says, "It is not in jest that We created the heavens and the earth and all that lies between them. We created them to reveal the truth."[28] In other words, we were created by God to live meaningful lives, and in particular, says the Koran, to live morally exemplary lives. For example, living a life characterized by justice and compassion in our dealings with others and responsible custodial care of the earth, God's created order, are paramount. Most important perhaps for this chapter, by fashioning themselves along these existential coordinates, secular analysands are less likely to experience their form of life as a drying up of a horizon of meaning. Rather, like the Muslim, finite existence is experienced as an opening out to infinitude, as an infinite expanse, a dimension of being that is saturated with transcendent meaning that positively animates everyday life.

THE DAY OF JUDGMENT

As I have insinuated, while there is a clear thrust in the Koran that supports a notion of predestination: "Nothing will befall us except what God has ordained," "There is no blessing you enjoy which does not come from God,"[29] Islam also has a strong emphasis on individual freedom and responsibility. In fact, while the tension between the notions of God's omnipotence and predestination, on the one hand, and man's freedom and responsibility on the other has not to date been satisfactorily resolved by Islamic theologians and philosophers, the Koran emphasizes time and again an uncompromising individual responsibility for one's behavior. The average Muslim in other words, lives with the paradoxical coexistence of God's absolute power and control of all happenings and the mindfulness that each person remains responsible for all his choices and actions. In other words, no human being can seek shelter in predestination by using the flimsy excuse, "God made me do it."[30]

It is precisely the belief in the responsibility and accountability of all human beings before a just, judgmental God that unites all Muslims. For if one believes in monotheism, in a God who is omniscient and who establishes the standards of ideal behavior for the world, there must be a time of judgment, otherwise the whole system implodes. In Islam, resurrection and Judgment Day refer more or less to the same idea and day, says the Koran: "The fate of each man We have bound about his neck. On the Day of Resurrection We shall confront him with a book spread wide open, saying 'Here is your book: read it. Enough for you this day that your own soul shall call you for account.' "[31]

The idea here is that God, at a time that is known only to Him, will judge every human being according to the record of his actions, which is etched in heaven. There is little doubt that there is an apocalyptic doom associated with Judgment Day for the average Muslim, though this sense of doom is counteracted by a belief that God is merciful and forgiving to the repentant sinner. Moreover, whether one takes this and other similar passages in the Koran literally or metaphorically, the main point comes through, namely, that while you can run, you cannot hide from God's judgment of your moral life. The Koran, with its fire and brimstone and paradisal imagery is using a stick and carrot approach that is meant to jolt the Muslim from his moral ignorance and spiritual sluggishness so as to live the straight path. It should be noted however, that the Koran also insinuates that a higher form of God-realization is reflected in those believers who though they are aware of Judgment Day, "give sustenance to the destitute, the orphan, and the captive, saying: 'We feed you for God's sake only; we seek of you neither recompense nor thanks.' "[32] In other words, acts of loving kindness and all good works should be done because they are what God expects from us; they are a form of worship to God, they are not to be done simply because we seek reward or fear punishment. Such an internalization of God reflects Islamic conscience and compassion at its best.

I am aware that the above notions only make sense if one believes in God for the whole system presupposes such a faith and a belief in Divine Judgment. However, I think there is an important insight that the Koran is getting at that is also serviceable to the secular analysand. I want to return to the last line of the quotation about resurrection and Judgment Day, "Enough for you this day that your own soul shall call you for account."

In contrast to the Koran's usual emphasis on God's role on Judgment Day, in this sentence, and there are others sprinkled throughout the Koran, the emphasis is on self-judgment and self-accountability. In other words, within the context of death, resurrection and Judgment there is the notion that the individual will judge his own life in addition to God doing so, this process being necessary to achieve salvation in the hereafter and personal happiness on earth. What I think the Koran is hinting at is this: in order for one to live an exemplary life, to be able to love and work with passion, to achieve Goodness and Wisdom, one must constantly reflect on and judge one's actions in terms of one's creatureliness, in terms of one's finitude, dependence, vulnerability and death. This self-judgment, especially in terms of one's moral and other lapses and weaknesses, is manifested in our dealings with others and in our limitations in giving and receiving love. In other words, the Koran is teaching the prudence of acquiring a particular relationship to oneself: one in which the self is diminished, actually humbled (ideally, extinguished or forgotten before God, as the Sufis say), as one's shortcomings and proclivity for selfishness and evil are acknowledged and one's finitude is accepted. Only after this, teaches the Koran, can self-transcendence begin, can the self begin to relate itself to powers beyond itself, to infinitude, to absolute transcendence, and by doing so create the surest basis for fostering the capacity for giving and receiving love, productive work, and peace of mind in this world.[33]

FINAL WORD

Islam is a religion that demands living a life characterized by passionate choice, that is, the acceptance of responsibility to do God's will as codified in the Koran and other sacred writings. The Koran promises to the believer that if he does God's will with a passionate inwardness, with love and devotion, if he acts as a friend, servant and perhaps most important, a viceregent of God on earth, he will be rewarded in this world or the next with deep and abiding happiness and serenity. Says the Koran:

> Such is the path of your Lord: a straight path. We have made plain Our revelations to thinking men. They shall dwell in peace with their Lord. He will give them His protection as recompense for what they do. [And elsewhere it is written:] As for those who have faith and do good works and humble themselves before their Lord, they are the heirs of Paradise, and there they shall abide forever.[34]

Moreover, although I have not emphasized this point in this chapter, as a religion, Islam is extremely oriented toward social responsibility and service to others, especially, though not only, the *ummah*, the Islamic community. Moreover, when lived at its highest level of spiritual development, Islam is a total way of life, one that does not separate the kingdom of God and the kingdom of Caesar, the sacred from the profane.

The Koran provides a number of passages that depict in accessible language the ideal person who lives Islam as a total way of life lovingly dedicated to God, that is, a life in which the transcendent, the Infinite, is a living everyday reality. In closing I want to give a sense of what such a person looks and "feels" like so that the reader of this book can concretize and thereby perhaps more easily internalize aspects of the spirit of Islam into their outlook. Says the Koran:

> Righteousness does not consist in whether you face towards the East or the West. The righteous man is he who believes in the God and the Last Day, in the angels and the Book and the prophets; who, though he loves it dearly, gives away his wealth to kinsfolk, to orphans, to the destitute, to the traveler in need and to beggars, and for the redemption of captives; who attends to his prayers and renders the alms levy; who is true to his promises and steadfast in trial and adversity and in times of war. Such are the true believers; such are the God-fearing.[35]

In my view, what the Koran is emphasizing perhaps more then anything else is the goal of man's moral perfection, a moral perfection based on unequivocal individual responsibility for one's actions that is entirely rooted in grateful, absolute surrender to God. That is, an acknowledgment of man's complete dependence upon the all-powerful, all-knowing, just and merciful God. Such a view is in a certain sense antimodern[36] in at least one important way and hence, it may be hard to appreciate by the secular analysand even though according to the Koran, it is the royal road to peace of mind.

Islam rejects the notion that man is the measure of all things and instead insists on the theocentric viewpoint; it situates God at the center of human life, nature and the cosmos. As Nasr further points out, such an outlook moves against the agnostic humanism of most secular analysands that puts humanity at the center of the cosmos, and according to Muslims, is threatening mankind's dignity, value and worth as well as his physical survival.[37] In other words, for the secular analysand to embrace the spirit of Islam means to radically transform one's angle of vision on life, to put the rights and wishes of God and most important, the responsibilities of humanity to God, before that of human rights and wishes. Pragmatically speaking, this means embracing with balance and compassion, according to Islam, an existential path that demands a high degree of passionate moral, ethical and spiritual commitment and refinement.[38] It means, says Nasr, choosing to live an inner and outer life that moves one closer towards the Ultimate Truth, the Supreme Good, the Infinite Beauty, that is, a life that is open to the transforming infinite grace of the Compassionate and Merciful Allah.

NOTES

1. This *hadith* (saying of the Prophet) is quoted in Abu Baker Siraj Ed-Din, "The Nature and Origin of Sufism," in *Islamic Spirituality: Foundations*, ed.,Seyyed Hossein Nasr (New York: Crossroad, 1997), p. 228.

2. Huston Smith. *The World's Religions: Our Great Wisdom Traditions* (New York: Harper San Francisco, 1991), pp. 235–236.

3. Seyyed Hossein Nasr, "Islam," in *Our Religions*, ed. Arvind Sharma (New York: Harper San Francisco, 1993), p. 429.

4. Textually speaking, Islamic spirituality is based on the Koran; the *Sunna*, the lifestyle of Muhammad and the first Islamic community, the *Hadith*, the collected statements of Muhammad that Muslims view as a crucial resource for understanding the *Sunna* and the first Islamic community; and *Shariah*, Islamic law, which is derived mainly from the Koran and the *Sunna*.

5. Quoted from John Esposito, *Islam: The Straight Path* (Oxford: Oxford University Press, 1998), p. 88.

6. N. J. Dawood, trans., " The Exordium," *The Koran* (London: Penguin Books, 1998), p. xvii.

7. Nasr, "Islam," p. 448. In contrast to Christianity, Islam does not believe in original sin. Rather, it has a more positive view of the human condition. While Islam is mindful of humanity's tendency toward "forgetting" God and doing evil, the work of Satan (*Iblis*), it views humanity as having a natural perfection or core of Godliness, which gets corroded and corrupted throughout life. Living according to the Koran is the antitdote to this corrosion; it is the way to be "saved."

8. Dawood, trans., *The Koran*, p. 70. See also Allahbakhsh K. Brohi, "The Spiritual Significance of the Quran," in Nasr, ed., *Islamic Spirituality*, p. 18.

9. Quoted in Charles Le Gai Eaton, "Man," in Nasr, ed., *Islamic Spirituality*, p. 369.

10. Smith, *Religions of the World*, pp. 239–240.

11. Victor Danner, "The Early Development of Sufism," in Nasr, ed., *Islamic Spirituality*, p. 266.

12. Dawood, trans. *The Koran*, p. 48.

13. Ibid., pp. 446, 78, 11. Psychoanalytically speaking, to "sit with bashful, dark-eyed virgins as chaste as the sheltered eggs of ostriches" implies more than just sitting with them. It seems that the Koran is insinuating that paradise includes having sexual relations with beautiful, chaste virgins.

14. Quotation in Abu Baker Siraj Ed-Din, "The Nature and Origin of Sufism," in Nasr, ed., *Islamic Spirituality*, 228; Ira G. Zepp, *A Muslim Primer*, 2nd ed. (Fayetteville: University of Arkansas Press, 2000), p. 85. "*Jihad* of the sword" can be implemented for self-defense, to protect one's family, nation, and religion, including to gain religious freedom, and to protect other Muslims who are defenseless and tyrannized. The criterion to wage a *jihad* of the sword are similar to those of the "just war theory" of Christianity. See Zepp, *A Muslim Primer*, pp. 96–97.

15. Quoted in Jean-Louis Michon, "The Spiritual Practices of Islam," in Nasr, ed., *Islamic Spirituality*, p. 285.

16. Quoted in Seyyed Hossein Nasr, "God," in Nasr, ed., *Islamic Spirituality*, p. 320.

17. Dawood, trans., *The Koran*, pp. 118, 358.

18. Quoted in S. G. Campion, *The Eleven Religions* (London: G. Routledge and Sons, 1944), p. 188.

19. John Swanson, "God and His Prophet: The Religion of Islam," in *Great World Religions: Beliefs, Practices and Histories, Part 2* (Course Guide) (Chantilly, Va.: The Teaching Company, 1997), pp. 15, 12.

20. Dawood, trans., *The Koran*, p. 148.

21. Dawood, trans., *The Koran*, p. 593; Allahbakhsh K. Brohi, "The Spiritual Dimension of Prayer," in Nasr, ed., *Islamic Spirituality*, p. 541.

22. Dawood, trans., *The Koran*, pp. 346, 336.

23. Ibid., pp. 262, 17, 413.

24. Smith, *The World's Religions*, p. 238.

25. Seyyed Hossein Nasr, "The Cosmos and the Natural Order," in Nasr, ed., *Islamic Spirituality*, pp. 345, 354.

26. Dawood, trans., *The Koran*, pp. 498, 520.

27. Nasr, "The Cosmos and the Natural Order," p. 355.

28. Dawood, trans., *The Koran*, p. 496.

29. Ibid., pp. 194, 271.

30. John Renard, *Responses to 101 Questions on Islam* (New York: Paulist Press, 1998), p. 42. Also see Renard's *Seven Doors to Islam: Spirituality and the Religious Life of Muslims* (Berkeley: University of California Press, 1996), pp. 12–13, 22, 89, 90.

31. Dawood, trans., *The Koran*, p. 282.

32. Ibid., p. 578.

33. Ernest Becker, *The Denial of Death* (New York: Free Press, 1973), p. 89.

34. Dawood, trans., *The Koran*, pp. 143, 223.

35. Ibid., p. 26.

36. Islam has probably been the least friendly of the three Abrahamic religions to the critique of the European Enlightenment, including resisting the critical-historical approach to its sacred writings: for example, "This Book is not to be doubted." See Dawood, trans., *The Koran*, p. 1. As Zepp has further pointed out (*A Muslim Primer*, p. 178), Islam has never experienced a period when

ultimate values were challenged and relativized as did Christianity in its engagement with Enlightenment rational, romantic, and revolutionary philosophy. This Enlightenment critique, which left its secular imprint on Western thinking, especially in its emphasis on individual freedom, ideological tolerance, and self-criticism, has hardly been embraced by most versions of Islam, though there have been a few exceptions. It is in part for this reason that there seems to be a potential for fanaticism in Islam that is probably greater than in either Judaism or Christianity.

37. Nasr, "Islam," pp. 529–530.

38. Balance or moderation is a key Islamic value. The Koran describes the true servants of Allah as "neither extravagant nor niggardly, but keep the golden mean." See Dawood, trans., *The Koran*, p. 364. There are many ways in which Islam demonstrates its commitment to balance and moderation. For example, in the Koran, God is described as both merciful and just. Islam also advocates an attitude toward sexuality that is against promiscuity, on the one hand, but is not prudish or repressive, on the other (at least relatively speaking). There is also a balance between the Islamic notion of predestination and individual freedom and responsibility and between this world and the hereafter.

10

Conclusion: Toward a Spiritually Animated Psychoanalysis

> One pole of any identity, in any historical period, relates man to what is forever contemporary, namely eternity.
>
> Erik Erikson[1]

My aim in this book has been, in part, to expose the psychoanalytic and psychological reader to some of the glorious wisdom of the great ancient religions of the world, East and West, within their vastly different sociointellectual realities. In doing so, I have attempted to lay the intellectual groundwork for my main claim: that psychoanalysis, a discourse, psychotherapy and profession on the wane, at least in American culture, could possibly benefit from a more serious intellectual engagement with ancient religious wisdom and spirituality (and its modern counterparts, though this was not my focus).

By psychoanalysis engaging and perhaps integrating into itself, some of the profound insights about the human condition, the art of living, the spiritual techniques to help bring about the enlightened or sanctified life as the religious often call it, and the implied ideal modes of being contained in ancient religious wisdom, then possibly, psychoanalysis may begin to be more in sync with the American spiritual zeitgeist and thus regain its once significant influence on cultural discourse. Perhaps most important, psychoanalysis may become a more compelling, relevant, and appealing life- and identity-defining narrative of the human condition and mode of self-transformation and form of psychotherapy.

Such a spiritually animated psychoanalysis, as I have called it, would be especially appealing to those potential analysands (usually but not always secularists) who are painfully alienated and adrift, if not trapped in a kind of spiritual ennui. Men and women of faith, inside and outside institutional religion, would also probably find psychoanalysis more in line with their spiritual needs, strivings, and worldview. These potential analysands and long-term psychotherapy patients—in religious terms, these spiritual aspirants, especially those lodged in a spiritual malaise—are often yearning to transform their consciousness and their way of being in order to live more meaningful, enlivened, creative, socially responsible and perhaps most important, contented lives. Unfortunately, this psychoanalytically underserved population often feels muddled and frustrated, believing there is no way out of their oppressive and painful existential reality, let alone through psychoanalysis or psychoanalytic-oriented psychotherapy. For when all is said and done, psychoanalysis, like all the religions discussed in this book, each in its own way and with its own emphasis, aims in part to foster self-transformation and transcendence. The goal is to help cultivate in the individual a mode of being which among other psychic changes, gradually increases and deepens the individual's peace of mind and sense of personal happiness, while at the same time making the needs of others and communal and relational processes a primary organizing principle of his or her life.

In this conclusion I want to suggest, in a rudimentary way, what a spiritually animated psychoanalysis might actually feel like. That is, I want to conclude this book with a thought experiment, by wondering what a psychoanalysis would feel like that, on the one hand, was open to transcendence, while on the other, maintained its self-declared mandate to be a critical, disruptive and demystifying discourse and practice.[2]

I am not going to review the specific ways in which each religious tradition I have discussed can enhance aspects of psychoanalysis. Each chapter in this book has tried to suggest how specific concepts and practices lodged in a particular religious tradition such as the Taoist notion of *wu-wei* (nonaction); Buddhist meditation techniques; Ecclesiastes' philosophy of life with his emphasis on resignation without despair, enjoying life in the present, and responsibility to the Other; the Confucian conception of the gentleman; and Saint Augustine's notion of ordered and disordered love can add something positive to psychoanalytic theory and clinical practice. Rather, I want to suggest in general, how ancient religious wisdom and spirituality taken as a whole, particularly as a way of being in the world, with all of its diversity, can possibly be integrated into psychoanalytic theory, practice and its worldview(s), at least in terms of embracing a more empathic and informed religious or spiritual sensibility. In this way, psychoanalysis can possibly become a discipline that has a greater spiritual attunement, vitality and depth, without becoming a dogmatic, moralistic, religiously, or otherwise unself-reflective, ideologically driven theory and practice.[3]

That spirituality, however defined, has become an important part of the spiritual zeitgeist in America and elsewhere has been supported by a number of surveys cited in the Introduction to this book. Moreover, there are many popular books, magazines and movies that pertain to the themes of spirituality and religion that have caught the attention of the American and international public in recent years. There also is a proliferation of alternative and traditional forms of spiritual and religious expressiveness and communities popping up throughout the land. Spiritual and religious themes have also of course, entered into mainstream political discourse, sometimes for the better (e.g., Martin Luther King, Jr.) and sometimes for the worse (e.g., Ayatolla Ruholla Khomeini).

THE WISDOM OF THE WISDOM WRITERS

Before I suggest how psychoanalysis can possibly benefit from ancient religious wisdom and spirituality toward becoming a more spiritually animated discipline and praxis, I think it is important that we first make some general comments about what many believe are some of the most worthwhile notions in the wisdom tradition, at least in terms of what constitutes the ideal form of conduct for life and perspective on reality. I am well aware that not everything that the wisdom writers wrote is praiseworthy, let alone applicable to our era. Moreover, there have been some monstrous things done in the name of God, religion, and spirituality. The bombing of the World Trade Center and the suicide bombings of the Islamic extremists in Israel, both of which involved the intentional murder of innocent men, women, and children, are perhaps the most recent dramatic examples of the perversion of the wisdom and beauty of a great world religion, Islam.

In his bold book *Psychoanalysis and Religion*, Erich Fromm perhaps best captured the underlying attitude common to the wisdom of the founders of all the great religions, East and West. Such a common attitude "is one in which the supreme aim of living is a concern with man's soul and the unfolding of his powers of love and reason."[4] Fromm believed, as do I, that this notion is entirely in sync with the spirit of psychoanalysis.

Extrapolating from Fromm's succinct, highly perceptive statement, there are a few pertinent general comments that can be made about how the wisdom traditions as a whole tend to conceptualize the ideal way of living one's life and construing reality. These ideas have some bearing on psychoanalysis, as I will suggest later.[5]

First, there are certain questions about what it means to be human and how to live one's life, that all the wisdom traditions, as well as psychoanalysis, grapple with. However, the wisdom traditions tend to be more direct in raising and answering these questions than psychoanalysis typically is, though as I have pointed out elsewhere, psychoanalysis has its own angle of vision on the world and philosophy of life.[6] Such questions are existential in nature in that they tend to deal with the ultimate problems of being human; in fact, they are questions that all of us face in our lives, one time or another, consciously or unconsciously: (1) What is the meaning and purpose of my life now, and as I go through the life cycle? (2) How should I relate and respond to others? (3) How should I come to terms with the fact that I am going to die? (4) How can I overcome my personal limitations and inadequacies?[7] And finally, (5) How can I endure, if not transcend the pain and suffering of life without giving into despair or falling apart?

In the areas of ethics, that is, how should I ideally relate to others, the wisdom traditions across the world believe, at least in terms of minimal standards, in the Decalogue (though all religions have a different name for the Decalogue and somewhat different emphases). For example, we should not murder, steal, lie, commit adultery, covet our neighbor, or disrespect our parents and elders. All religions consider these and other basic ethical precepts to be a prerequisite for any authentic, transcendent spiritual or religious life. Psychoanalysis, in general, considers these ethical precepts which have been thoroughly integrated into Western and to some extent Eastern ethical and psychological discourse, as reflecting healthy superego development and object relationships.

From this basic ethical framework, the question that next emerges is, what kind of people should we struggle to become? According to Smith, the ideal form of life-conduction emanating from the wisdom traditions is one that is based on three key virtues: humility, charity and truthfulness. Briefly, humility is the ability to view oneself in the presence of others as one, but not more than one. Charity is to regard one's neighbor as also one, as fully one as oneself. Truthfulness not only means telling the truth, it also involves a high degree of impartiality and objectivity, that is, the ability to view things exactly as they are, to live according to the Reality Principle as analysts might say. Most religions, perhaps especially the Asian ones, stress the difficulties that must be mastered in order to appropriate these virtues into one's life and worldview. The Buddha, for example, called these impediments to acquiring the three virtues the "three poisons," that is, greed, hatred, and delusion. To the extent these poisons are mastered, transformed, if not eliminated, selflessness (humility), compassion (charity), and seeing things in their "Suchness" (truthfulness) replaces them.[8]

Conclusion: Toward a Spiritually Animated Psychoanalysis

According to the wisdom traditions, how does the ideal person view reality, that is how does he conceptualize the ultimate nature of things? First, says Smith, the wisdom traditions begin by declaring that if we could see the full picture, if we had a glimpse of eternity as it were, we would conclude that the world is more integrated and harmonious than we usually assume. In other words, we have only a limited angle of vision on life and what we see and take to be reality is greatly colored by our wishfulness and by our own self-interest. Thus, the world frequently looks more chaotic, fragmented, out of control and downright cruel than it may actually be, at least from the long-range perspective of the wisdom tradition. From the human perspective the wisdom traditions represent the human wish to imagine the whole pattern of the universe, the grand design as the religious conceive it, which gives meaning to the specific parts that make up one's individual experience and world of meaning. To the extent that we are able to apprehend the beauty and harmony of the design, we are then able to give meaning to the parts that we perceive and experience, including the difficult times. This apprehension of the whole, and how the parts relate to the whole, fosters the feeling of "at-one-ment," of the interconnectedness and interrelatedness of all beings and things, and thus greater peace of mind, a goal of all the wisdom traditions and for that matter, psychoanalysis.

The second assertion of the wisdom traditions as it pertains to construing reality is suggested by the first. If the world is animated by a hard to apprehend grand design, it is not only more integrated and harmonious than it appears to be, but it is also better than it appears to be. In other words, the world is a better place than we can normally perceive from our limited perspective. The Tao, Brahman, nirvana, God, and Allah all insinuate a perfect realm or being. This leads the wisdom traditions to generate an ontological enthusiasm that is hardly found elsewhere. This enthusiasm is expressed, for example, in how the human self is conceived, in the way that the world's unity suggests that selves are lodged in and belong to the world; its worth implies that selves share in the world's exalted stature. The Hindu notion of the atman and the Buddha nature are good examples.

Finally, following the wisdom traditions' insights into the unity and integration of things and the tremendous intrinsic worth of things, that is, things are better than they seem, comes the claim that the world is also more mysterious than it seems. That is, says Smith, "we are born in mystery, we live in mystery and we die in mystery."[9] A mystery, in the sense of the wisdom traditions, means that the human mind cannot fathom an answer to the mystery no matter how much knowledge we have. The more we understand the more we realize how little we understand about the world and being.

From these three claims—that the world and things are more unified and integrated than they appear to be, better than we can discern, and more mysterious than we can comprehend—comes a new insight. That is, when we build on these three claims, the basis for ethical behavior and their conception of human virtues, one begins to imagine that the wisdom traditions are on to a wiser way of living life and construing reality. That is, says Smith, at the heart of the religious mode of being is a specific kind of joy and enthusiasm for life, the prospect of a happy ending that unfolds from seemingly necessary painful beginnings, the promise of difficulties faced and overcome. When this joy arrives we are not sure whether our happiness is the rarest or the commonest thing on earth, for in all earthly things we find joy, give it, and receive it, but cannot usually sustain our happiness. When these intimations are ours, it appears that it is normal to be so happy, but in hindsight we wonder how such happiness could have been ours. As Smith points out, the human opportunity, the ancient religions tell us, is to change our flashes of insight and happiness into abiding, bright light, that is, to a life, a self-world relation characterized by integrity, wisdom and transcendence.

In closing this section, it is worth noting that a comparative study of the major world religions showed a remarkable agreement on many of the main aspects that constitute the nature of reality and the ideal life. In a sense, one wonders why there is so little cooperation among religions when they have so much in common. For example, Heiler's study of seven of the world's major religions concludes that they all believe that the ultimate reality is love, compassion and mercy; the most effective modality for humans to merge with, mirror or imitate the divine requires sacrifice, discipline, and prayer; that as a spiritual aspirant seeks God or the divine this must also include helping their neighbors and community's well-being, even looking after the welfare of their enemies; and finally, while religious experience is forever diverse and multiform, the royal road to God is love. However, all of the major religions believe that ultimately, we humans lack the capability to fully grasp let alone understand the infinitude and transcendence of God, though at times we can sense His infinite nearness and immanence.[10]

SOME ELEMENTS OF A SPIRITUALLY ANIMATED PSYCHOANALYSIS

As I suggested in the Introduction to this book, in general, psychoanalysis has been more focused on the psychological in religion, such as the psychodynamic and developmental basis for religious experience, and the meaning of religious behavior, and much less on what ways religion, conceived in part, as one of the great narratives on subjectivity, can enhance psychoanalysis. For example, in general, psychoanalysis has either ignored or downplayed the religious answers to some of the important existential questions that are embedded in the psychoanalytic encounter, such as the nature of the human condition, human suffering and coming to terms with man's rather harsh destiny, as Ecclesiastes has made so poignantly clear.

In a certain sense this is surprising in that, as psychoanalyst Joel Kovel has noted, "the essential spiritual space of psychoanalytic work cannot be displaced."[11] Put somewhat differently, psychoanalysis is one of the great Western spiritual exercises, a Western form of meditation that awakens individuals to ask themselves some key existential questions such as why they often generate their own psychic pain and suffering. At the same time, it suggests a way out of the suffering, towards autonomy, compassion, a sense of interdependence and to some extent, a radically different way of being in the world, one that moves toward ultimate inner freedom and self-transcendence. However, as I have argued throughout this book, what is needed is a further elaboration of how psychoanalysis can possibly integrate into its theory and practice some of the often overlooked and underemphasized spiritual and religious insights and practices, that are rooted in the ancient religious wisdom traditions. While this subject is worth a book in itself, in this conclusion I simply want to insinuate some of the points of entry into this exciting and potentially important addition to psychoanalysis, one that I hope can complement, not replace, traditional psychoanalytic wisdom.

PSYCHOANALYSTS AS VALUES AGENTS

Psychoanalysis is not a unified theory; there are many versions of psychoanalysis, each with its own spin on how it conceptualizes the human condition, psychopathology and treatment.[12] Given the function of this conclusion, I will mainly be referring to Freudian psychoanalysis as my focus though I will mention other forms of psychoanalysis as well. Nevertheless, what all of these versions of psychoanalysis have at least in common is that they, like all forms of psychotherapy, have a value-informed perspective. That is, while psychoanalysis is regarded as a secular and moral encounter, it has an implicit worldview and value assumptions, which are unfortunately often obfuscated by the use of highly technical and theoretical jargon.[13]

Psychoanalysts, in my view, would be enhanced by wholeheartedly embracing the idea that they are value agents, that they consciously or unconsciously sanction certain values and lifestyles that they prefer and believe will strengthen psychological health and well-being. For example, psychoanalysis has its implied views about what constitutes the ideal human life, which includes, for instance, being healthy, integrated and whole, autonomous, capable of so-called mature love and work, and being realistic and rational. It also has a perspective on what works against creating an ideal human life, namely, to be pathological, infantile, emotionally blunted, closed-off, aggressive to oneself and others, and living a life that is based on lies and self-deception. Psychoanalysis is also wedded to a scientific worldview as Freud described it, and it tends to draw its analysts and analysands, and other adherents, from the middle and upper classes of society, suggesting that these groups find something in psychoanalysis that is in sync with their general sociointellectual outlook. All of this is rather important in light of the finding that assisting patients to delineate and make clear their own values may be the most crucial element of successful psychotherapy.[14] That is, as Bergin notes, in order to empathically understand patients' mode of being, their world of meaning, it is necessary to comprehend their values, beliefs, their moral outlook, and their core assumptions about life and the world.[15] This of course means that an analyst must be informed, knowledgeable and culturally sensitive to the conscious and unconscious spiritual and religious values and strivings of our patients, who come from a wide variety of religious cultures, just as we strive to be culturally sensitive to race, gender, ethnicity, and other kinds of differences among our diversified caseload, one that reflects our pluralistic society.

The issue of values and psychoanalysis has been kicking around the discipline since it inception, and I have no intention in this conclusion given the scope and complexity of the subject, to enter the debate in any depth or detail. Rather, my point is a simple one, at least at first glance. There are certain key values that are embedded in every ancient religious or spiritual wisdom tradition discussed in this book, and their modern counterparts. Psychoanalysis would benefit from creatively integrating these values, at least to some extent, into its theory and practice, for they personify what, in my view, is most noble in the human enterprise, and most likely to bring about individual and communal survival and well-being, at least as conceived by every major religious culture for thousands of years. These values also seem to point toward what constitutes the royal road to peace of mind or at least, more than a modicum of happiness, which seems to be about the best that most thoughtful people, religious or otherwise, say they can hope for in our troubling world and distress-filled existence. Such an addition to the psychoanalytic outlook would tend to reorient psychoanalysis somewhat, at least when psychoanalysis is conceived as a secular moral encounter. In other words, a psychoanalysis that is to some extent spiritually animated would involve embracing some different notions and attitudes on the part of the psychoanalyst that may at first glance seem far-fetched or "unpsychoanalytic." However, psychoanalysis should always try and think and imagine beyond itself. Thus, these notions and attitudes are aimed less at fundamentally changing psychoanalytic theory and practice and more about augmenting psychoanalysis so that it can better engage the analysand's world of the spirit while at the same time the analyst and psychoanalysis are more in sync with the American spiritual zeitgeist. That is, as I have said, my aim is to help psychoanalysts begin to cultivate a new sensibility, one that is open to transcendence. Space limitations allows me to only outline some of the important themes that in part constitute this new sensibility, themes that require additional study and elaboration.

THE ARTS OF SERVICE

As I have emphasized throughout this book, every religious tradition encourages its adherents to engage in service towards others, especially selfless service within one's own community, to members of other communities and the wider world.[16] Given the fact that the wisdom traditions regard selfishness, excessive self-interest, ego consciousness, and inordinate narcissism as the fundamental human problematic that needs to be mastered, if not overcome, it is not surprising that the wisdom traditions regard altruism and selfless service to others as a potent antidote. For such behavior is an essential humanizing activity, one that is rooted in a life-long engagement with a transcendent source that is both personal and intimate and yet entirely Other. While there are of course different emphases and requirements within and between each religious tradition, the notion that one becomes more humane, more compassionate, more spiritually developed, and therefore closer to God (or a Higher Power, Realm, etc.) when one acts altruistically and selflessly, is axiomatic. For example, every religious tradition emphasizes charity and acts of loving-kindness as in part what constitutes living a genuine life of the spirit, an authentically religious life devoted to God. This view is probably based in part on the assumption that there seems to be a universal human need for companionship and friendship, mutual social support, and solidarity, and service to others. To the spiritual aspirant, companionship, social support, and service toward others have an obvious benefit in terms of, for example, reinforcing one's spirituality when one's faith is assaulted and strengthening one's determination against selfishness and other evil influences in one's heart and in the external world, as the spiritual aspirant conceives it.

What this means for psychoanalysis is that while humanity, at least according to Freud, is basically driven by pressing selfish desires and other infantile and narcissistic needs and wishes, as well as a basic wish to destroy (in reality and/or in fantasy) that which stands in the way of these gratifications, we also have the need and desire to enhance others and not only ourselves, that is, to make the world a better and more beautiful place in part through serving and supporting others without expecting or demanding reciprocity. I will not reiterate in detail the empirical findings on this point. I will only remind the reader that there is quite a bit of hard evidence that altruistic service and acts of loving-kindness, especially when rooted in a wider religious belief system and like-minded spiritual community, have beneficial psychological and physical effects including decreased mortality rates.[17]

While the typical analyst is not likely to recommend that patients volunteer to work in a soup kitchen or with severely handicapped children as part of their analysis (though I wonder if that wouldn't be a good idea), it is, I think, important for analysts to somehow incorporate into analysis the notion that serving others, sacrificing for others and giving to others, and not just to one's immediate family and close friends, and without mainly instrumental motives such as a return from one's wife, husband, or friend, is, in and of itself, therapeutic. That is, the arts of selfless service is one of the best counterpoints to our culture of narcissism, and the narcissistic pathology that characterizes the garden-variety analysand these days. Analysts would be wise to acknowledge the healing power of altruism and introduce this notion in creative and subtle ways to those analysands who are responsive to such a service value. I believe analysands would be receptive to such a service value when they grasped and internalized the notion that probably the main dynamic root of their human suffering (and evil, for that matter) is inordinate human narcissism in one form or another.

Moreover, empirical studies have suggested that altruistic activity may give one a strong sense of transcendence. For example, in a survey of thousands of volunteers throughout the United States, Luks reported that the greater majority of respondents indicated that helping others gave them an enhancement of consciousness, a rush, including a physical sensation of sudden warmth, greater energy, a feeling of euphoria, and increased calmness.[18] In other words, altruistic behavior in part, helps to undo the "eclipse of the transcendent soul by the ego," or to put it in less religious terms, it transforms ego-consciousness into a more for-the-Other mode of being that one experiences as mind and soul enhancing.[19]

What I am thus suggesting is that psychoanalysis help analysands develop a more open, inclusive, interdependent non-self-centered subjectivity, in which the reasonable needs and desires of others, including

Conclusion: Toward a Spiritually Animated Psychoanalysis 187

one's fellow citizens and the wider community, become central organizing notions for living one's life at a higher level of psychological, moral and spiritual development. According to the assumptions of this book, that is, from the point of view of ancient religious wisdom, this requires developing the capacity to imagine a moral order beyond oneself, one that is rooted in a transcendent reality that is experienced as ultra real, ultra intense and ultra personal and perhaps most important, brings one closer towards God's infinite reality. Such a transcendent moral order creates the psychological, moral and social context for putting responsibility for the Other above one's narcissistic needs and wishes and self-interest. This is no easy personal achievement, for it requires the transformation of one's self-world relation from a primarily for-oneself existential orientation, as Emmanuel Levinas describes it, to a for-the-Other stance in which "responsibility for the other" is taken to be "incumbent on me exclusively, and what humanly, I cannot refuse."[20] This Levinasian view, which is in part rooted in his Hebraic outlook (he was a practicing Orthodox Jew), is not merely some abstract theoretical notion with no relevance for one's actual life; in fact it can determine the difference between remaining or not remaining human, and between living and dying. As I have noted earlier in one or two chapters and shown in other publications, in the Nazi concentration camps the most effective way of staying relatively psychologically intact (e.g., autonomous and integrated) and remaining human, was to embrace a for-the-Other orientation.[21] As Auschwitz survivor Hermann Langbein noted, "the struggle for the life of one's fellow prisoners had to be kept alive, because otherwise the strength to resist would atrophy and disappear completely." Another camp inmate said, "In order to hang on, each one of us has got to get out of himself, he's got to feel responsible for everybody."[22] Many other quotes could be cited from the survivor literature that indicate that caring for others (a form of responsibility), especially selflessly, was the best way to retain one's humanity, autonomy and integration in the camps as much as it was possible in such a horrid, terrifying and dehumanizing world. In other words, an ontological conviction that emphasizes responsibility to the Other, altruism, selfless service, especially when rooted in the strong belief in the presence of a reality of the Godly or divine at the center of the human condition and experience, can bring about perhaps the main goal of psychoanalysis: the creative transformation of the individual's existential reality. This includes developing those humane and morally praiseworthy qualities to their highest potential possible, as stressed in every major religious/spiritual wisdom tradition.

Thus, the major paradigms in psychoanalysis could benefit from including a radically different version of human being and human striving into its understanding: Freud's "guilty man," who continuously struggles towards fulfillment of his drives; Kohut's "tragic man," who struggles to fulfill the aims of his nuclear self; and the Object Relational emphasis, such as W. R. D. Fairbairn's conviction that "mature dependence"—the individual's ability to sustain intimate, mutual connections to other people—is the ideal state of emotional health, all certainly describe important parts of the human condition and human striving.[23]

However, following most of the ancient religious/spiritual wisdom traditions, what needs to complement these above mentioned psychoanalytic paradigms, is an image of man that lives by a very different existential orientation. Perhaps, this new mode of being was best conveyed by Elie Wiesel, who said somewhere in another context (I am paraphrasing from memory), that after the Holocaust man's existential orientation and fundamental commitment in life should be replaced by a much less narcissistic and self-referential fundamental principle than, say, Descartes' monumentally influential "cogito, ergo sum" ("I think, therefore I am").[24] As is well known, this statement was Descartes' attempt to prove the existence of the self in any act of thinking or doubting as the only "certainty," a pathbreaking view that, in part, made Descartes the founder of modern philosophy. Rather, after Auschwitz, suggests Wiesel, "I think, therefore I am," and I would add, Freud's guilty man, Kohut's tragic man, Fairbairn's emphasis on "mature dependence," and other such egoistic psychoanalytic versions of the human condition, should be augmented beyond the quest for certainty and self-centric satisfaction to include the quest for wisdom. In this context, wisdom means an existential affirmation that implies a radically new self-world relation, one that can be aptly suggested in one sentence: "I suffer, therefore you are." That is, the development of a subjectivity that is characterized by responsibility to the Other, especially the willingness to suffer for the other, altruism and loving-kindness as its foundational principle of living.

TO BE OR NOT TO BE IN CONTROL OF OUR LIVES

As I have indicated in previous chapters, the issue of control is one of the most common ones in psychoanalytic treatment. Analysands and psychotherapy patients are frequently complaining about feeling out of control, of being controlled by others, or wanting to control others. This is especially the case in contexts that are stressful, painful and require endurance such as coping with extended suffering.

Psychoanalysis, like most Western forms of secular psychotherapy, has embraced a certain overarching attitude to the problem of control, one that I feel animates the way this issue is dealt with in treatment, especially as it relates to coping with life's hardships and troubles. As Pargament has pointed out, much of one's everyday life is concerned with efforts to master big problems and small worries and troubles.[25] Agency, control and efficacy, Pargament suggests, are guiding notions in coping with stress, particularly in Western culture where individual effort and accomplishment are highly valued. As most people intellectually realize, though many do not fully internalize, the fact is that some, perhaps many problems are not controllable, let alone correctable. Psychoanalysis, like other forms of Western psychotherapy, have little to say about this, except to state the obvious. As my analyst must have told me hundreds of times over my ten-year analysis (and I have told my analysands!) "you must learn to accept reality whether you like it or not." Of course, I basically agree with this notion. However, what a religious/spiritual sensibility and intervention have to offer, adds, I think, something possibly more helpful, at least in certain contexts and with certain types of patients.

The mechanisms of religion, unlike a purely Western secular psychoanalysis, provide the suffering analysand with a potentially helpful "language of the sacred," as Pargament calls it. For example, notions of mystery, forbearance, suffering, finitude, surrender, hope, divine meaning, and redemption,[26] when creatively, gently and judiciously introduced into the analytic situation, have a power to them that "accepting reality whether you like it or not," as my analyst suggested to me, lacks with certain patients. What religious wisdom has to offer the suffering analysand is a different language, the symbolic resources that helps make difficult and painful situations "interpretable" (understandable, intelligible) and "sufferable" (i.e., endurable) as Geertz points out.[27] That is, where a secularist might feel utterly overwhelmed by a terrible situation, like the random murder of a child, a situation that for most people is "at the limits of their analytic capacities, at the limits of their powers of endurance, and at the limits of their moral insight,"[28] the religious/spiritual angle of vision on such matters, its sacred language and its protective, overarching "sacred canopy,"[29] helps give the suffering analysand the symbolic resources to better "manage" their psychic pain. As Geertz further suggests, as well as according to most of the religious traditions discussed in this book, intense, relentless brute pain can be sustained in part, by giving a precision and definition to a person's strong and complex feelings. That is, a religious/spiritual angle of vision gives the suffering analysand the possibility of situating his pain into a meaningful and purposeful context, it provides a mode of action and behavior through which the pain can be expressed, by being expressed comprehended, and by being comprehended endured.[30]

My point, following Pargament, is simply that while a Western-based psychoanalysis aims to assist people to gain control of their lives, or at least give them the illusion that they are in control, a religious/spiritual approach assists people to come to terms with the limits of their control. That is, when it comes to nearly every major aspect of living, birth, who your parents are, and as Freud noted, who you fall in love with and the kind of work you choose (advised Freud, weigh the options, but ultimately, let your unconscious decide), how your children fare in the world, illness, and death to name a few examples, by and large, especially as one gets older and more reflective about life, one realizes that the deeper and more decisive issue than trying to control one's life and world (though that is important, too), is learning to come to terms with the fact of how little control we actually have regarding things that really matter. A religious/spiritual sensibility on the part of the analyst helps the analysand internalize this rather harsh truth about reality while at the same time offers him some hope through a sacred language, especially when embedded in a sacred canopy. For example, by living in the present, moment by moment, even amid intense pain as the Buddha taught, as opposed to getting stuck in the past and dwelling on the future as is so common with secular analysands and others, the analysand can better endure his suffering. Suffering, says the Buddha, like all emotional experiences follows the same pattern, one that requires patience and a transcendent perspective. Suffering arises, dwells, changes and ultimately fades away.

Briefly, for example, as Pargament notes, there are a number of studies that indicate that religious forms of coping with bad things that happen in one's life are particularly helpful to people who feel these situations are unmanageable, uncontrollable and difficult to cope with (which is just about everyone).[31] In a two-year longitudinal study of a community sample, it was found that attendance at religious services protected the sample against the negative impact of increased numbers of undesirable life events on later psychological discomfort. Another study showed that spiritual support was connected to less depression and increased self-esteem among those who had to bear the death of a child in the past two years. Similar correlations were not found for those whose child had died more than two years before the study was commenced. Says Pargament, these and many other studies suggest that the language, outlook and traditions of the sacred can be quite helpful in very bad situations. "Vested with unlimited strength and compassion, the sacred offers a source of solace, hope, and power" when other resources, particularly when secular resources have been depleted and people must look beyond themselves, to a transcendent source for assistance. That is, the strength of religion/spirituality is the amalgamation of the sacred with the human in search for ultimate meaning, purpose and significance, that is, the use of ultimate resources to potentiate, support and satisfy infinite longings of the finite spirit.[32]

TO ERR IS HUMAN, TO FORGIVE, DIVINE

To the secularist, the word forgiveness is saturated with religious connotations and meaning and therefore is generally not a crucial part of the dialogue between the typical secular analyst and analysand, nor in general, is it usually part of scholarly psychoanalytic discourse.[33] However, ancient religious/spiritual wisdom and its modern counterparts, especially theistic-based religions, emphasize the importance and benefits of forgiving those who have harmed you as well as to seek forgiveness for hurtful actions that one has intentionally or unintentionally perpetrated against others. There are, as one would imagine, differences in emphasis on how each religion conceptualizes the dynamics of forgiveness, that is, differences on how forgiveness should be implemented in real life, such as under what circumstances, to whom and when forgiveness should be expressed and received. Within the religious context, in Christianity for example, forgiveness is conceived as an important part of one's spiritual evolution with important spiritual ramifications such as repairing one's relationship with God, showing one's faith and loyalty to God, and increasing one's chances of being saved. In Judaism, obtaining forgiveness usually requires that the offender fully admit his hurtful act, repent for his wrongdoing, and make efforts to repair the damage done before forgiveness can be granted.

Forgiveness has not been adequately studied in the empirical psychological, psychoanalytic or general psychological literature. However, from a psychological, nonreligious viewpoint, authors have suggested that forgiveness has major psychological benefits. As Richards and Bergin note, forgiveness can foster positive changes in one's emotional life such as reducing one's anger, resentment and retaliatory wishes; it can improve one's mental and physical health such as changing one's Type A coronary-prone behavior pattern and heart disease[34]; it can renew a person's sense of efficacy, control, and power in that one is taking a more active and compassionate role in changing how one views one's sense of being mistreated or having done the mistreatment; and of course, forgiveness can possibly lead to the reconciliation between the perpetrator and the offended. In addition, by forgiving, individual's enlarge their options, autonomy and freedom to grow, develop and flourish. Forgiveness also encourages people to take responsibility for their wrongdoing, which makes it somewhat easier for the offended to reduce his hurt and perhaps begin the healing process. Richards and Bergin further note that fostering forgiveness, for example, of one's abusive or neglectful parents or others who have mistreated them, for ones own personal shortcomings and mistakes, and forgiving God for what may appear to be His injustice, is one of the most often used spiritual techniques by psychotherapists of all persuasions.[35]

As is well known to experienced analysts, a rush toward forgiveness can be viewed as the analysand's attempt to prematurely protect him- or herself from the narcissistic hurt and injury of having been mistreated. However, forgiveness is a much more complex psychological experience. Forgiveness also includes rage, resentment and animosity, what seem to be typical reactions when one feels grossly mistreated or victimized. Moreover, by forgiving someone who has mistreated you, you in effect, give up the right to hit back at the offender, this being one of the main reasons it is so hard to forgive. That is, it requires giving up the thoroughly gratifying rage, resentment and animosity, as counter-intuitive as that may sound, as well as the shame that is often associated with being offended. The negative impact of this rage, resentment, animosity and shame on one's psyche and life is well documented and need not be detailed. To forgive therefore demands a radical transformation of one's mode of being, of who one is emotionally, cognitively, interpersonally, and spiritually. In other words, forgiveness moves one out of the web of pain, outrage and felt injustice towards a future of more satisfying relationships and greater inner peace, though as I have said, to forgive is no easy psychic accomplishment.

While I am tempted to discuss forgiveness as a general psychological concept in much more detail, our focus is on whether the ancient religious/spiritual wisdom traditions discussed in this book can offer anything in addition to what we know about forgiveness from a secular point of view, one that can be useful in the psychoanalytic encounter. According to Pargament, religion can add to forgiveness in at least two ways. It can add meaning and significance to the act of forgiving and it can provide a set of models and techniques to foster forgiveness.[36]

Nearly all religious/wisdom traditions discussed in this book assume that human relationships are meant to be opportunities to help perfect one's relational capacities in order ultimately to actualize the ideal relationship, namely, between man and God (or the divine, Higher Power, Force, Realm, etc.). From this spiritual point of view, the rupture in a relationship with a person has a cosmic meaning in that it is also a rupture in one's relationship with God or the transcendent Other, however defined. Therefore, forgiveness in the spiritual context offers the opportunity to achieve greater "at-one-ment" within oneself, with the other person one is in conflict with, and with God.

To the spiritual aspirant, the meaning of developing the capacity to forgive is that the individual can get his own forgiveness from God, as many scriptural sources from the world religions demonstrate. In other words, if you forgive others who have offended you, God will forgive you for your own similar offenses. In addition, by being forgiving an individual has the chance to live a spiritual/religious life that is guided by empathy and compassion for others' shortcomings and flaws. Finally, forgiving allows the individual to possibly find greater intimacy with others, greater spiritual fellowship within one's community and elsewhere, and greater closeness with God.

It should be mentioned that in psychoanalysis the notion of forgiveness in order to achieve greater "at-one-ment" and to improve human relationships can be seen in the concept that the harshness with which one views others reflects the harshness which analysands turn on themselves, including their actions, thoughts and wishes. The technique of helping analysands diminish the severity of the superego toward themselves is considered the means by which the analysands will improve their connection to the other. In other words, the psychoanalytical view, dynamically speaking, views forgiveness from a different standpoint compared to the religious devotee, though they both seek the same goal of fostering forgiveness.

The ancient religious/spiritual wisdom literature contain many narratives of remarkable people who had the capacity to transcend their own suffering and reach out to others in an empathic and compassionate manner. For example, as Pargament further points out, the conflicted and dysfunctional family can model the example of Joseph, who was able to forgive his brothers even though they were jealous of him, hated him, nearly killed him and sold him into slavery. The wife whose husband has been unfaithful and disloyal can look to the story of Hosea to reduce her sense of outrage and betrayal. The victim of a brutal assault can look to Jesus Christ, who forgave his tormentors while being slowly and painfully murdered on the cross. "Father, forgive them; for they know not what they do" (Luke 23:34).

In other words, a religious/spiritual angle of vision and techniques can help analysands to forgive others and themselves more easily. Religion can help analysands articulate their pain, hurt and anger to the offender. Whether one "turns the other cheek" as in Christianity or passionately argues with God as Job did about the injustice of how he was being treated by God, such models encourage analysands to express their emotions associated with being victimized. A religious/spiritual outlook can also help a person make the decision to forgive, such as when one takes the gamble to forgive the offender, conceptualized by Pargament as a kind of "leap of faith." While a leap of faith implies no guarantee of success, the act of forgiveness is situated in a spiritual context of faith and trust in what is conceived as ultimately an ethically caring universe, hope, and good intentions. Religion can also foster a degree of empathy, compassion and humanization of the offender. There are of course many references that can be cited from sacred literatures that support such a view, though this aspect of forgiveness is a extremely difficult psychic achievement.[37]

What I am getting at is that psychoanalysis could benefit from including into its understanding of forgiveness the religious/spiritual insight that the process of forgiveness, whether as the offended or the offender, can be enhanced by embracing the notion that we all have done wrong and require forgiveness, and we all need to be forgiving of others, ourselves and if it applies to the analysand, forgiving to God. Such a sensibility can be very helpful as the analysand works through the anger, rage, hurt, bitterness, grief, and shame often associated with being offended and the haunting guilt, need for punishment and sometimes masochistic position often associated with having been the unforgiven and unpunished offender (sometimes this is also true of the offended). Of course, forgiveness as an intervention must only take place at the right time, when the analysand is ready to make such an emotional, cognitive, behavioral, and spiritual shift in outlook. Premature forgiveness blocks the analysand's ability to work through the painful emotions that need to be worked through and this ultimately obstructs the healing process. As I tell my analysands, following the insights of the religious/spiritual wisdom literature, one of the keys to learning to live with having been mistreated by someone or God, that is, after working through all of their painful emotions, is to sublimate their hurt and anger into something more healthy, life affirming, and hopeful. This mainly involves as insinuated by the wisdom writers, developing the self-transcendent capacity to forgive, but never to forget. As the Baal Shem Tov said, forgetfulness leads to exile but memory is the secret of redemption.

THE QUEST FOR TRANSCENDENCE

One of the key points that I have been stressing throughout this book has been the importance of adding a spiritual dimension to the psychoanalytic understanding of the human condition and clinical practice. As I have tried to show, such an addition would be a most useful complement to the discipline and would be another resource from which analysts can help their analysands, including those with and without serious, conscious spiritual or religious convictions. Psychologically speaking, the spiritual dimension includes many elements, for example, the striving for integration, wholeness and balance, generating a creative life that is saturated with meaning and significance, a capacity for unity, integration and sense of interdependence in one's self-world relationship, especially as it relates to the many relationships, responsibilities and commitments throughout one's life.[38]

Most important, the spiritual dimension seems to be rooted in man's need to create an overarching framework of ultimate meaning, significance and purpose, that is, a symbolic world, one that gives one the sense of transcendence. As Fowler has pointed out, humanity has "evolved with prepotentiated capacities that underlie the structuring activities of faith and that equip people for their ontological callings to relatedness and partnership with God."[39] According to Smith, writing in another context, what this means for psychoanalysis is that the discipline needs to progress beyond the current materialistic, relativistic and scientistic understanding of existence and acknowledge, and be continually mindful of, the fact that consciousness, not matter, is the ultimate basis of the universe.[40] Put somewhat differently, it seems as if psychoanalysis has replaced the transcendent with the ego and self, such that in a certain sense humans have become god-like (I discuss this point in the Islam chapter). To the spiritually attuned analysand, not only is the sacred regarded as a reality, that is, the religious search for the transcendent is not illusory, nor is spirituality a manifestation of more basic infantile psychological motives and desires as analysts tend to think, but rather, the sacred must also come before the profane as the life-guiding force in one's life.[41] Such a view no doubt will trouble some secular psychoanalysts.

For psychoanalysis what this implies is that the discipline needs to develop a more sophisticated, nuanced and less reductionistic spiritual hermeneutics, one that acknowledges that the mind fundamentally has a spiritual cast. Moreover, the way to help the secular or religious spiritually questing analysand to accomplish the ultimate goal, namely self-transformation and transcendence, requires that the analyst decenter the ego and self, not gratify its desires and wishes. This view is highly emphasized in Buddhism and Hinduism but also all of the major religious traditions in one way or another. Freud, however, thought that whatever was "non-self" or "non-ego" was not an enhanced kind of consciousness reflecting a transcendent self, but rather a form of the spiritual, which he regarded as a avenue of flight from reality. This, of course, follows Freud's commitment to an ideology of egoistic individualism, which contributed to the despiritualization of contemporary culture. In addition, to help the analysand acquire a sense of self-transformation of his mode of being and transcendence means a reorganization, or at least augmentation, of the explicit and implicit values in every version of psychoanalysis not only toward using the secular and naturalistic notions in its theories, but also to a focus on the ontological, spiritual, and moral struggles that affect the existential reality and mental health of analysands. In other words, continues Shafranske, psychoanalysis, conceived in part as a moral enterprise that is saturated with values, can help fill the moral vacuum and spiritual malaise that is so common these days among analysands and others.[42]

It should also be emphasized that an analyst can only take an analysand, conceived in part as a spiritual aspirant, as far as the analyst him- or herself has spiritually progressed. This therefore requires that the analyst have an understanding of his or her own religiousness/spirituality and comfort level with it, a subject that is frequently not dealt with in much depth in one's psychoanalytic training or training analysis, from my experience and from what I have read. In other words, psychoanalytic treatment includes the conscious and unconscious spiritual and faith commitments, spirituality and conflicts of both the analysand and the analyst. It therefore is incumbent on the analyst to view the religious/spiritual dimension of the analysand as an important force to be reckoned with, and this requires the analyst to have an educated and respectful view of a wide range of religions and modes of religious/spiritual experience in both their conventional and unconventional forms. This is especially important as it relates to the overlap (which fosters greater peace of mind), or lack of overlap (which fosters greater conflict), between what one's beliefs, values, and faith commitments are compared to how one actually lives life. This, of course, does not preclude the analyst doing what he or she ordinarily does, namely, exploring the personal meaning of religion and spirituality, such as how God is represented on a psychodynamic level and developmentally, religious/spiritual conflicts, and transference/countertransference ramifications. I would suggest as others have, that part of an analyst's intake procedure, that is, history gathering, should include a religious/spiritual history as well as the usual personal history.

One other point which I think is very important to spiritually educated and attuned analysts (not necessarily formally religious) who treat secular analysands with no conscious religious/spiritual/ transcendent yearnings. I am referring to the fact that such analysands can be unconsciously religious/spiritual, though these spiritual yearnings may be symbolized and manifested under many disguised forms. That is, as Frankl has pointed out,[43] if you believe as Freud did that there was unconscious instinctuality, "proven" largely based on clinical data and cultural analysis, one can just as well assume that there is in the unconscious an unconscious spirituality, which has also been clinically and culturally "proven."[44] By spiritual Frankl means that which is uniquely a human phenomenon (compared to the subhuman characteristics that we have in common with other animals).[45] The essence of such unconscious spirituality, according to Frankl, goes further than his famous "bottom-line" human motivation and representative phenomenon of human reality, "man's search for meaning." It also includes

Conclusion: Toward a Spiritually Animated Psychoanalysis   197

"man's search for ultimate meaning." As Frankl points out, it was Albert Einstein who suggested that to be religious is to have discovered a satisfactory answer to the question, What is the meaning of life? If this statement seems true, which I think it does, though with qualifications, then religiously animated belief, faith and spirituality can be viewed as "trust in ultimate meaning."[46] This "Unconscious God" as Frankl calls it, suggests that there is a religious sense profoundly rooted in every man's unconscious depths. It is the analyst's job, in collaboration with the willing analysand, to access this repressed spirituality and make it conscious, and therefore a potentially positive resource for living one's life with greater spiritual vitality, moral and ethical development, responsibility to the Other, and self-transformation and transcendence. Psychoanalysis is well aware that the unconscious has powerful evil and devilish aspects to it, but what Frankl is suggesting, as am I, is that also within the unconscious there exists somewhere a "repressed angel."[47]

Finally, I believe that despite Freud's rhetoric of rejection regarding the realm of the Spirit as a living, compelling reality in people's lives, that is, his despiritualization of man and culture, I think Freud also insinuated in his writings an awareness, conscious or unconscious, that there was a sacred aspect to the work of the psychoanalyst. In fact, as Bettelheim has pointed out in *Freud and Man's Soul,* Freud described the psychoanalyst as a "secular minister of souls."[48] Moreover, as I have said, this sacred aspect of psychoanalysis is probably most representative in other quasi-religious features of psychoanalytic treatment. In particular, I am referring to the role of values, purpose and ultimate meaning in people's lives that help the analysand maintain his arduous and, at times, frustrating and seemingly hopeless personal struggle for self-transformation and transcendence. This includes making the necessary changes to achieve a higher degree of integration, autonomy, integrity, wisdom, transcendence and of course, peace of mind. Most important, perhaps, both the psychoanalytic encounter and spiritual quest require that the analysand and spiritual aspirant surrender, as Islam demands in another context, that is, to cultivate the "capacity to experience and yield to that mysterious occurrence called being."[49] As St. Augustine noted, such a surrender, which can lead to self-transformation and transcendence, can occur as an act of grace. That is, as all analysts probably have asked themselves at one time or another after conducting a successful analysis, "What exactly was the mechanism of change"? "What made this analysand decisively change the way he lived his life and develop a new mode of being in the world?"

As in my case, while most analysts have a notion about what was the mechanism of change in psychoanalysis that brought about a successful analysis, there is often a sense that there was an intangible, ineffable, almost "magical" aspect to the process. To answer the question of what was the mechanism of change more satisfactorily, perhaps analysts have to go beyond psychoanalytic interpretation and so-called scientific explanation. That is, to be open to the mystery of being, the mystery of human identity and the mystery of life itself. This includes developing the sensibility that religious and spiritual modes of knowing also provide authentic knowledge of reality, as the prominent psychoanalyst Hans Loewald noted.[50] It also means being open to the possibility that God, by whatsoever name, has graciously, lovingly, and mysteriously helped make the successful analysis a soul-saving reality for the analysand. To quote Loewald:

> As the unconscious becomes transformed into ego-freedom . . . the images and concepts of this relatedness {to the dynamic unconscious} also change into higher forms. The deepest inner knowledge of such relatedness is the experience of relation to a universal being. . . . The mature individual, being able to reach back into his deep origins and roots of being, finds in himself the oneness from where he stems, and understands this in his freedom as his bond of love with God.[51]

NOTES

1. Erik H. Erikson, *Dimensions of a New Identity: The Jefferson Lectures in the Humanities* (New York: Norton, 1974), p. 41.

2. Joel Kovel, "Beyond the Future of an Illusion: Further Reflections on Freud and Religion," *Psychoanalytic Review*, 77, no. 1 (Spring 1980): 85.

3. In recent years an increased sympathetic interest in spirituality and religion has developed within the psychoanalytic community, in keeping with the spiritual American zeitgeist, as well as for other reasons. There have been a number of conferences and lectures that have, in part, discussed these subjects. There have also been some good books published recently that attempt to deal with religion and psychoanalysis in a more mutually respectful manner. Some of these books do not explicitly or implicitly assume that, compared to religion, psychoanalysis is a superior mode of knowing and understanding. See, for example, Polly Young-Eisendrath and Melvin E. Miller, eds., *The Psychology of Mature Spirituality: Integrity, Wisdom and Transcendence* (New York: Routledge, 2000); Charles Spezzano and Gerald J. Gargiulo, eds., *Soul on the Couch: Spirituality, Religion and Morality in Contemporary Psychoanalysis* (Hillsdale, N.J.: The Analytic Press, 1997); Jeffrey Rubin, *Psychoanalysis and Buddhism* (New York: Plenum Press, 1996); Moshe H. Spero, *Religious Objects as Psychological Structures* (Chicago: University of Chicago Press, 1992); Mark Finn and John Gartner, eds., *Object Relations Theory and Religion: Clinical Applications*. (Westport, Conn.: Praeger, 1992); James W. Jones, *Contemporary Psychoanalysis and Religion: Transference and Transcendence* (New Haven: Yale University Press, 1991); J. H. Smith and S. A. Handleman, eds., *Psychoanalysis and Religion* (Baltimore: Johns Hopkins University Press, 1990); Julia Kristeva, *Tales of Love* (New York: Columbia University Press, 1987); W. W. Meissner, *Psychoanalysis of Religious Experience* (New Haven: Yale University Press, 1984); and A. M. Rizzuto, *The Birth of the Living God* (Chicago: University of Chicago Press, 1979).

4. Erich Fromm, *Psychoanalysis and Religion* (New York: Bantam Books, 1950), p. 96.

5. In this section I have drawn liberally from Huston Smith, *The World's Religions: Our Great Wisdom Traditions* (New York: Harper San Francisco, 1991), pp. 386–39.

6. Paul Marcus and Alan Rosenberg, eds., *Psychoanalytic Versions of the Human Condition: Philosophies of Life and Their Impact on Practice* (New York: New York University Press, 1998).

7. C. Daniel Batson and W. Larry Ventis, *The Religious Experience: A Social-Psychological Perspective* (New York: Oxford University Press, 1984), p. 8.

8. Smith, *The World's Religions*, p. 387.

9. Ibid., p. 389.

10. F. Heiler, "The History of Religions as a Preparation for the Cooperation of Religions," in M. Eliade and J. M. Itigawa, eds., *The History of Religions: Essays in Methodology* (Chicago: University of Chicago Press, 1959), pp. 132–160.

11. Kovel, "Beyond the Future of Illusion," p. 81.

12. Marcus and Rosenberg, *Psychoanalytic Versions of the Human Condition*.

13. Allen F. Bergin, I. Reed Payne, and P. Scott Richards, "Values in Psychotherapy," in *Religion and the Clinical Practice of Psychology*, ed. Edward P. Shafranske (Washington: American Psychological Organization, 1996), pp. 297–325.

14. H. Smiley, "Values and Empowerment," *Hakomi Forum*, 3, 1985, 10–13.

15. Bergin, Payne, and Richards, "Values in Psychotherapy," p. 301.

16. I am aware that, psychoanalytically speaking, even the most seemingly selfless act has a degree of narcissistic gratification. Mother Theresa, for example, did some remarkable selfless acts, yet one can argue that on some level, she got a certain amount of narcissistic gratification, such as from living in accordance with her religious values and beliefs. It is also interesting to note that in Jewish tradition, at least according to Maimonides, the second highest form of charity is to give anonymously to an anonymous person in need. (The highest form is to give a needy person a means of supporting himself, a job, so that he or she doesn't need charity.) This personifies the religious insight that narcissism and self-interest are the main adversaries of living the holy life.

17. Kenneth I. Pargament, *The Psychology of Religion and Coping: Theory, Research and Practice* (New York: Guilford Press, 1997), pp. 275–314.

18. A. Luks, *The Healing Power of Doing Good* (New York: Ballantine Books, 1993); cited in P. Scott Richards and Allen E. Bergin, *A Spiritual Strategy for Counseling and Psychotherapy* (Washington: American Psychological Association, 1997), p. 219.

19. Quoted in Richards and Bergin, *A Spiritual Strategy for Counseling and Psychotherapy*, p. 279.

20. Emmanuel Levinas, *Ethics and Infinity*, trans. Richard A. Cohen (Pittsburgh: Duquesne University Press, 1985), p. 101.

21. See, for example, Paul Marcus, *Autonomy in the Extreme Situation: Bruno Bettelheim, the Nazi Concentration Camps and the Mass Society* (Westport, Conn.: Praeger, 1999), pp. 175–184.

22. Falk Pingle, "The Destruction of Human Identity in Concentration Camps: The Contribution of the Social Sciences to an Analysis of Behavior under Extreme Conditions," *Holocaust and Genocide Studies* 6, no. 2 (1991): 178; Tzevetan Todorov, *Facing the Extreme: Moral Life in the Concentration Camps* (New York: Henry Holt and Company, 1996), p. 88.

23. Marcus and Rosenberg, *Psychoanalytic Versions of the Human Condition*, pp. 2–3, 163.

24. St. Augustine anticipated René Descarte's "cogito, ergo sum" in the *City of God*: "If I am deceived, then I exist," cited in W. L. Reese, *Dictionary of Philosophy and Religion* (Atlantic Highlands, N.J.: Humanities Press, 1980), p. 96.

25. Kenneth I. Pargament, "Religious Methods of Coping," in Shafranske, ed., *Religion and the Clinical Practice of Psychology*, pp. 232–233.

26. Ibid., p. 232.

27. Clifford Geertz, "Religion as a Cultural System," in his *The Interpretation of Cultures* (New York: Basic Books 1973), pp. 100, 105.

28. Ibid., p. 100.

29. Peter L. Berger, *The Sacred Canopy* (Garden City, N.Y.: Anchor Books, Doubleday, 1967).

30. Geertz, "Religion as a Cultural System," p. 105.

31. Pargament, "Religious Methods of Coping," p. 232.

32. Ibid., p. 233.

33. In this section I have drawn liberally from Richards and Bergin, *A Spiritual Strategy for Counseling and Psychotherapy*, pp. 211–214, and Pargament, *The Psychology of Religion and Coping*, pp. 260–269.

34. Dean Ornish, *Dr. Dean Ornish's Program for Reversing Heart Disease: The Only System Scientifically Proven to Reverse Heart Disease without Drugs or Surgery* (New York: Ballantine Books, 1990).

35. Richards and Bergin, *A Spiritual Strategy for Counseling and Psychotherapy*, p. 212.

36. Pargament, *The Psychology of Religion and Coping*, p. 264.

37. Ibid., pp. 265–266.

38. Seymour W. Applebaum, "The Rediscovery of Spirituality Through Psychotherapy," in *Psychotherapy of the Religious Patient*, ed. Moshe Halevi Spero (Springfield, Ill.: Charles C. Thomas, 1985), p. 152.

39. J. Fowler, "Pluralism and Oneness in Religious Experience: William James and Faith Development Theory," *Psychology of Religion Newsletter*, 19, 1994, 182–183.

40. Huston Smith, *Why Religion Matters: The Fate of the Human Spirit in an Age of Disbelief* (New York: Harper San Francisco, 2001), pp. 3, 255–271.

41. Pargament, *The Psychology of Religion and Coping*, p. 45.

42. Shafranske, Introduction, in Shafranske, ed., *Religion and the Clinical Practice of Psychology*, pp. 12, 5.

43. Viktor E. Frankl, *The Unconscious God* (New York: Simon and Schuster, 1975).

44. Ibid., p. 25.

45. Ibid., p. 23.

46. Ibid., p. 13.

47. Ibid., p. 59.

48. Bruno Betttelheim, *Freud and Man's Soul* (New York: Vintage Books, 1982), p. 35.

49. Roger Brooke, "Emissaries from the Underworld: Psychotherapy's Challenge to Christian Fundamentalism," in Young and Miller, *The Psychology of Mature Spirituality*, p. 156.

50. James W. Jones, "Hans Loewald: The Psychoanalyst as Mystic," *Psychoanalytic Review*, no. 88, 6, (December 2001): 805.

51. Ibid., pp. 807–808, quoting from Loewald's essay, "Psychoanalysis and Modern Views on Human Existence and Religious Experience," *Journal of Pastoral Care*, 7, 1953, 1–15.

Selected Bibliography

THE *BHAGAVAD GITA*

Easwaran, Eknath. *The Bhagavad Gita*. Tomales, Calif.: Nilgiri Press, 1985.
Miller, Barbara Stoller. *The Bhagavad Gita*. New York: Bantam Books, 1986.

BUDDHA

Molino, Anthony, ed. *The Couch and the Tree: Dialogues in Psychoanalysis and Buddhism*. New York: North Point Press, 1998.
Price, A. F., and Wong Mou-lam, trans. *The Diamond Sutra and The Sutra of Hui-Neng*. Boston: Shambhala, 1990.
Rubin, Jeffrey B. *Psychotherapy and Buddhism: Toward an Integration*. New York: Plenum Press, 1996.

THE ANALECTS

Tu Wei-ming. *Confucian Thought: Selfhood as Creative Transformation*. Albany: State University of New York Press, 1985.
Waley, Arthur, trans. *Confucianism: The Analects of Confucius*. New York: Quality Paperback Book Club, 1992.

THE *CHUANG TZU*

Mair, Victor H., ed. *Experimental Essays in Chuang Tzu*. Honolulu: University of Hawaii Press, 1983.

Watson, Burton. *The Complete Works of Chuang Tzu*. New York: Columbia University Press, 1968.

MARCUS AURELIUS'S *MEDITATIONS*

Aurelius, Marcus. *Meditations*. Translated by Maxwell Stanforth. Middlesex, U.K.: Penguin Books, 1964.

Hadot, Pierre. *The Inner Citadel: The Meditations of Marcus Aurelius*. Translated by Michael Chase. Cambridge, Mass.: Harvard University Press, 1998.

ECCLESIASTES

Gordis, Robert, trans. and commentator. *Koheleth—the Man and His World*. New York: Jewish Theological Seminary of America, 1951.

Perry, T. A. *Dialogues with Kohelet: The Book of Ecclesiastes*. University Park: The Pennsylvania State University Press, 1993.

SAINT AUGUSTINE'S *CONFESSIONS*

Augustine, Saint. *Confessions*. Translated by Henry Chadwick. Oxford: Oxford University Press, 1991.

Cary, Philip. *Augustine: Philosopher and Saint*. The Great Courses on Tape. Chantilly, Va.: Teaching Company, 1997.

THE KORAN

Dawood, N. J., trans. *The Koran*. London: Penguin Books, 1998.

Nasr, Seyyed Hossein, ed. *Islamic Spirituality: Foundations*. New York: Crossroad, 1997.

GENERAL READING

Finn, Mark, and John Gartner, eds. *Object Relations Theory and Religion: Clinical Applications*. Westport, Conn.: Praeger, 1992.

Jones, James W. *Contemporary Psychoanalysis and Religion: Transference and Transcendence*. New Haven, Conn.: Yale University Press, 1991.

Marcus, Paul. "The Religious Believer, the Psychoanalytic Intellectual, and the Challenge of Sustaining the Self in the Concentration Camps." *Journal for the Psychoanalysis of Culture and Society*, 3, no. 1 (Spring 1998): 61–75.

Meissner, W. W. *Psychoanalysis of Religious Experience*. New Haven, Conn.: Yale University Press, 1984.

Pargament, Kenneth I. *The Psychology of Religion and Coping: Theory, Research and Practice*. New York: Guilford Press, 1997.

Richards, P. Scott, and Allen E. Bergin. *A Spiritual Strategy for Counseling and Psychotherapy*. Washington: American Psychological Association, 1997.

Rizzuto, A. M. *The Birth of the Living God*. Chicago: University of Chicago Press, 1979.
Shafranske, Edward P., ed. *Religion and the Clinical Practice of Psychology*. Washington: American Psychological Association, 1996.
Sharma, Arvind, ed. *Our Religions*. New York: Harper San Francisco, 1993.
Smith, Huston. *The World Religions: Our Great Western Traditions*. New York: HarperCollins, 1991.
Spero, Moshe H. *Religious Objects as Psychological Structures*. Chicago: University of Chicago Press, 1992.
Spezzano, Charles, and Gerald J. Gargiulo, eds. *Soul on the Couch: Spirituality, Religion and Morality in Contemporary Psychoanalysis*. Hillsdale, N.J.: Analytic Press, 1997.
Young-Eisendrath, Polly, and Melvin E. Miller, eds. *The Psychology of Mature Spirituality: Integrity, Wisdom and Transcendence*. New York: Routledge, 2000.

Index

Adawiyah (Al-), Rabiah, 163–164
Adharma, Hinduism, 27
Adler, Alfred, 108
Adversity, Islam, 167
Aesthetics: Chuang Tzu, 90; Confucian philosophy, 65–66
Agency, definition of, 104
"Allegory on Old Age," 126–127
Ames, Roger T., 59
Analects, The: description of, 60; purpose of, 63; and religion, 69; self-integration, 74–75
Angels, Islam, 163
"Anthropocosmic vision," 69, 73–76
Anxiety, mindful meditation, 45–46, 49
Aristotle: Golden Mean, 67; happiness, 139–140
Arjuna: *Bhagavad Gita* role, 16, 17; *Bhakti* yoga, 27–29; *Jnana* yoga, 19–22; *Karma* yoga, 22–24, 26
"Art of living," 102
Atman, Hinduism, 18, 19, 20, 21, 26, 32n.11
Attachment, Buddhism, 40
Attitude, Stoicism, 103, 104
Augustine (Saint): inner conflict, 146; life of, 139
Aurelius, Marcus: Stoic philosopher, 101, 102–103, 105, 106, 107, 109, 110; wisdom tradition, 6, 10
Autonomy, Stoicism, 101, 104, 114–115

Avatara (descent), Hinduism, 27

Basham, A. L., on *Bhagavad Gita* composition, 15–16
Bass, Alan, 129–130
Bavel, Tarsicius J. van, 143–144
Bellah, Robert, 73
Berger, Peter, 151
Bergin, Allen F., 184, 191–192
Bettelheim, Bruno, 104, 197
Bhagavad Gita, aim of life, 17–18; *Bhakti* yoga, 17, 18, 27–29; composition of, 15–16; description of, 15; *Jnana* yoga, 18–22; *Karma* yoga, 22–27; and psychoanalysis, 16, 17–18, 19, 29–31; spiritual cartography, 31
Bhakti yoga (devotion), Hinduism, 17, 18, 27–29
Bion, Wilfred, 45, 50
Bobrow, Joseph, 52
Body, Hinduism, 21
Book of Mencius, Confucian tradition, 67
Brahman, Hinduism, 17, 21, 25, 26, 32n.7
Brotherhood, 108
Brown, Peter, 146
Buber, Martin, 145
Buddha, wisdom tradition, 6
Buddhism: Eightfold Path, 37, 41, 52; Four Noble Truths, 39–43; and Hinduism, 16, 32n.11; human condition, 36–39; mindful meditation,

43–44, 55n.31, 105, 178; and psychoanalytic theory, 46; three poisons, 180

Cary, Philip, 140, 150, 157n.27
Caste system, Hinduism, 16, 33n.33
"Catalogue of the Times," 123–124
"Centered responsiveness," 84
Ch'i (breath), Chuang Tzu, 88
Chan Wing-Tsit, 84
Chinese culture, early religions of, 69
Chinese wisdom, Confucian philosophy, 59
Christianity: gratitude, 145; humility, 149. *See also* Augustine (Saint)
Chuang Tzu: life of, 82; philosophy of, 81, 82–95; in wisdom tradition, 6
Chun-tzu (gentleman), Confucian philosophy, 61. *See also* Gentleman
City of God, Augustine (Saint), 153–154
Compassion, Chuang Tzu, 86
Complete Works of Chuang Tzu, The, 81, 82, 95
Confessions of Saint Augustine: as autobiographical work, 139; on happiness, 156; "interiority" of, 140–141; on love, 144
Confucian philosophy, critical view of, 82
Confucian tradition, in Confucian philosophy, 61
Confucius: Chinese wisdom, 59–60, 61, 62–63; wisdom tradition, 6
Control: Chuang Tzu, 92–93; psychoanalysis, 188–191; Stoicism, 103, 104
Cox, Harvey, grace, 145
Creel, Herrlee G., 68
Cua, A. S., 62, 65

Dalai Lama, 43, 54n.4
de Barry, William Theodore, 81
Death: Chuang Tzu, 88–89; Ecclesiastes, 127, 128; mindful meditation, 48–49

Decision-making, Stoicism, 104–105
Depression, mindful meditation, 46–47, 49
Descartes, Rene, 188
Detachment: Chuang Tzu, 83–84, 87, 88; Hinduism, 22, 23–25; Stoicism, 104
Determinism, Ecclesiastes, 128, 129, 136n.13
Dhammapada, Buddhism, 44
Dharma: in *Bhagavad Gita*, 22; Hinduism, 16–17
Disciplines, Hinduism, 17
Discriminative wisdom, Hinduism, 19–20
"Disordered love," 142–145, 148, 178
Divine Providence, Judaism, 128
Divine reality, unity of, 9
Divinity, Stoicism, 108
Doctrine of the Mean, Confucian philosophy, 66, 67, 68
Dreams, Chuang Tzu, 85
Dualism: Buddhism, 37, 38; Chuang Tzu, 84, 91
Dukkha (suffering), Buddhism, 39. *See also* Suffering

"Earthly City," 153
Ecclesiastes: on change, 37; composition of, 120–121, 136n.5; enjoyment of life, 132–136, 178; on suffering, 41; wisdom tradition, 6, 119–122
Eck, Diana, on dharma, 16
Edelson, Marshal, on psychoanalysis, 2
Ego: in Buddhism, 38, 50–51; in Confucian philosophy, 71; in Hinduism, 19, 25; Lacan's view of, 56n.44; in psychoanalysis, 40, 50–52
Ego psychology, description of, 51
Eightfold Path, Buddhism, 37, 41, 52
Eliot, T. S., 15
Emerson, Ralph Waldo, 15
Emotions, Chuang Tzu, 90, 91. *See also* Feelings
Emptiness, Chuang Tzu, 87, 88

"Enlightened One, The," 36
Enlightenment, in Buddhism, 37–38; in Hinduism, 31; Western view of, 37–38
Epictetus, 103, 107–108
Epicurean hedonism, Ecclesiastes, 132–133
Epicureans, Roman philosophy, 103
Epstein, Mark, 39
Equanimity: in Chuang Tzu, 92; in Hinduism, 20, 21, 23
Erikson, Erik, 89
Ethics: Buddhism, 42; Confucian philosophy, 61, 62; Wisdom literature, 180, 182
Ethics of the Fathers, gratitude, 145
Europe, religious belief, 2–3
Evil: Augustine (Saint), 149, 150; Stoicism, 106
Existential concerns, wisdom literature, 180

Fairbairn, W. R. D., 154, 188
Family, Confucian philosophy, 67–68
Fatalism, Islam, 167
Fear, mindful meditation, 45–46
Feelings, Confucian philosophy, 76. *See also* Emotions
Fertile void, Chuang Tzu, 87
Fetishization, 133–134
Filial piety, Confucian philosophy, 67, 72
Five Constant Relationships, Confucian philosophy, 66, 67, 68
"Five Pillars of Islam," 160, 161, 162
Floating, Chuang Tzu, 87–88
Flux, Chuang Tzu, 84
"For the Other," 8, 43, 51, 52, 53, 72, 148–149, 155, 165, 178
Forgiveness: in psychoanalysis, 191–194; in religious traditions, 191
Fortitude, Augustine (Saint), 144
Foucault, Michel, 7, 39
Four Families, religions, 10
Four Noble Truths, Buddhism, 39–43
Fowler, J., 195
Frankl, Viktor E., 196–197

Freedom: Chuang Tzu, 82–83; Stoicism, 103, 107, 114–115
Freud and Man's Soul, 197
Freud, Sigmund: and Augustine (Saint), 141, 146, 149; on drives, 186; and Ecclesiastes, 121–122; on egoistic individualism, 195; on fatalism of, 92; on goal achievement, 36; on the human condition, 29, 59, 187–188; on the inner discourse, 103; "masternarrative" of, 53; as mystical thought, 82–83; and "oceanic feeling," 155; on religion, 4; on suffering, 39; scientific view, 184; skepticism of, 94
Fromm, Erich, 179
Fung Yu-lan, 68, 89

Gallup, George, Jr., 3
Gallup Organization polls, religious belief, 2
Gandhi, Mahatma, on *Bhagavad Gita*, 16, 24
Geertz, Clifford, 189
"Gentleman," Confucian philosophy, 61, 64, 66, 69–70, 75, 178
God: Augustine (Saint), 132–144; in Ecclesiastes, 129, 131; Hinduism, 17, 21, 25, 26, 32n.7; Islam, 164–167
Golden Mean, 67, 120
Golden Rule, Confucian philosophy, 63, 77–78n.11
Goldstein, Joseph, 42, 44, 47, 49
Gordis, Robert, 120, 127, 132
Grace: Augustine (Saint), 144, 145, 155; in Hinduism, 28; and psychoanalysis, 152
Graham, A. C., 90–91
Gratitude: Christianity, 145; psychoanalysis, 111
Greek philosophers: on actions, 92; and Augustine (Saint), 140
Greek rationalists, wisdom tradition, 6
"Guilty man," 29, 39–40, 187–188
Gunas, Hinduism, 25

Index

Hadot, Pierre, 7, 102, 103, 105, 107, 109, 115n.10
Hale, Nathan, on psychoanalysis, 1, 1–2
Hansen, Chad, 85
Happiness: Aristotle, 139–139–140; Augustine (Saint), 140, 152–153, 155–156; Ecclesiastes, 132; and psychoanalysis, 154; Stoicism, 103, 106
Hatha yoga, 20
Health, and forgiveness, 191
Heaven, Confucian philosophy, 62, 68, 72, 73, 74, 76
"Heavenly City," 153–154
Hebrew Wisdom, Ecclesiastes, 120, 121
Hegel, Georg, 84
Heiler, F., 182
Heraclitus, 37
Hinduism: and *Bhagavad Gita*, 15–18; *Bhakti* yoga, 17, 18, 27–29 and Buddhism, 16, 32n.11, 55n.25; and *Jnana* yoga, 17, 18–22, 25, 28; *Karma* yoga, 17, 18, 22–27, 28; psychoanalysis, 16, 17–18, 19, 29–31
Hinton, David, 82
Human beings, and religion, 3
Human condition: Augustine (Saint), 139–140, 146; in *Bhagavad Gita*, 16; in Buddhism, 35, 36–39; in Chinese tradition, 81; Chuang Tzu, 81–82, 92; Confucian philosophy, 59, 75–76; Ecclesiastes, 119–120, 121–128, 132; Hinduism, 29–30, 31; 161; psychoanalysis, 29, 35, 76, 177; Stoicism, 102
Human nature, Confucian philosophy, 64, 74
Humility: Christianity, 149; psychoanalysis, 111
"Hundred Schools of Thought," 82
Huxley, Aldous, 15

Idolatry, Islam, 160
Ihsan (virtue), Islam, 163
Illness, mindful meditation, 47–48
"Illusory wish fulfillment," 129
Iman (faith), Islam
Individualism, Western concept, 71
"Inner sage and outer king," 61
"Inner world of representations," 140
Insight meditation: Buddhism, 43–44; and psychoanalysis, 44–45
"Intraworldly mysticism," 82, 84, 89–92
Intuition, Chuang Tzu, 92
Islam, and Christianity, 159, 160–161; core beliefs, 160; on creation, 168–170; God, 164–167; and Judaism, 159, 160–161; Judgement Day, 163, 170–171; Koran, 159; and modernism, 172–173, 174–175n.36; recent history, 179; spiritual development, 162–164; as surrender, 162–163. *See also* Koran
"I-Thou" relationship, 145

Jesus, roles of, 141
Jihad (struggle), Islam, 165–167, 174n.14
Jnana yoga (cognition), Hinduism, 17, 18–22, 25, 28
Job, Wisdom literature, 121
Judaism: subordination to God, 148; Wisdom tradition, 6; *See also* Ecclesiastes
Judgement Day, Islam, 163, 170–171
Jung, Carl, unconscious, 1
Justice, Augustine (Saint), 144

K'ung F-tzu, 60. *See also* Confucius
Kabat-Zinn, Jon, insight meditation, 43, 44, 47–48, 55n.31
Kant, Immanuel, 108
Karma (moral law), 17, 23, 25
Karma yoga (action), Hinduism, 17, 18, 22–27, 28
Kernberg, Otto, 42–43
Klagsburn, Samuel, 3
Klein, Melanie: human condition, 76; unconscious, 1
Knowledge, Ecclesiastes, 124–125
Koheleth, 119, 124, 136n.5. *See also* Ecclesiastes

Index

Kohut, Heinz: Augustine (Saint), 154; human condition, 29, 39–40, 76, 188; "masternarrative," 53, 76; mature narcissism, 43

Koran: composition of, 160; on creation, 168; in Islam, 159, 161, 168–169, 172, 173n.4; and predestination, 170; straight path, 164–166

Kovel, Joel, 7, 183

Krishna: in *Bhagavad Gita* role, 16, 17; *Bhakti* yoga, 27–29; *Jnana* yoga, 19–22; *Karma* yoga, 22–26

Kunz, George, 53

Kurzweil, Edith, on psychoanalysis, 2

Lacan, Jacques, 51, 56n.44

Langbein, Harmann, 187

Language: Chuang Tzu, 85; Confucian philosophy, 66–67; psychoanalysis, 114, 189

Lao Tzu, Chinese wisdom, 81, 86

Lau, D. C., 59

"Leap of faith," 193

Leibowitz, Yeshayahu, 148

Levinas, Emmanuel: ethics of, 8; on happiness, 52; "masternarrative" of, 53; on the Other, 53, 134, 148, 187; on self/ego, 51; on social responsibility, 111–112, 187; on totalizing, 129

Li (rules of propriety), Confucian philosophy, 64, 65–68, 69–70, 72, 74, 75, 76

Life, Ecclesiastes, 121–128

Loewald, Hans, 198

Logos, Stoicism, 103, 108, 109

Love, Augustine (Saint), 141–145, 178

Luks, A., 186

Mahabharata, and *Bhagavad Gita*, 15

Mahayana Buddhism, 40

Marcel, Gabriel, 151

"Masternarratives," 53, 76

Meaning, search for, 2

Meditation: Buddhism, 42–44, 91; Chuang Tzu, 87; Hinduism, 20–21

Meditations: composition of, 101, 102; as spiritual exercise, 102, 109, 112–114; and Stoic philosophy, 101, 102, 105

Meissner, William W., 4

Mental health, and spirituality, 3

Merton, Thomas, 15

"Middle Way," 41

Miller, Barbara Stoler, on *Bhagavad Gita*, 22, 26

Mind, Hinduism, 21

Mindful meditation: anxiety/fear, 46; Buddhism, 43–44, 55n.31, 105, 178; and psychoanalysis, 47

Mindfulness: Chuang Tzu, 90; Stoicism, 105–107

Mirror: Chuang Tzu, 87; Zen Buddhism, 87

Moksha (liberation), Hinduism, 17, 32n.6

"Monkey mind," 91

Monotheism, Islam, 160, 170

Morality: Augustine (Saint), 139–140; Confucian philosophy, 59; Islam, 161, 164–166, 169, 172, 175n.38; search for, 2 Stoicism, 103–104, 108; and transcendence, 8–9

Muhammad (Prophet), Koran, 160, 165–166

Mysticism: "intraworldly," 82, 84, 89–92; Hinduism, 31, 32n.7

Nagarjuna, on nirvana, 40, 55n.19

Nakamura, Hakime, 38

Narcissism, and anxiety, 45; and depression, 46–47; and pain, 48; and suffering, 40; transformation of, 42–43, 75

Nasr, Seyyed Hossein, 159–160, 173

Natural law, Stoicism, 108

Nature: Chuang Tzu, 83, 86, 92; Confucian philosophy, 73, 75; Ecclesiastes, 122, 123; Stoicism, 104, 108, 110

Neurotic anxiety, mindful meditation, 45–46, 49

Neurotic depression, mindful meditation, 46–47, 49

Neurotic suffering, Buddhism, 40
Nirvana, Buddhism, 37, 40–41, 52
Nivison, David, 83
"No-mind and no-feeling," 87
Nonattachment, Chuang Tzu, 92
Nondirectedness, Chuang Tzu, 84
Nonself: Buddhism, 38–39; psychoanalysis, 52

Object relations, 1
"Objective," Stoicism, 113
"Observing ego," 49
"Oceanic feeling," 155
Original sin: Augustine (Saint), 146–147, 156–157n.19; Islam, 173n.7

Pain, Stoicism, 106
Paradise, Islam, 168, 174n.13
Pargament, Kenneth I., 189–190, 192, 193
Pattison, E. Mansell, 147
"People of the Book," 160
Perry, T. A., 123–124
Personal freedom, Chuang Tzu, 82–83
Philips, Adam, 110
Physical pain, mindful meditation, 47–48, 49
Postmodernism, and Buddhism, 55n.32
"Practice of the self," 7
Prayer, Islam, 167
Predestination, Islam, 163, 166, 170
Predetermination, Ecclesiastes, 122–123
Present, Stoicism, 105–107
Pride, Augustine (Saint), 147–148, 155
"Primordial awareness," 60
"Profound malaise," 2, 4
Prophets, Jewish Wisdom tradition, 6
Proverbs, Wisdom literature, 121
Prudence, Augustine (Saint), 144
Psychiatrists, and religion, 5
Psychoanalysis: anti-systematization of, 129–130; and Augustine (Saint), 144–145, 152, 154–156; and *Bhagavad Gita*, 16, 17–18, 19, 29–31; and Confucian philosophy, 70–72; 74–75; contemporary crisis of, 1, 3–5, 177; current theory, 4; definition of, 6–7; and Ecclesiastes, 120, 128–132; and forgiveness, 191–194; goals of, 30–31, 61; and Islam, 159,162, 164–165, 173; and insight meditation, 44–45; and religion, 4, 9; service to others, 185–188; and spirituality, 198n.3; spiritually animated, 177–179, 182–183; and Stoicism, 101–102, 104, 108–111, 112, 113–114; and Taoism, 82, 89, 90, 93, 94–95; theoretical framework, 2; value agent, 183–185
Psychoanalysis and Religion, 179
Psychoanalysts, mindfulness, 50, 52, 111

Rajas, Hinduism, 25–26
Ramadan, Islam, 160
Reality, Wisdom literature, 181–182
Reason, Stoicism, 104, 108, 109, 113
Rectification of Names, Confucian philosophy, 66–67
Reincarnation, Hinduism, 18
Religion: Confucian philosophy, 68–69; and coping, 3; definition of, 8; and forgiveness, 191; four families of, 10; monstrous behavior, 179; and spirituality, 3; unity of, 10–11
Religious beliefs: Europe, 2–3; United States, 2
Ren, Confucian philosophy, 62–65, 66, 68, 69–70, 72, 74, 75, 76
Repetition: Ecclesiastes, 123; *Meditations*, 112–113
"Repressed angel," 197
Restraint, Chuang Tzu, 86
Revelation, Hinduism, 30
Rig Veda, on truth, 9, 30
Rigby, Paul, 146–147
Rise and Crisis of Psychoanalysis in the United States, The, 1–2
Ritual, Confucian philosophy, 65
Roland, Alan, on spirituality, 3
Rolland, Romain, 155
Roth, Paul A., human condition, 76
Rubin, Jeffrey B., 46, 51

Rumi (Al-din), Jalal, 161–162, 163–164

"Sacred canopy," 151, 189
Salvation: Augustine (Saint), 146; Islam, 166
Salzberg, Sharon, 42, 44, 49
Samsara (life cycle), Hinduism, 17
Sattva, Hinduism, 25
Schafer, Roy: "masternarratives" of, 53, 76; unconscious, 1
Schopenhauer, Arthur, 15
Schuhmacher, Stephen, 25
Schuon, F., 9
Scott, R. B. Y., 121
Self: Augustine (Saint), 140; in Buddhism, 38–39, 50–51; in Confucian philosophy, 70, 71, 73; in Hinduism, 21; Islam, 169; psychoanalytic view, 50–52, 70
Self-analysis, Augustine (Saint), 140–141
Self-awareness, *Bhagavad Gita*, 18
Self-control, Stoicism, 107–108
Self-cultivation, Confucian philosophy, 59–60, 62, 69–72, 74
Self-determination, Greek philosophy, 92
Self-esteem, depression, 46
Self-improvement: Buddhism, 35; Confucian philosophy, 69–70; psychoanalysis, 61
Self-judgement, Islam, 171
Self-knowledge, psychoanalysis, 31, 61
Self-mastery: Buddhism, 35; Stoicism, 101
Self-psychology: description of, 51; happiness, 154
Self-realization, Confucian philosophy, 69–70, 73; psychoanalysis, 61
Self-reliance, Stoicism, 101
Self-transcendence, 2, 3, 5
Self-transformation: Buddhism, 35; Chuang Tzu, 83, 84; desire for, 2, 197; Ecclesiastes, 120
Self-understanding, *Bhagavad Gita*, 17
Seneca, 107–108

Sensual pleasure, Ecclesiastes, 124, 125, 133
Service: psychoanalysis, 186–188, 199n.16; Wisdom literature, 185
Shahaada, Islam, 160, 161
Shang-ti, Chinese religion, 69
Shariah, Islamic law, 162–163
Shruti (revelation), *Bhagavad Gita*, 16, 61
Siddhartha, Gautama, life of, 36. *See also* Buddhism
Silver Rule, Confucian philosophy, 63, 77–78n.11
Sin, Augustine (Saint), 143, 146–149
Smith, Huston: on Confucian philosophy, 67; on creation, 168; on Hinduism, 26; on Jesus, 154; on life conduct, 180; on mystery, 181; on religion, 3–4; "Religion's Four Families," 10; on the religious mode, 182; on Ren, 63; on the spiritual nature, 195; on surrender, 162
Smriti (remembered text), *Bhagavad Gita*, 16, 61
Social duty, Stoicism, 108, 111
Social feeling, 108
Social responsibility: Islam, 172; Levinas, 111
Soul, Augustine (Saint), 140; *See also Atman*
Spinoza, Baruch, 95, 108
"Spiritual exercise," *Meditations*, 102, 109; psychoanalysis of, 7
Spirituality: definition of, 7–8, 10–11; and psychoanalysis, 183; 198n.3; in wisdom religions, 3
Staniforth, Maxwell, 101
Stoicism: Ecclesiastes, 132; philosophy of, 101, 102–111, 112; spiritual exercises, 112–114; and transcendence, 10
"Straight path," 161, 164
Stumpf, Samuel Enoch, 108
"Subjective," Stoicism, 113
Subjectivity, reconfiguration of, 36
Sublimation, and suffering, 41
"Sufferable," 151, 167

Suffering: Augustine (Saint), 149–152, 157n.27; Buddhism, 35–36, 37, 39–41; Chuang Tzu, 88, 89; Confucian philosophy, 77n.4; Islam, 166–167; Stoicism, 106
Sufism, 161–162, 166
Superego, in Hinduism, 19
Surrender, Islam, 162–163
Svadharma, Bhagavad Gita, 19

T'ien (Heaven), Chinese religion, 69
Tamas, Hinduism, 25–26
Tao (the Way): Chuang Tzu, 83–85, 86–87; Confucian philosophy, 61–62, 64, 68, 77n.8
Taoism, and Buddhism, 55n.25
Tawhid (unity), 161
"Technique of the self," 7, 120
Theodicy, Augustine (Saint), 150, 151
"Therapeutic of the passions," 102
Thoreau, Henry David, 15
"Three in the Morning," 94
"Three poisons," 180
Tibetan Buddhism, enlightenment, 37
Totalizing, and psychoanalysis, 129–130
Tov, Baal Shem, 194
"Tragic man," 29, 39–40, 188
Tranquillity: Buddhism, 35, 44; Chuang Tzu, 86
Transcendence: Augustine (Saint), 140, 142–145; concept of, 7–8; Hinduism, 31; and psychoanalysis, 194–194
Truth: Ecclesiastes, 124; search for, 2
Tu Wei-ming, 60, 70, 73, 75–76

Ummah (community), Islam, 172
Unconscious: belief in, 196–197; in Hinduism, 21; self-transformation, 198; views of, 1
United States, religious belief, 2–3, 5
Upanishadic doctrines, Hinduism, 16, 32n.7

U.S. News/PBS's Religion and Ethics Newsweekly poll, religious beliefs, 2

Values, psychoanalysis, 183–185
Vedic rituals, Hinduism, 16
Vipassana (clear seeing) meditation, 43, 49. *See also* Insight meditation, Mindful meditation
Virtue: Augustine (Saint), 143–144; Confucian philosophy, 62; Islam, 163; Stoicism, 108, 109
Vishnu, Hinduism, 28

Warring States: Chuang Tzu, 82; Confucius, 60
Water, Chuang Tzu, 87, 97n.40
Watson, Burton, 81, 86
Watts, Alan, 87, 92
Weinstein, Fred, 1
Western society, and control, 189
Wiesel, Elie, 188
Will of Heaven, Confucian philosophy, 64, 68, 69, 74, 76
Wilson, E. O., 3
Wing-tsit Chan, 64, 66–67
Wisdom: Ecclesiastes, 124–125; Stoicism, 103, 110
Wisdom literature: description of, 6; Ecclesiastes, 120–121; wisdom of, 179–182
"Wise discrimination," 47
Woerner, Gert, 25
Women, Confucian philosophy, 78n.23
Work, Hinduism, 24, 26
"Worldview," and Ecclesiastes, 128
Wu-wei (nonaction), Chuang Tzu, 85–86, 92–93, 96n.29, 178

Yearley, Lee, Chuang Tzu, 89–90
Yoga, Hinduism, 17, 20–21. *See also Bhakti* yoga, *Hatha* yoga, *Jnana* yoga, *Karma* yoga

Zen Buddhism: enlightenment, 37; mirror symbol, 87

ABOUT THE AUTHOR

PAUL MARCUS is a supervising and training analyst for the National Psychological Association for Psychoanalysis. He is the author of *Autonomy in the Extreme Situation: Bruno Bettelheim, the Nazi Concentration Camps and the Mass Society* (Praeger, 1999).

Warning: Replacement cost for this book is over $75. if it is lost or damaged.